To Pat — I do hope y··· ···
this! love from M···

RETURN TO
MUCK

Matador
Unit E2 Airfield Business Park,
Harrison Road, Market Harborough,
Leicestershire. LE16 7UL
·   Tel: 0116 2792299
Email: books@troubador.co.uk
Web: www.troubador.co.uk/matador
Twitter: @matadorbooks

ISBN 978 1803132 198

British Library Cataloguing in Publication Data.
A catalogue record for this book is available from the British Library.

Printed and bound in the UK by TJ Books Ltd, Padstow, Cornwall
Design and typesetting by Hawk Editorial Ltd, Hull

Matador is an imprint of Troubador Publishing Ltd

RETURN TO MUCK

A JOURNEY AMONG SOME LESSER-KNOWN SCOTTISH ISLANDS

MARG GREENWOOD

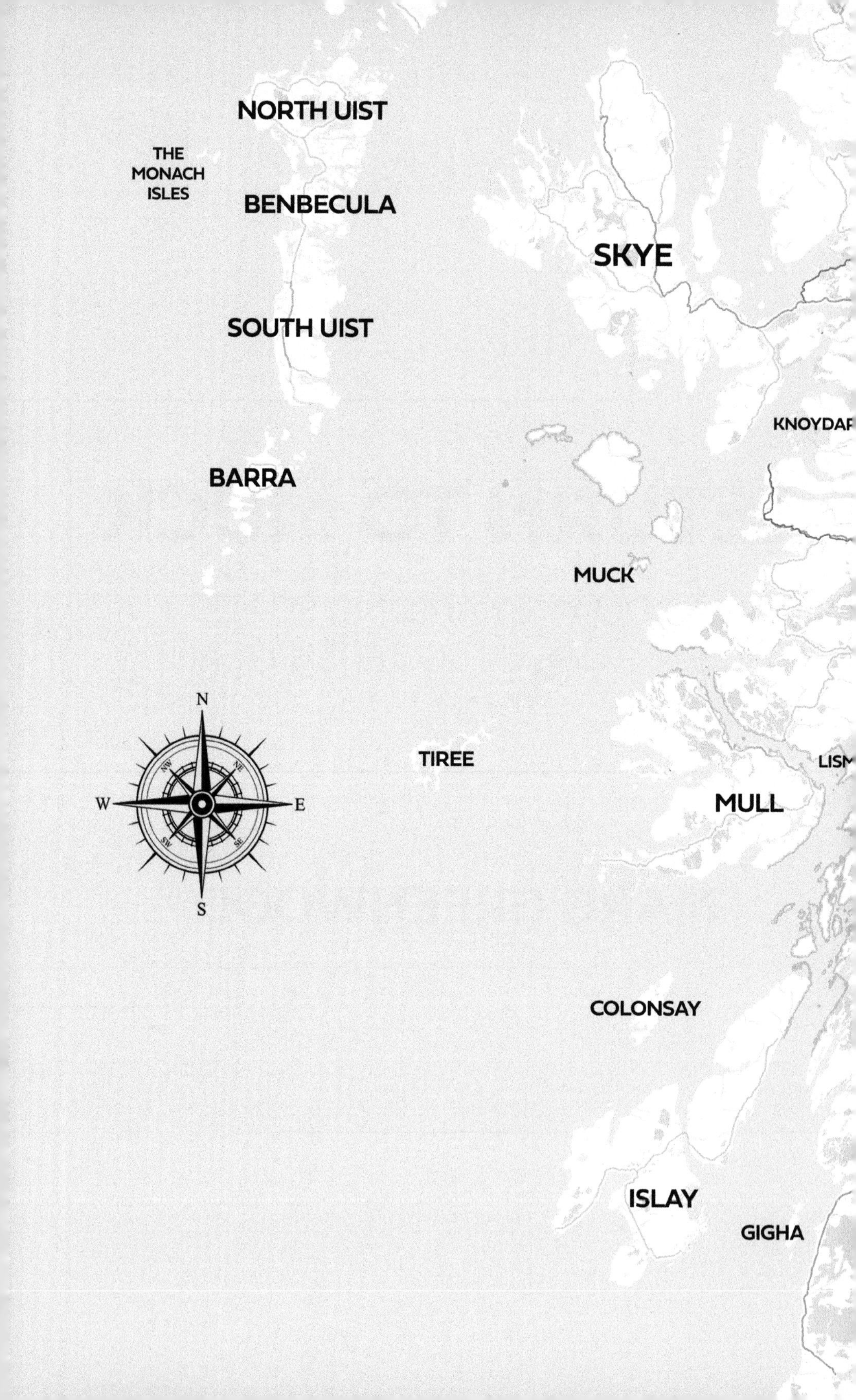

NORTH UIST

THE
MONACH
ISLES

BENBECULA

SKYE

SOUTH UIST

KNOYDAR

BARRA

MUCK

N

NW NE

W E

SW SE

S

TIREE

LISM

MULL

COLONSAY

ISLAY

GIGHA

CONTENTS

PREFACE

Johnson said, 'I cannot but laugh, to think of myself roving around the
Hebrides at sixty. I wonder where I shall rove at fourscore!'
– James Boswell.[1]

'**W**hat's there to do on Muck? It's only a tiny island, isn't it?'
This is a typical question put to me by friends when
they realise I am about to set off for this small Hebridean
island. When my great-nephew asked me why I travel to the Scottish Isles
every year, I found myself saying, 'Because there's a surprise around every
corner.'

As an answer it's as good as any. I've been exploring the islands, mostly
by myself, almost every year for about twenty years since very early
retirement as a teacher. I continued to work part-time as a teacher and

Gallanach farm with Skye and Eigg in the background

counsellor/psychotherapist for a few more years. Now past the age of seventy, I still hope to be 'roving around the Hebrides' at eighty, and not think of laughing about it, like Johnson.

Unlike Boswell and Johnson, who often stayed with local lairds who treated them like royalty, I stay, wherever I can, in hostels and bunkhouses and self-cater. This cuts down costs of long trips, and meets my needs for living simply. Hostels are in my genes. My father was one of the pioneers who, in the 1930s, helped set up the Youth Hostels movement in England and Wales. He lived in Leeds and was, for many years, secretary of the Yorkshire West Riding branch, responsible for opening several hostels, and according to one history of the YHA, member number one of that organisation.

I enjoy being on my own, but am also greatly attached to family and friends. When in Leeds I gallivant off on local walks, attend writing classes, and go to the cinema and theatre (often with my partner), and feel Leeds is my true base. But I have found another base, or even home, in Muck – and from there I travel to other islands, most of which are not popular tourist destinations.

Friends ask me if I get lonely as a solo traveller. The answer is no. Spending the daytime reflecting, looking for – and at – birds and otters through my binoculars, flower-spotting, beachcombing, walking, meeting people by chance and chatting – these are meditative pastimes happily spent alone. But coming into a hostel or bunkhouse each evening meets my basic need for social interaction. If I were to wild-camp solo every night instead of going to hostels I probably would get lonely, and devoured by midges.

I'm not insistent on being alone in the islands. Occasionally I've been with family or friends when we've rented a cottage for a week or so. I can then see the advantages of sharing these treasured isles with others. I'll never forget my granddaughter Helena, aged about twelve months, inspecting daisies in Hushinish on Harris, or Isabelle, then aged eight, listening with rapt attention to a talk at the Callanish stones in Lewis.

The obvious advantage of solo travelling is that you can please yourself. You can do what you like, choose where to go, and eat your stewed lentils with a tin of sardines without anyone complaining. As for the question, 'An older woman walking on your own – are you safe?' the answer is possibly not always. I have few inhibitions when meeting other walkers, and greet everyone I come across if they don't greet me first. This has led to some interesting chats in out of the way places, and a fair bit of serendipity too.

There's also a pragmatic and possibly morbid motive to greet everyone, especially in lonely places. I want people to remember what I look like and where they saw me – just in case I have a fall or accident. But this must be true of all solo travellers, including men, although many men might disagree. Awareness of my vulnerability keeps me on the moderate 'B' walks, lifted off pocket walk guides (wherever they exist) rather than the strenuous 'A' ones that might land me in trouble. I scrutinise the OS maps for distance, difficulty of terrain and safety. If a path looks, on the map, as if it disappears, I will not go down it. Usually.

Do I have an underlying motive, like escape or enlightenment? Mariella Frostrup wrote in the *Times*: 'Why did the man climb Everest?' 'Because it was there.' 'Why did the woman climb Everest?' 'Because she was divorced or having a mid-life crisis.'[2] I have not been on the islands in the middle of a divorce or in crisis, mid- nor end-life. But over the years I have discovered more about myself, as you will find out.

*

Why 'Return to Muck'? Muck is small, beautiful and safe. Each time I have walked up to the trig point, or stood gazing at Rum among the cows on Gallanach beach, I remind myself how special this island is. And Muck is particularly special because of its community, and the history of having had a benign, live-on-the-island farmer and owner, Lawrence MacEwen and his family. You cannot wander around the island for half a day without meeting one of the family at work around the farm or attending to shoot-related activities. The family have also worked tirelessly to enable residents to pursue their own destinies, while committing themselves to the ethos of a small community, which is stable at about forty people.

As well as accounts of my experiences on Muck, you'll read here about Gigha, Colonsay, Tiree, Islay, Knoydart and Lismore – all in the Inner Hebrides. Chapter 6 describes my explorations in the southern islands of the Outer Hebrides. When I've come across an archaeological feature of one island, for example, or heard some intriguing folklore, I'm often reminded of something similar on another. This book attempts to capture these 'finds' in accounts, folk tales, poems, songs and photographs that are peppered throughout my narrative.

My poem 'Walk on the Isle of Muck' in the last chapter describes a walk that is neither linear nor circular. I've used poetic licence; the actual walk on the ground would be somewhat zigzag. This reflects how I've visited the Scottish Islands; no particular thought or aim, going backwards or forwards as the whim takes me, just as the CalMac ferries take zig-zag routes between islands on the western seaboard of Scotland.

*

The first time I went to Muck was the day of the Queen's Golden Jubilee. That same afternoon I was invited to, and made welcome at, the island's beach party. This was a wonderful affair, where I was somewhat embarrassed by my own offering of cooked lentils, as the barbecue food was meaty and delicious. I was able to chat with, and start to get to know some of the islanders, unaware that I would be back several times in the years to come. After more visits I undertook a project to enable the school children and some adult islanders to sing, play instruments, start or continue to read music, and formed a choir to which visitors were welcomed. This experience made me feel part of the community, and gave me encouragement to invite myself to other island primary schools, to offer one-off music sessions to the children.

I keep on returning to Muck because I want to see the people I've got

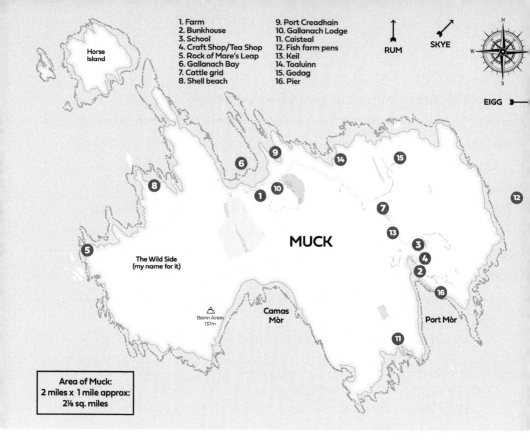

1. Farm
2. Bunkhouse
3. School
4. Craft Shop/Tea Shop
5. Rock of Mare's Leap
6. Gallanach Bay
7. Cattle grid
8. Shell beach
9. Port Creadhain
10. Gallanach Lodge
11. Caisteal
12. Fish farm pens
13. Keil
14. Toaluinn
15. Godag
16. Pier

RUM

SKYE

EIGG

Horse Island

MUCK

The Wild Side
(my name for it)

Beinn Airein
137m

Camas Mòr

Port Mòr

Area of Muck:
2 miles x 1 mile approx:
2⅛ sq. miles

to know, and to revisit my favourite corners where I rarely come across anyone else. So not only the people, many of Muck's lovely corners have become like old friends. They are 'my' secret spots; Shell Beach; Middle Wood, Beinn Airein, Rubh' Leum na Làraich. I go to see what's changed since my last visit. Is the barrister's bothy still tied up with tape? Has the red phone box been blown down? Is Ewen's new house finished after ten years in the building? How many children are in the school now?

There will never be a time when these questions peter out, and there are always surprises.

*

The biggest surprise has been the coronavirus lockdown in early 2020, just at the time of my trying to book the Muck bunkhouse once again, and starting to plan another visit to the Western Isles for later in the year. What if I don't manage to get to Muck for the foreseeable future?

CHAPTER 1
MUCK: THE EARLY YEARS

The Small Isles, seen from Muck
Now you see Rum, now you don't;
vanished into thick air; a clever trick.
Hey presto; back it comes,
snowy peaks startling in April..
Eigg's skyline's bold and bumpy,
scrambled, good Eigg!
Canna keeps a low profile,
oyster-like, hiding its gem from the world.
Yet the best-kept secret, pearl of pearls,
is Muck.

Rum, as seen from Muck

started my solo island-hopping in 1999, travelling with my bike through the Western Isles, but went to Muck for the first time in 2002. I begin this book by describing a typical journey to Muck in my early years, after 2005. After a long car journey from Leeds, I drove west from Fort William for about forty miles, to Mallaig, and stayed overnight. Mallaig is the port for the Small Isles, from where I took the Caledonian MacBrayne (CalMac) ferry next morning for Muck.

I needed to carry on to the boat not only my bags and rucksack, but also food, as I was self-catering in the bunkhouse. I loaded the car with a large supply of groceries from the Mallaig supermarket, drove the short distance to the quay, and off-loaded my shopping and other bags labelled *Muck*, in a neat pile next to the Small Isles van.

A CalMac man with yellow wellies and a big smile who was standing by the van asked me if I was a passenger. I told him that I was just going to park the car in the long-stay car park up the road, and then hurry back. There was no need to worry about baggage security – nothing ever got stolen on the quay – but luggage and food were in danger of getting soaked if it rained.

After locking the car, I ran back to the boat and asked the van driver to put my stuff in the van, which in those days he was allowed to do. (On subsequent journeys I'd have to carry the bags myself, often helped by friendly strangers, on to the car deck.)

*

The ferry journey from Mallaig to Muck has always been one of my favourite experiences, and I'm aware of an extra frisson of excitement when I'm poised to board the boat. I and about twelve other passengers watched the van board the ferry – it was one of two vehicles on the car deck, and we followed it on foot. I heard the Gaelic welcome and safety notices on the tannoy, then the English translation. The word for skipper in Gaelic was the same as the English, I noted.

We set off on time. Down below in the cafeteria I had a cup of tea, and noticed that the islanders spent the whole voyage chatting to each other. They rarely went on deck. But I trundled up and down the decks just like a toddler, never settling in one seat for a moment. I could have a choice of plenty of seats. Out on the windy deck with my binoculars, I spotted gulls, terns, porpoises and the occasional minke whale, while the mainland slowly shrank away. During the two and a half hours' journey there was plenty of time to enjoy the sea life.

The boat first called at Eigg. I stayed on deck and watched Eigg people and a couple of cyclists disembark, and new passengers embark. The CalMac van moved up the slipway to unload the Eigg luggage, and then reversed back again. I looked up at the crazy skyline of Eigg, its Sgurr, and wondered if I would ever climb up it.

Just a half an hour's voyage from Eigg we arrived at the Muck pier. From the deck I could see a huddle of people who were there to greet friends, family and visitors. Others had come to pick up their own supermarket orders or building materials in a tractor or Land Rover, and there was Rosie, the bunkhouse warden, waiting for me with her wheelbarrow, the most eco-friendly method of carrying luggage.

Muck is a small island off the west coast of Scotland and is only two miles long and a mile wide. It has a school, but no church, pub or shop, and a population of just over forty people. I have visited the island around twelve times for up to five and a half weeks at a time, so have happily got to know many of the islanders.

The island is one of the four Small Isles, together with Rum, Eigg and Canna, all to the south of Skye, and all of which I have visited. There are a few holiday cottages, and other places to stay, from a small hotel to a yurt. There is one road of less than a mile long, and in the early days, just a couple of Land Rovers and tractors, but no cars; definitely no visitors' cars. Mobile phone reception is rare. So the island feels remote.

*

The van now drove off the car deck up the slipway, and disgorged the Muck luggage and boxes, then drove back on board again. Rosie helped me load her barrow with my stuff and I walked with her on the only road, stepping around a cattle grid. (Cows were not allowed anywhere near the pier.) There was a motley collection of boats in the harbour, and the slippery old stone pier was tucked away below the road. We turned the corner at Pier House. And almost immediately the bunkhouse appeared on our left.

*

Rosie was the first island resident with whom I made a friendship, which is still going strong. She led me to the bunkhouse. A beautiful setting with its back windows facing the tiny estuary at Port Mòr, it became what child psychologist John Bowlby would call a 'Secure Base' from then on.[1]

It was a green and white painted building with a corrugated iron roof. We skipped over a long-standing puddle in front of the unlocked door which led to the tiny kitchen, one and a half yards square. There was a window that rattled, as did the tin roof, in a gale; a bottled gas cooker,

View of the old bunkhouse looking back towards Pier House and the old pier

a sink and some cupboard space. A small fridge was just outside in the dark hall, where you took off your wellies or boots, and which led to other rooms. 'Very little food needs a fridge,' Rosie said, who hadn't a fridge in her own cottage.

I wasn't the only guest. She introduced me to a young man whom I will call Niffy Neville, for obvious reasons, so I was pleased to hear he would be away on tomorrow's boat. After a spot of lunch, I went out for a four-hour walk up Beinn Airein, and saw two herons, two shelduck, one buzzard, and oystercatchers galore. The singing seals at Gallanach made me feel extra happy. But it was getting cold.

Coming back to the bunkhouse I was welcomed by the Rayburn in the main sitting-cum-dining room, sat next to it and toasted my elbows on the black metal. The walls of this room had white-painted wood panelling and a crammed bookshelf lined the length of two of the walls at door-height. Red linoleum, cracked in places, covered the floors. There was no TV, no wi-fi and no phone signal. As for sleeping space, three bedrooms, with beds, not bunks, slept about seven. There was a bathroom with one toilet. 'My' room was a small sparsely furnished bedroom overlooking the estuary, with a double bed, and most importantly the bed lamp was excellent to read by. I was touched to see a 'hottie' placed on the bed.

The Rayburn was lit all year round, contributing greatly to the cosiness of the bunkhouse. It took me several visits before I got used to the cooking and heating benefits of a Rayburn. It was a great way to cook jacket potatoes, and it kept pots and pans hot, but you had to check the hob kettle every so often so that it didn't boil dry. And it saved on gas. But normally I used the kitchen, and made use of the Calor gas cooker to cook lentils and other basic food. I am not very interested in cooking. I am not a vegetarian, but rarely buy meat to eat on my travels, and there is no shop on Muck. I ate all kinds of beans and fish from tins. I could have bought fresh crab from Sandy the fisherman, but I wouldn't have been able to cook them. I was sometimes able to buy fresh bread and a bottle of milk from the Craft Shop – which at that time was really a cafe/restaurant – but on long stays when I ran out of milk, I had to piggy-back on Rosie's supermarket order from Mallaig. Sometimes it was possible to buy island-grown

Old Bunkhouse kitchen

vegetables and eggs when they were available.

When other travellers were staying, there was rarely a problem sharing the kitchen and bathroom. (Neville was an exception.) You just took it in turns. No one played the radio or music to disturb others. There was one notable exception to this statement, but that incident could have happened anywhere.

During quiet times I often had the bunkhouse to myself, and in the early years, periods of no electricity led to quiet early nights with a book and a good torch. Occasionally, because of booking issues, I wasn't able to stay in the bunkhouse, so I stayed in another resident's house, or B&B. I went to Julie's, at Godag, on the north of the island, for example, swapping views of the estuary and its heron, for views of Rum.

Rosie gave much of her time to bunkhouse visitors who wanted to talk and find out things about the island. As I kept on returning and we got to know each other, she and I would often share meals and put the world to rights.

I'll always remember Rosie and her wheelbarrow and seldom saw her without it. It served as a handbag, shopping bag, bag to carry bunkhouse residents' luggage to and from the pier, as well as many other uses. I'm surprised other islanders aren't often seen with one. (On a visit to Easdale off the Argyll coast, the sight of about twenty brightly coloured wheelbarrows – each one belonging to a different resident – greeted me as I landed on this tiny car-free island.)

*

Once I accompanied Rosie and her barrow on a hunt for driftwood on the shore at Camas Mòr. This involved at least half a mile of road walking, and another half-mile of negotiating hummocks, ditches and hillocks on fields and foreshore. Arriving at the shore, I was intrigued to see five different piles of driftwood. They 'belonged' to residents who would come and add to their pile regularly, or not. Rosie and I made for her pile, loaded the wheelbarrow until it could take no more, and bumped back to her cottage with loads of wood for her wood-burning stove.

She was meticulous about the bunkhouse waste disposal, and gradually I learnt how much she cared about environmental issues. She was in charge of the island's wheelie bins (and later skips) for different types of rubbish, located near the pier and clearly labelled. She told me about discovering a huge bag of rubbish dumped into the 'residual' (non-recyclable) skip by some yachtsmen. The skips were only emptied a few times a year. This particular bag contained a mixture of rubbish and food waste. Rosie separated out, in situ, the remains of the stomach-churning slops, dumped them in her wheelbarrow, and burnt them in an appropriate place. Not many people would do that. 'Leaving the messy food waste in that skip will encourage rodents and flies,' she told me.

*

The bunkhouse forms part of a collection of buildings at Port Mòr (locals call it 'Port'), which include residents' houses, the school and the Craft Shop, all overlooking, at different heights, the small V-shaped estuary. Above on a small hill there were two wind turbines and a turbine tower. There was a long stretch of time when these lay idle, due to the windpower company calling in the receivers. This resulted in electricity from the island's one generator twice a day – between 8.30am and 11am and then between 5.30pm and midnight.

Across the estuary is Port Mòr House, which in my early years was the home of Ewen MacEwen and his wife Judy. This has always had a very pretty garden, including a large vegetable patch. Ewen is the brother of Lawrence MacEwen, the laird. Soon after my first visit, Ewen started to build, mostly by himself, another house higher up the hill, which I inspected at a distance each time I went to Muck. It took him years.

In those early years I didn't pay much attention to boats on Muck. However, *Wave* was an exception. On my very first visit the Small Isles CalMac boat wasn't equipped for docking at Muck. This was before the new pier was built in 2005. *Wave* was the hugely important 'flit boat' that

Wave's MOT (built 1954). It was from this boat that I disembarked on my very first Muck visit

was used for conveying passengers and goods between the big boat and shore, and/or for similar short-distance transport. I had been helped on to *Wave* from the big boat that had anchored off Muck in a heavy swell. I sheltered from the spray in the prow of *Wave*, together with a gang of excited children, as it chugged into the estuary and towards the old pier.

A few yards up from the bunkhouse, set a little away from the road, was the Craft Shop, a building converted from the ruins of an old thatched house. It was always called this, although it was primarily a cafe/restaurant, with superb home baking as a speciality. Rosie would often suggest to me that we have lunch there on my arrival day, as the boat conveniently arrived at lunch time. The soups were delicious.

It also sold island-made crafts, books, gifts and cards, and materials for crafts, but its chief function was a hub for residents and visitors to gather and natter.

Jenny MacEwen, Lawrence's wife, ran the Craft Shop for more than twenty years, with the help of a few residents, putting in huge amounts of energy, always with a smile, offering a warm welcome to all comers. For many years during the summer season she would get up at five in the morning to do the baking for the day. On fine days people sat outside at the wooden tables, while children ran up and down the steep knoll just outside the shop. On top of this knoll was one of the few places where you could get a mobile signal. On the other side of the knoll was the island generator, another signal opportunity. This also afforded a tiny bit of shelter from teeming rain when I ran from the bunkhouse to make a call.

Just after the head of the estuary the road turns right, and climbs slightly. Port Mòr Wood is a collection of pine trees on the left. Over the years some of the trees have succumbed to the gales and now there are a lot fewer than before, but a child's swing attached to one of the branches has survived them all.

One May morning, after passing the wood, before the road turns left to Gallanach, I noticed a gigantic hole in the stone wall on my right near the cattle grid. The hole struck me as incongruous; there wasn't a reason for it. The rest of the wall was in excellent condition. I never did meet 'the waller who knits', whom the islanders sometimes talked about. All I

View of Eigg from wall

know is that he was not a resident. I wonder if he had been attempting the start of a lace pattern?

By kneeling down, I managed to keep the island of Eigg looking like an island. Eigg is so close to Muck that you often get views with no sea between them.

The hole stayed there for years, and then suddenly it wasn't there any more. I searched for new stones that could have been put in to fill up the hole, but to no avail. It was as if I'd dreamt the whole hole. I've never remembered to ask about it.

I didn't keep to the road on my wanderings, and would seldom plan my walks ahead of time. I hardly ever saw anyone, resident or visitor, on what I call the Wild Side of Muck, which you can reach by following the coast westwards past Gallanach. I loved to climb up Beinn Airein, and to the Rock of Mare's Leap. Once I asked a resident youngster if he ever went to the Wild Side. 'Only to gather sheep,' he said.

*

I was always on the lookout for flowers in bloom and birds. Just as I cannot tire of the landscape and views of Muck, I never tire of listening to birdsong. I hear birds better than I can identify them by sight, and since my retirement I've become very interested in the musical qualities of birdsong. One day I gave my full attention to trying to distinguish a pipit's song from a wheatear's, but despite my serious study, I still find that difficult.

I have my own mnemonics for particular birds. The willow warbler's song descends from on high for about an octave, without a hiccup. So I think of a 'weeping' willow tree with its descending branches. This is in contrast to the chaffinch's song which has a hiccup, or a 'tipple-over,' to quote my granddaughters' parlance, at the end of its phrase. These two bird species regularly nest on Muck. Few people can mistake the piercing shrieks of the oystercatcher; most readers will know it is a big black and white bird with a red beak, which shouts at all and sundry to get out of the way. Once I was driven away by a pair of very aggressive oystercatchers, one of which made a neat flight curve about six inches from my face. Scary. These birds, like gulls, have, during my lifetime, started to patrol many inland sites, such as Malham Tarn in Yorkshire.

The cliffs at Fang Mòr, just next to Camas Mòr, are home to gulls and fulmars. Geologists are drawn to this bay with its impressive rock formations on the shore exposed between tides. Big grey boulders and two Jurassic Age limestone pavements like small jetties or crocodiles jut out into the sea. This has resulted in Camas Mòr being designated a Site of Special Scientific Interest (SSSI). This was the bay where Rosie and others had made piles of driftwood.

The beach at Camas Mòr showing limestone and boulders of dark grey basalt

Another of my favourite beaches is Shell Beach on the north coast where you can find the odd cowrie shell. I learnt, when I lived in Africa, that these shells used to be used as currency. On my many tramps along the path to the bothy nearby at Bagh, a traditional cottage sometimes occupied by a mainland dweller, I've seen and heard stonechats. I like the russet-pink colour on their chest. Their call reminds me of tapping on stones with a walking stick. I heard someone doing just that, walking behind me, on the island of Kerrera, near Oban. Turning around, I said, 'I thought you were a stonechat!' The man, who turned out to be an archaeologist, was amused.

I've often seen eider duck at Port na Luce, at Gallanach, as well as behind the bunkhouse at Port Mòr. Its song or call is a loud hum going up and down in the manner of a woman, or man, saying 'ooooh' when she/ he finds out something scandalous about their boss. The estuary is the favourite patch of a lone heron too, and a pair of curlews and shelduck nosey around the back of the bunkhouse quite frequently.

In the summer I've heard one or two corncrakes in the grassland on the east side of the road, but have never seen them. They are ventriloquists and are never in the place where you think their call is coming from. Once or twice I have mistaken a mallard's croak for a corncrake, but that was wishful thinking. I'm always thrilled when I hear the call of a corncrake in the islands (even once on the mainland in Sutherland), and always annoyed I can't catch sight of it. I also love to hear the sound of a snipe at dusk, making its eerie drumming noise, sounding a bit like a wobble board. I've rarely seen one but they are plentiful on the island.

Great skuas aren't common on Muck, but a pair of these birds nest each year above Seagull Rock. I was bullied by one at the Devil's Cauldron (Sloc na Dubhaich). The Gaelic name of this secluded rocky bay means 'the sad and gloomy hollow'. Perhaps that's why this bird chose to lurk there. Skuas are aggressive predators and dive-bomb any passer-by they think is going to steal their chick, like oystercatchers and terns. Skuas think nothing of laying into a gannet while it is in the air, and forcing it to relinquish its beakful of food. They can attack lambs: Hugh MacDiarmid writes in this poem, The Bonxie: 'In its presence even the eagle… forbears to pounce on the lambs.'[2]

The beaches at Gallanach at the end of the road on the north of the island are wonderful for bird watching. In spring 2009 I invited my old school friend Ali to stay with me on Muck for a few days. She is a very keen birder. She discovered a new bird species for the island – a sedge warbler. I could hear it but couldn't see it. At Gallanach we noted fulmars, gulls, oystercatchers and shags. My binoculars picked up a posse of ringed plovers following each other parallel to the edge of the water. They were doing exactly like Norman McCaig writes – 'they/ sprintayard (like that) and/stop.'[3]

Birds are only one element of the fascinating natural world of Muck. Ali's speciality is botany. We saw plenty of stunted early orchids, and she was thrilled with the lichen we discovered on the rocks at Am Maol. In *The Isle of Muck – A Short Guide*, written by Lawrence, the laird, he reminds us that owing to heavy grazing by sheep, wild flowers are not so abundant, but he cites a list including crowberry, club moss, pyramidal bugle and dwarf juniper.[4] I have noticed juniper taking hold on the wild side of the island.

As for mammals, small animals such as shrews, field mice and voles can be found. These creatures don't make a habit of showing themselves, but no visitor can miss the spectacle of Muck's resident grey Atlantic seal population. They laze on rocks near the pier as if to greet new arrivals, but they are even more numerous near Gallanach on the extensive low rocks just offshore at Rubha Port na Creadhain.

Seals at Gallanach

If you are in luck, you can hear them sing. I give myself a pat on the back if I can watch them lie around without any of them heaving themselves up to splat into the water – it means that they don't feel under scrutiny.

RETURN TO MUCK

Singing seals
Under the cliff breakers crash,
shingle deafens as it's dragged.
The deep bass
of grinding, scouring,
out of tune with cormorants
and keening of kittiwakes.
Herring gulls screech,
high-pitched, discordant,
their sullen faces mock.

In a soft hiatus,
on the far rocks
I hear singing seals,
choirboys humming
in harmony and counterpoint
under the cloud-bossed roof
of the blue cathedral.

I close my eyes and wait

wait

for the most precious moment:
a chord of resolution.

Seals with Rum in the background

Tramping over the island, waterproof trousers were often de rigueur and I was always shod in my walking boots. Normally I didn't get my feet wet despite the odd soggy bog. The weather could be a fierce challenge. One very rough day it took me ten minutes to don my boots, overtrousers and Gore-Tex raincoat, not to mention stashing my heavily protected music books in the rucksack.

Children made full use of their one-piece waterproofs and wellies on rainy days as they walked to school, and the first things you would notice if you entered the school building were the wellies and waterproofs on pegs, benches and the floor.

I was always impressed by the heroic tasks parents had to undertake just to clothe their young children for rough weather. An account of one such moment is described in the following poem.

Wellies

Going out, coming in, wellies on, wellies off.
Mum bends, arms and legs in and out,
toddler squiggles,
undertrousers, overtrousers,
waterproof jacket.

Mum's hand grips the dog's lead,
one arm for the baby-seat,
one arm for her own right boot,-
one arm for toddler's left foot.

Not quite making it,
toddler topples
onto the wet floor.
Springs up like that rubber toy
you push from the base,
paddles in the hallway,
sodden socks,
falls over dad's boots.

Wellies in school porch

Dog lurches from the loosened lead,
licks him better.
Mum grabs dog, child, lead,
one leg in her overtrousers, trips
over, splat,
all fall down,
except the baby, asleep in her seat.

Waterproofs became a familiar sight during my regular visits to the school as a music teacher. In the early years I had discovered that regular piano tuition had never been available on Muck, and after talking with many residents and the school teacher, the idea was born of a project to offer some musical input to children and adults. This was to include classroom music sessions, individual lessons and an adult choir. I ran two five-week phases; the first in the spring of 2009 and the second in the summer of 2010. Both parts were of five weeks' duration. So those years, when I disembarked from the ferry, I had extra baggage for Rosie's wheelbarrow – my keyboard and lots of sheet music.

Deciding the location and timetabling of these individual lessons was tricky. Finding out which pupil (or adult) had access to piano or keyboard for practising purposes brought interesting challenges. There were only four pianos on the island. The children's individual lessons had to take place after school, but it was necessary to timetable lessons on

School session, 2009

keyboards when there was electricity. The school had its own generator but it was not failsafe. Once the electricity went off in the middle of a child's keyboard lesson. I encouraged him to continue playing and scrutinised his fingers. We both enjoyed the fun of silent sight-reading and playing.

During the second phase the following year I was thrilled to discover that one or two keyboards had been bought by the parents. This meant that practice at home between lessons was possible. Generally the children did not practise much – they were too busy playing or helping out with farm activities such as sheep-shearing – but the adults were more motivated. Being peripatetic was good for my exercise regime. Setting out one stormy day, to teach Jenny piano and singing at the farmhouse, I trudged through gateways, over a cattle grid, avoiding cowpats and sheep dung on the track, and was nearly blown over by the wind. I had to dodge the waves at Gallanach beach which came over the road itself. Yet on another much quieter day, the sight of the sea around Rum in a purple hue and the eerie drumming sounds of snipe accompanied my walk home in the dusk.

View of Rum in a purple glow

The children were very keen on singing, two boys having lovely musical voices. One of these left the island and auditioned successfully for the Highland Youth Choir, and much later he studied music at university. During my project a film-maker, who was also working with the children, needed a musical score. We used a tune I had composed many years before and encouraged the children to make up a song about ecological issues, praising the clean and safe Muck environment. 'We've no need for keys, we've no burglaries.'

The choir – the one activity where visitors were welcome – met for an hour and a half once a week, and was great fun. Attendance improved gradually and by the end of the second phase we had nineteen people; always a good core of islanders, but not enough men, which is a characteristic of amateur choirs. I tried to recruit the reluctant men of Muck, so on my tramps, if I came across a man on his own, I asked him if he'd like to join the choir – 'I can't sing!' was the stock reply.

Two choir sessions were memorable. At one, four hefty 'yachties' burst into the school hall late and noisily, encumbered by their yellow waterproof gear (despite it being a fine evening), and announced they couldn't stay long. However, they stayed and sang lustily until the end. At another session a closet chorister who was 'just visiting' arrived. He had a wonderful voice. Three or four youngsters sidled in as well, declaring they wouldn't sing, but my old inner-city classroom tactics put paid to that idea; they too settled down and sang well.

We worked towards a musical performance at the end of both phases. All the islanders were invited, as well as visitors. The programme included pupils playing or singing solos, pieces from a guitar and clarsach (a Gaelic harp), and an adult recorder duet. The children's group sang 'Kalinka' and danced with as much gusto as the Red Army Choir. The adult choir sang a sensitive 'Dona Nobis Pacem' and then gave a rowdy rendition of 'Any Dream Will Do.'

At the end of the performance, the choir, children and audience all sang a 'round'. I had made up new words to a Canadian folk song, and the tune and lyrics were very easy for all to pick up. Half of the audience sang 'Isle of Muck' (or 'I love Muck') while the rest sang the main lyrics at the same time. A rich texture of sounds emerged, the words summing up the island community spirit; 'This is the Isle of Muck/wonderful people/ We're one big family/Join us today!' (See appendix for musical score.)

One of these 'wonderful people' was Catherine, who had helped me enormously with logistics to do with timetable organising. Going to her house on the wooded hill at Dùn Ban was a treat. I accompanied her singing, on her piano, and gave lessons to two of her four children. On school days they had about half a mile to walk to and from school and I would often meet them coming or going as I've described in the following poem.

After school
Catherine collects them right on time,
but they wander, dawdle,
play on the swing,
Oliver's minuscule bike parked on the ground,
minuscule helmet on his head.
He climbs the wall
to wait for big brother Edward at the cattle grid.

Edward's supposed to only use the road
but sometimes he takes a long short cut
jumping over bogs and stones and tufts and cowpats, through the wood and beyond.
Catherine gives up, off home for a cuppa,
knowing they're safe.
Perhaps Ty the farm dog will round them up.

One Saturday in June 2012 I rode the bike that I had borrowed from the farm to Gallanach, and left it against the barn wall. I walked across to the west side of the island, had a rest at the lovely viewpoint at the Rock of Mare's Leap (Rubh' Leum na Làraich), then followed the shore southwards, on sheep tracks. Taking the steep path from the south up to Beinn Airein, with a sheer drop to my right, I reached the trig point.

On the way back I made my way to Gallanach past Camas Mòr, admiring again the amazing limestone pavements on the shore. Muck has a thin 'waist' in the middle, so that you can walk from the main south bay (Camas Mòr) to the main north bay (Gallanach) in about fifteen minutes. Back near the farmhouse I was greeted by an unexpected and wonderful sight: 190 sheep were being sheared. Lawrence and Jenny's son Colin, and his wife Ruth, had by now taken over most of the responsibility of running the farm, but the older couple were still

Cattle grid, with Canna in the distance

very much 'hands on'. Colin, together with Dave, Barnaby and Sandy, were doing the shearing. Ruth was pulling the sheep from the front of the 'race' and dragging them one by one to the next free shearer. I marvelled at her strength; the sheep were heavy.

Lawrence was the chief fleece folder, as befitted the laird, and stood in the middle of the action. He was making a very neat job of it. He was aided by Catherine and Patrick (a relative newcomer), who were putting the folded fleeces into huge bags. When one of these was full, Catherine sewed up the bag with twine. The young boys, some of my pupils – Archie, Alexander, Edward and Oliver – were larking about in the sheep pen squashed up with the waiting sheep, pulling them by the ears and pushing them one by one into the narrow 'race'. The race held about four sheep at a time and they were prevented from escaping at the front end by a plank of wood. The children, excited and laughing, were having the time of their lives. Ben was on the far side of the shed watching the other boys and using the bags as a slide. Isobel played the older sister and was attempting to tell the boys what to do.

I just smiled and, like Ben, watched.

After this treat, I left them, rode my bike back towards the bunkhouse, and passed another bike at the Green Barn halfway to Port. For several years this old green ladies' bike was propped against the barn wall and never moved. Quaint, or just normal? After all, I have several important sticks of various sizes that have been propped up next to my side gate for ten years.

Visitors have no need to know
Green bike propped against the wall,
next to the green barn
where Geoff and Ros are plotting veggies.
Ladies' V-shaped frame, hugely rusted.
I'm not going to ask who owned it.

Eight pink piglets in the byre
snuggling head to toe,
like sausages with faces,
one splotchy, open-eyed.
Perhaps they know their fate.
I'm not going to ask about it.

People are often curious or amused that the island is called Muck, so I did some research. It was customary in Samuel Johnson's time for lairds of islands to be addressed as the name of their island. For example, to greet the laird of Coll you would say, 'Good evening, Coll.' James Boswell wrote of himself and Johnson meeting Isle of Muck. Boswell relates, 'It was somewhat droll to hear this laird called by his title. Muck would have sounded ill; so he was called Isle of Muck, which went off with great readiness.'[5] Boswell went on to write that this laird insisted that Isle of Monk was its proper name. Even these days people are not used to the name, and seemingly this laird was embarrassed by his being addressed simply as Muck, as I would be.

Piglets in the byre. It is possible that the name Muck is derived from the Gaelic 'muc', meaning 'pig'

But many sources explain that the name of Muck (Gaelic muc) refers to the Gaelic for pig, or swine. *Muc na mhara* means sea-pig, a generic name for whales and dolphins. Historically the island was known as a favourite haunt of the wild pig and it was said that Muck's shape was that of a pig. In the Highlands, the boar's head and flesh were eaten with relish, but the domestic pig's meat was deemed inedible. Muck was seen as a sanctuary for the wild boar. Folklore tells that whenever their number grew too many for the small island they were pushed off the coast to swim to Eigg and from there to Skye, and back to the mainland. The idea was to improve hunting. How the pigs were prevented from swimming back to the Muck shore as soon as they were pushed into the water is not explained.

Staying with the pig or boar reference, I recount a tale about a certain boar with lethal bristles, resident on Muck. Fionn is a well-known hero of many a Gaelic romance, and his band of heroes are known as the Feinn. The better-known English form of Fionn is Fingal (as in Fingal's Cave, on the island of Staffa). One of the Feinn, a friend of Fionn, was the Scottish and Irish hero Diarmad. Most stories of Diarmad are set in Ireland but as the Feinn hunted boar it doesn't seem too far-fetched for a Diarmad/Fionn story to be associated with the Isle of Muck, in addition to many other islands that have adopted the story.

Once there was a young man called Diarmad who was irresistible to women, and (or because) he had a love spot on his forehead. Seeing him, every woman immediately fell in love with him. He and his friend Fionn decided to go to Muck to hunt boar, accompanied by Grainne, a beautiful woman. Grainne and Fionn had been lovers until Grainne had seen Diarmad's love spot and changed allegiance.

Among the Muck boars, there was one that had poisonous bristles. Diarmad knew of a prophecy that he would be killed by a boar but he was a brave man and went hunting undeterred. He came across the bristly boar, a struggle ensued, and he was fatally wounded by its spikes. Fionn ran up to him, saw that the boar was dead, and Diarmad mortally wounded. Fionn's first instinct was to race to the Well of Healing, in an unspecified place, to gather magic water to save Diarmad.

But Fionn was in two minds. He was torn between wanting to save his friend, and anger that Diarmad had stolen Grainne's love from him. Fionn came back to the dying Diarmad with well water in the cup of his hands, but he changed his mind about helping him and poured the water on the ground. Then his conscience pricked; he recalled how Diarmad had been a true friend, so he ran back to the healing well again. This happened three times. The third time he knelt by his wounded friend, poured the well water into a cup, and held it to his lips. But it was too late; Diarmad fell back dead from the boar's poison bristles.[6]

We are not told what Grainne felt, said or did, but I am curious to look for more versions of the story to flesh out the details. I even found a very fancy one written in German, but, alas, my knowledge of that language has declined, and I didn't get very far.

In comparison with many of the larger Scottish islands, there are sadly very few folktales associated specifically with Muck and, as will be apparent, I've had to dig deep and use author's licence to link the Diarmad and Grainne story with Muck. According to John Hunter,[7] during the time of eviction and emigration (the Clearances) in the first part of the 19th century, many island families and social groups left their homes, usually for Canada, which led to reduced populations. When incomers eventually started to settle in these small islands, the social structures, traditions, folklore and customs that had developed over hundreds of years became gradually forgotten.

Yet not all traditional customs are lost. In most of the Scottish islands, the gales and wind often result in damage, so the custom lives on, of tying down, or up, or round, even large and heavy objects. On other islands newly renovated blackhouses' thatched roofs are tied down with rope and large stones, and on Muck I found at least three objects that had been made wind-proof with rope or strong tape.

Two tied-up objects

*An old Land Rover above the bunkhouse
has the best view over to the mainland.
Doors and bonnet bundled with sturdy blue rope;
the wind might expose the engine otherwise.*

*The turf-roofed bothy near Shell Beach,
posh white-striped tape around its middle,
door and windows barred,
inviting nosey-parkers.*

The bothy near Bagh was tied up with tape for many years

*A puzzle this – perhaps one day
the owner will charter a helicopter
to hoist the whole structure
and deposit it in his Edinburgh back garden.
While he's at it, he could take the Land Rover
and phone box too,
and charge mainland folk to view.*

In my wanderings around the island I discovered two small areas where I could get a phone signal. In the early years I didn't have a smartphone and was dependent on my mobile unless I asked a resident to borrow their landline. There was a computer with internet access in the Craft Shop, which I used to email family. A lone telephone box stood just up the slope from the bunkhouse and, unlike so many public booths, it was clean inside, despite an obvious history of an ill-fitting door that was upside down.

Phone call
The phone box door, upside-down,
says llnd instead of pull.
A big stone used to stop it from flapping open.
Now, its blue string not quite thick enough to call rope,
is tied, fraying at the corner,
a girdle for the booth's waist.

Phone booth with upside-down door

It works,
they told me.
Coat tightly done up against the cold,
I try phoning.

First, undo the blue rope
wrapped around it like a belt.
No need to stand on my head
to open the door.
Lift the receiver, a dialling tone!
Hopes rise and then collapse.
'This phone for emergency calls only.'
Nothing for it, use the mobile.

I tie the rope up again.

There's just a small half-sheltered spot
a hundred yards from the bunkhouse,
where there's a signal good enough.

Facing the worn-out generator
I cower in the gale.
Wind-chill factor minus twenty,
horizontal sleet and snow.
No response.

Tributes and memories of my early years
She who gave me tea and cake when her baby was poorly,
he who showed me a newly hatched corncrake,
she who cut hair in return for bartered services,
he who could play tunes on the piano by ear
but struggled with reading music,
he who roamed the land always clad in a tattered jacket.
She who, nurse-trained, inspected my tick bite,
she whose painting Ken bought and which adorns his fireplace,
he who dug across a track to lay a pipe to his new house,
and put up a MAN AT WORK sign.
She who gifted superior cakes on numerous occasions,
she who sang, kept bees, had four children and organised my timetable,
she who cared.

The sweet sound of the turbine blades,
duck nests in the barn,
the shortcut to school past the horses,
the first goslings seen that spring,
different methods of lighting gas
according to electricity status,
wind blowing down Jasper.

At the end of each visit I like to do a farewell climb. This time I've walked up the steep eastern side of Beinn Airein. There haven't been many birds – a pair of stonechats, some wheatears. After sitting with my back against the trig point, I stand up, not knowing which view I want to see more of; a difficult decision.

*

From the sea or from neighbouring islands Muck looks like a low-lying plank with a small bump, but views from Muck are magical. I enjoy the 360-degree view in bright hazy sunshine. The Beinn is just 137 metres above sea level. Some of Muck's features, including Port Mòr, are hidden behind crags and low-lying tree plantations.

I gaze at the spiky Cuillin of Skye in the far north, and Rum, Eigg, Canna, Mull, and of course the mainland towards the south, nicely defined by the just-about-visible lighthouse at Ardnamurchan Point. Rum and Eigg have such distinctive skylines; Eigg's Sgurr with its knobbly crest looks almost unnatural, and Rum's triangular mountains could have been designed by a child. On showery days you can watch Rum disappear and reappear in the space of a minute, as its higher mountains attract rain and clouds. Canna has a low table-shaped silhouette.

View of Eigg from trig point

From the same spot on a much clearer day, I can make out a lighthouse to the west of Canna and discover it's Hyskeir. I can even see Tiree peeping up behind Coll. Five triangular bumps on the horizon to the far west are the hills of the Western Isles, and, with screwed-up eyes, another lighthouse – is it an illusion? No, someone tells me later it's Barra Head lighthouse.

This time I've noticed a small plane coming over from the south-east, high but dark against the blue sky. Keeping my eyes fixed on its progress, it seems to be heading straight for Muck, but as it approaches it doesn't start to dip. I'm glad of that as there is nowhere for even a small plane to land. I suddenly realise that the plane is no plane, but a huge bird flying very swiftly. It's most likely a sea eagle on its way from Mull to Rum.

My gaze falls on the road now, winding past the farmhouse at Gallanach. I will be down there in twenty minutes or so. And I wonder which island I feel most drawn to next.

1. Cuddyport
2. Achamore House
3. South End Pier
4. Tarbert
5. The Twin Beaches
6. Gallachoille
7. Càrn Bàn
8. Beach of the Fish Trap
   (Camas Nàireach)
9. Ardlamy
10. Sloc an Leim
11. The Twin Stones
    (Bodach & Cailleach)
12. Kilchattan Church
13. Cara House
14. Brownie's Chair
15. School
16. Church
17. Ogham Stone
18. Water Mill
19. Giant's Tooth
20. Wind farm

N
W E
S

Creag Bhan
100m

GIGHA

Ardminish

Sound of Gigha

Achamore
Gardens

Gigha

Gigalum

Cara

Area of Gigha:
6 miles long x 1½ miles
wide, approx

CHAPTER 2
GIGHA

’m always fascinated by the lack of certain mammals in small islands. On Gigha there are no squirrels, hares, foxes, moles, stoats, hedgehogs or weasels. But rabbits, mice and rats abound, even feral cats. Minks, escapees from mink farms, can be a problem in parts of Scotland, and sadly one mink found its way to Gigha recently. The islanders thought it had sneaked onto a ferry, with or without human help. This mink played havoc with a large collection of chickens, and killed forty of them. Mink traps have been set to stop this happening again.

You can take a few routes to get to Gigha, depending on your start point and inclination. It's a small island just off the west coast of the Kintyre peninsula, so you need to get to Kintyre somehow, which isn't straightfor-

Pier at Cuddyport

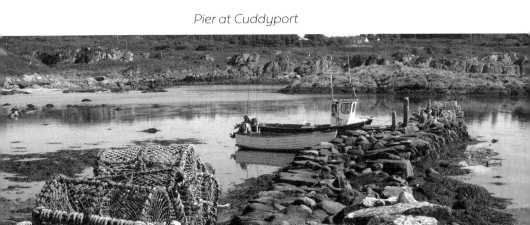

ward. As regards public transport, there is no train service into Kintyre and a bus journey from Glasgow to Tayinloan could take you three or four hours. You take the ferry from Tayinloan over to Gigha, either with your car or not, but best check if there is a mink on board.

Gigha, pronounced Ghee-a, is not well known, partly because it's so small, but it was once an important commercial route up and down the west coast of Scotland, because of its geographical location. It has been inhabited since prehistoric times. In the 18th century there were about 700 people – it currently has a population of 160.

*

The scenic route from Ayrshire, travelling by car, involves three ferries. My journey could have gone wrong at any point. In July 2017 I boarded the CalMac ferry from Ardrossan on the Ayrshire coast to Brodick on Arran, and drove from Brodick to Lochranza, with fond memories of last year's stay with my family on the island. I waited in the hot sun at Lochranza for the modest boat to Claonaig, a tiny unheard-of place on the east coast of the Kintyre peninsula. There were very few cars on this ferry. It was a short wild drive on a B road to the main Kintyre road, where, an hour after the left turn, I arrived at Tayinloan.

I left the car in the Tayinloan car park and walked on to the ferry from Tayinloan to Gigha; just a twenty-minute trip. The island is seven miles long and about a mile and a half at its widest point. Cycling is the best option for Gigha; there's a cycle hire shop near the ferry terminal.

This poem shows the romantic names of the seas I crossed that day – the Firth of Clyde, Kilbrannen Sound, and the Sound of Gigha.

Musical Waters: three ferries to Gigha
The first, the Firth of Clyde,
a lisping motion, pizzicato
as befits a hissing puffer
in the Para Handy days.*

Kilbrannen Sound, low pitched,
cool murmurs in Eb minor.
A lullaby cantabile
in six smooth quavers to the bar.

The Sound of Gigha, freer,
F major moderato,
a twenty-minute piece,
a brighter, higher pitch.

White horses swish
like grace notes,
rise above my excitement,
reaching the finale.

*Para Handy, novel by Neil Munro.[1]

There being no hostel or bunkhouse on the island, I stayed that first visit in a B&B with Alasdair MacNeill, a much-respected resident, who met me at the ferry. Up the short road from the ferry we passed the school, post office-cum-shop, church and a hotel at the tiny village of Ardminish. The MacNeill family has been on the island since around 1493, and even now there are numerous family members on Gigha, some of whom I was to meet.

Alasdair and I had some fascinating talks about Gigha. One morning we sat in his living room. 'I had a marvellous childhood,' he said, 'there was always more time to talk to each other. People in general were much gentler.'

I asked him about his school days. 'I remember the day I went to the Gigha primary school in 1948. We had slates and a slate pencil; this was long like a biro. As it wore down it was much easier to work with!'

I was interested in this, as I remember using slates, but not slate pencils.

'The teacher could be very strict; she had red hair and a tawse!'

She had the children listen to records on a wind-up gramophone, and played the piano.

'Uncle Donald played the fiddle. The kids imitated him by pretending to play the fiddle with rulers.'

He remembered James Horlick (of bedtime drink fame) who bought Gigha in 1944, and in particular Horlick's generosity to the islanders. 'Farms were done up, he employed people, every household had at least one jar of Horlick's in their cupboards, and he put on parties for the workers,' Alasdair told me.

*

I could tell from Alasdair's memories of Sir James Horlick that he had a great deal of respect for him. This is not surprising when you look into Horlick's life history. Born in 1886, Horlick went to Oxford, developed a passion for cricket, and took six wickets for 90 runs against Harrow at Lords. He also played cricket for Gloucestershire as an amateur. In the First World War he joined the Coldstream Guards, and served in France, the Balkans and South Russia. He was mentioned in dispatches four

44

times and awarded the Military Cross (British), the Légion d'Honneur (France) and the White Eagle of Serbia. With his brother, in 1908 he set up the factory of Horlick Malted Milk in Slough, Berkshire, where the famous malted drink was made for around 100 years. He was the Conservative MP for Gloucester between 1923 and 1929.

Having never drunk Horlicks, I think I'd better start, as a different advert says it's for the aged and travellers.

*

As I have noted, in 1944 at the age of 58, Horlick bought Achamore House and Gardens. He had been searching around the west coast of Scotland for a suitable place to buy where he could indulge in his passion for rhodo-dendrons and azaleas. Gigha was that place. Sir James was an enthusiastic plantsman and wanted a garden where he could grow exotic shrubs, especially the more tender rhododendrons that flourish in the relatively mild and frost-free climate. In the 1940s the gardens already contained mature trees planted by previous owners which made for a luxurious canopy over a large area. Thanks to Horlick's intense enthusiasm, the gardens became a wonderful kaleidoscope of rhododendrons, camellias, azaleas and other subtropical shrubs. He was awarded the Victoria Medal of Honour as a rhododendron breeder in 1963. He lived in the house until he died in 1972, and is buried in the new graveyard of Kilchattan church.

We can deduce from this potted history of some of his achievements that James Horlick threw himself into everything he set his mind to do. On his death he left much of his plant collection to the National Trust for Scotland and a small endowment to fund the propagation of rare species, but sadly the gardens slithered into a decline and the house was uninhab-ited for some years. The house is now in private hands and can't be visited. But the gardens can.

*

Gigha was completely treeless in the 17th century. The first chronicler of island travels, Martin Martin, wrote in 1695, 'This isle affords no wood of any kind, but a few bushes of juniper on the little hills.'[2] However, Hamish Haswell-Smith writes in *The Scottish Islands* that Gigha 'has more trees than many Scottish islands', and cites 'scrub willow, prostrate juniper, sycamore, thorn, alder, birch and hazel' as thriving.[3]

It was a grey, drizzly day when I wandered around the gardens on that first visit, the trees sheltering me from the nippy wind. The magnificence of the exotic trees, bushes, plants and peacocks was in marked contrast to the rest of the island which is a mixture of farmland and moorland.

Peacocks in Achamore Gardens

I picked up a map of the gardens. Peacocks stood in small groups behind the main kitchen garden, where old greenhouses and sheds were waiting for much TLC. I sat on a bench with camomile tea in a flask, and ate a banana. A cat wanted to sit with me, but I warded him off. He came back; he was probably lonely. I met no gardener in the hours I was there. There was a recruitment notice for volunteer gardeners; a massive amount of work was required. I discovered that I couldn't shake off a low mood, as seeing all this unintended neglect of what was once a magnificent garden was depressing. It made me think that if I'd had a companion with me, it might have lightened the moment.

After negotiating a bamboo maze rather too easily, I climbed an old flight of steps up a steep slope and had a surprise view of the west side of the island. I breathed into the fresh breeze. Climbing back down the steps, I passed the house, and into the wilder part in front of it. I saw a spindly plant I'd not seen before, growing in the marshy area around the rim of a pond. I looked it up; it was a primula candelabra. This discovery lightened my mood.

Primula candelabra, species planted by Horlick

*

I discovered the Gigha wind farm after I left Achamore Gardens, and walked slowly south to the end of the road in Gigha, noticing some of the colourful shrubs and bushes at the edge of the gardens. Gigha Renewable Energy Ltd (GREL) is Scotland's first community-owned grid-connected wind farm, and is an excellent success story. Like Eigg, Knoydart and other islands or part-islands, Gigha is owned by its residents. The largest community buy-out of an island in British history happened in 2002, islanders forming the Isle of Gigha Heritage Trust (IGHT) and within four years the population increased by more than 50 per cent.

The trust was working on many projects, including the restoration of the gardens, as well as the refurbishment of housing, restructuring of farmland and the creation of new businesses. Brandon Clements, a 19-year old, had just become a director of the trust. His vision for the next five years was 'to see Gigha with no debt, with a lower age average and new houses and community buildings for the islanders'.[4] He had hopes to persuade others of a similar age to build their lives on Gigha to counter its ageing profile.

As I walked, a blaze of red blossom at the roadside momentarily brightened the drizzly day. Just before South End pier, the end of the seven-mile road that dissects Gigha from south to north, I came across the gate leading to the wind farm. I am all in favour of wind farms, as long as there are not too many bunched up in otherwise wild, unspoilt moorland areas. A display board at the gate gave me digital information that included wind speed energy output as well as other current (!) readings. £31,345 sounded a goodly figure for that month's income. Belatedly I realised that the digits on the panel wouldn't come out on my camera photo. I forgot the video function.

It was an east wind – no surprise – I'd had to wrap myself up. In the summer Gigha is a net exporter of electricity, generating 25 per cent more energy than it uses throughout the year. There are four wind turbines, three of them having names: Faith, Hope and Charity, the Dancing Ladies. The fourth turbine, built later than the other three, is called Harmony.

Some things on my travels remain a mystery... including this sign

NO SOCKS AND SANDALS BEYOND THIS POINT

As I walked away from the information board, I noticed a stile over a fence leading into a field full of weeds and wildflowers. I saw no path on the other side, but a notice on the fence caught my attention. I pondered long and hard. The terrain in the field behind looked boggy so it might have been asking me to walk barefoot, or conversely to put on formal dress. I did neither, and continued walking on the road. I never found out the answer to this puzzle. Some things I've encountered on my travels remain a mystery.

Reaching the small harbour and rickety fishing pier at South End, I felt a little sad, just as I'd experienced in the kitchen gardens earlier. There was no one there except Alasdair's brother John, a tall, quietly spoken elderly man, who was tinkering with his hauled-up fishing boat, and we exchanged a few words.

From the pier I could see a tiny island. I was impressed by its name – Gigalum – it made me think of schoolgirls (including my younger self) giggling, unable to stop. The bigger island further away was Cara Island, which I write about later.

*

I was yet to meet other MacNeills, relatives of Alasdair. From the end of the road I accepted a lift from a couple in a car and they dropped me off where there's a turn to the right to South Druimachro. Perhaps a nice beach to explore along there, I thought, as the rain had let up a little; so I wandered along the unmade track, pausing to inspect a purple spotted orchid on the verge, and eventually found not a beach, but a sign saying Caroline's Wee Shed. I was nosy and found Caroline pottering outside her house, and we fell into conversation. She told me she was a niece of Alasdair. She had been crafting small gifts for about five years, selling tourist mementos from Gigha, such as brooches, Christmas decorations, knitted chickens and bears. Inside her Aladdin's cave of her 'shed', I inhaled with delight the lovely smell of soaps, incense sticks and bath bombs. I bought a pair of Celtic cross earrings.

From her I learnt that the family of Mcneill, or MacNeill, made up a sizable proportion of the present island population. Caroline often received visitors from the diaspora. Visitors walk up from the ferry terminal and say, 'I'm Walter MacNeill, what's your name?' She told me: 'MacNeill people come from Texas or other places in the States, to chase their ancestors. It's like closure for them when they find their relatives up in the graveyard.' The MacNeills have family gatherings both in the States and on Gigha. Caroline was looking forward to another family get-together soon.

Her grandfather was Duncan MacNeill. 'He was a fisherman; he was very tall and had huge hands like shovels. He worked in Keills in Islay. And my uncle John, who is in his eighties, still goes out fishing.' I told her I'd come across him at the South End pier.

*

Determined to explore Gigha as much as possible, one hot morning I wandered along the road northwards. Because the road is narrow, and this was high summer, the verges were strimmed, but tall bracken had been left along what would be the field edge, so as to look like a hedge. Purple loosestrife, brambles, dock leaves, meadowsweet and umbellifers, some quite tall grasses, Yorkshire fog, and the huge giant hogweed all adorned the verge.

This blue tractor was parked for good, throttled by nettles, grasses, tufted vetch, the Gigha version of knapweed, and thistles. Harebells in Scotland seem to be a deeper, more purple colour than in Yorkshire. A very fresh green fern caught my eye; the fronds were not opposite each other and I made a mental note to look it up, which I did, but still couldn't identify it. Massive clumps of bell heather were flaming.

Tractor parked for good

I took a track to the left towards Ardailly and after cresting the watershed I was now able to see the sea on the west side of the island; the islands of Islay and Jura are so close together that you can't always tell where one ends and the other begins. I looked out for the Paps of Jura, three conical hills that are Jura's icons.

On my way towards the old water mill near Port an Duin, I happened upon a couple who were hard at work building a cluster of eco buildings. The main living house was already up, but not yet running. They invited me in to have a look and I was particularly taken with the skylight in the roof that gave extra light to the whole house. The man was Tony Philpin, of the Gigha Coast and Countryside team. He told me that the team, which included John Bannatyne, a ferry skipper, were working towards making Gigha landmarks more accessible to the visitor. A little later I took my leave of the Philpins, and continued my walking.

The old mill, which was in the gardens of a private cottage, was down by the shore.

The old water mill

As no one was around, I climbed over the fence to inspect more closely the ruins of this 18th-century oatmeal mill. Water was supplied to it by two artificial lochs, Mill Loch and Upper Loch, which I'd noticed earlier. The huge rusty wheel was still firmly attached to the roofless building, whose interior was gutted and strewn with millstones and machinery. Despite the sea being extremely close to the mill, the vegetation between mill and coast was high and impenetrable-looking. I wondered if it was easier to negotiate in the winter. I used my arms to 'swim' through the tall rushes, and my boots squelched through puddles and stream-water, until I came to firmer ground, which was the grassy, rocky sea-edge. A small rest, listening to the lapping waves. No birds – they were hiding from the heat. Retracing my steps to the watershed, I took the path to the top of Creag Bhan, the highest point of Gigha at 100 metres, following a path from behind the covered reservoir. I skipped over stones and tufts of heather, but the path was not too steep, and there was a wondrous blue-sky view from the top, with a trig point and a viewpoint indicator giving me pointers to nearby and faraway islands, as well as the Kintyre coast. A mouthful of tea from my flask was in order.

Summit of Creag Bhan

This walk to Creag Bhan had been easy to follow from the map with the help of a few signposts, so hats off to the Coast and Countryside team.

*

The very narrow small loch called Tarr an Tarbh (tail of the bull) is on the west side of the island, not far from the old mill. The loch is supposed to hide a shy bull-like monster that Hamish Haswell-Smith 'may have actually seen', according to his book, *An Island Odyssey*. He tells of a cycle trip with his son Peter, near Mill Loch. A bull stood in the middle of the track, blocking their passage but not in a threatening way. He wouldn't budge to let them pass. They greeted him in a polite way (like you do with the Brownie on Cara, of whom more later), and rode past on either side of him.[5]

An earlier account of the bull story is made by R. S. G. Anderson. An islander came across the shy bull, leapt into the air with surprise, and landed a mile away in the sea at Ardlamy Bay, in a pool known as Slubha an Tarbh Uisge, Pool of the Water Bull. I wish there were more details in this story, so I'm left wondering if, and how, he swam back.[6]

*

On another sunny day, I walked from Alasdair's, passing the Giant's Tooth stone, which is in a very obvious spot on the narrowest part of the island. It's also known as the Hanging Stone and probably the best known of Gigha's prehistoric monuments. It looks like an enormous incisor thrust in the ground, and is thought to have been used as a place of execution. If it looks familiar it's because it's part of the Heritage Trust's emblem.

The Giant's Tooth stone

Frantic hay-making near Tarbert was taking place and I admired the wide strips of ground suddenly changing colour as the mowers moved. I was walking slowly because of the heat, but wanted to reach the top of the island in time for a bit of exploration, so I decided to try for a lift. Apart from the hay-makers none of the 160 inhabitants, not to mention a tourist, was about, so I carried on walking on the road for about two miles. I had misjudged my liquid needs and was very thirsty, so I went into Tarbert Farm and asked for water. The busy farmer showed me their kitchen, and left me to gulp down quantities from the tap and refill my flask. He was in work mode and probably didn't want to waste a second of hay-making time by chatting with me.

To the east of Tarbert Farm lies an important well that features in many a tale, but I wasn't looking for it this time. Tobar a'Bheathaig, or Bheathaig's Well, is on the northern slopes of Cnoc Largie, and Martin Martin wrote that it had healing waters, a catholicon for diseases.[7] More recently Hamish Haswell-Smith writes that only residents were allowed to lift up the capstone, so if you were a master of a foreign boat and were held up on Gigha because of bad winds, you could ask a local person to open the well up, and give him or her a piece of money. Then they would throw the well-water in the required direction, and the wind would follow suit.[8] Other offerings besides money were common: a needle, pin, or even a brightly coloured pebble. A. A. MacGregor wrote that 'the MacNeills would go to the well when their galleys were wind-bound, and by stirring the water with a cane, a favourable wind arose and conducted them whither they wished to sail.'[9]

In Catherine Czerkawska's book *The Way it Was*, she describes impressively how, after much searching, but with a local man's help, they found the well hidden in the undergrowth, complete with running water and a capstone.[10] Perhaps this important treasure needs to be waymarked, so that friendly visitors like me can find it easily and enjoy it. It would save a great deal of fruitless searching and ankle-breaking trampling in bracken and rough ground.

After a while of trudging on the road past the thinnest part of the island, I finally saw a car park near a signposted path pointing towards an impressive isthmus: Eilean Garbh and the twin beaches, a tiny island linked to Gigha by a spit of land. As the track reached some bushes it became very muddy, and upturned plastic containers had been placed for stepping 'stones'. I was delighted to discover water forget-me-not in a large puddle.

One or two people were around before me, picnicking or exploring the area. The sandy beach facing north, Bàgh na Dòirlinne, is backed by a pebble beach facing south, Bàgh Rubha Ruaidh. This beach, in contrast to its twin, sadly collects all kinds of flotsam and jetsam. I was desperate for some shade, and managed to find a spot under some big rocks on the north-facing litterless beach with its fine hot sand. Bliss. As usual the only dog within three miles' radius found me and asked me to play with him – I declined. But a solo paddle was in order, so off came my boots and socks, and into the water I went; more bliss. It was hard to imagine on this windless day that the sea could ever breach the isthmus.

This was the end of my exploring for this day, and I regained the road. I didn't have time to go up to the most northern part of Gigha. If I'd done so, I'd have passed an old quarry, taken a path through the bracken and reached the very old North Cairn from which there are wondrous views towards Knapdale, Jura and Islay. (I did get to the North Cairn eventually.)

'You can't do everything,' I said to myself, and this time I was lucky trying for a lift; a friendly couple on holiday took me back to Alasdair's before I expired with the heat. Later I heard that it was the hottest day on Gigha that summer.

*

I stayed at Mary's B&B on my second visit to Gigha a year later, in September, when I took the car. There was still no bunkhouse on the island! One morning at breakfast, I watched the birds at Mary's bird table, where she'd put a lot of scraps as well as seeds. The birds were having a bonanza. My own feeder in Leeds has a baffle to deter squirrels, and birds are always on the look-out for interlopers. Here in Gigha there was no need for a wire feeder with a baffle; only small friendly birds visited their table – no greedy magpies or pigeons. It was Mary who told me about the marauding mink.

I was out early for a walk, passed Caroline's house and wandered to the end of Druimachro Road where I came across yet another old pier, at Gallochoille Port. There was John the fisherman again! He showed me a small queue of oyster bags in the shallows near the pier – they had nothing to do with him, but would be collected later and taken to a nearby shed to be graded.

We also spoke about creel making. He told me he was the last lobster-creel maker on the island, and pointed out its features, including a heavy stone at the base. It takes some doing to bend the hazel stems to the correct arch-shape for the two ends of the creel.

Lobster creel

As we were chatting, a trio of calves were picking their way across the rocks and shallow water between a small island just across from where we were standing. They seemed to prefer to keep their legs on the sandy bits and not to step on to the rocks, so their passage was somewhat zigzag. John told me that the calves never got stranded – he had watched them swim across at high tide when their mother had summoned them. I would love to see that.

I revisited Achamore Gardens that year after my first visit. This time there were people there and the kitchen garden was in a much tidier state. I congratulated Helen, the newly appointed main gardener, who was hard at work shredding garden waste, aided by two volunteers. The dull mood that I had experienced from the garden's neglect the previous year wasn't there this time – it was so good to see it being tended.

*

Later I met a cousin of Alasdair's, Malcolm. We spoke just inside his house not far from the gardens. Malcolm MacNeill had been the head gardener in the Horlick years and still mourned the once wonderfully kept gardens. He proudly showed me a framed photograph of himself in a group of seven full-time gardeners of Achamore House.

Horlick's gardeners, 1971-2. Horlick on the left; Malcolm, the tallest gardener, in the middle

I'd bought a smart yellow map (scale 1:16000) from the post office. It is part of the series of *The Yellow Walk Maps* that I've used before in Yorkshire. I took the car and parked at the top of the island, and tried Walk number 1, which leads to Càrn Bàn near Port Mòr on the north of the island and had been labelled wrongly as 'Viking graves'. The 'graves' are not Viking at all but Neolithic stone cists, as Tony Philpin had told me. A small number of new waymarks had been vandalised, one of which I saw that day, on my attempt to find the cists.

I was not able to reach them. The main problem was that after following a few waymarks on the north shore, a post was lying on the ground ambivalently just where I calculated I had to go inland. Confusion. Did I need to follow the shore a little more, or dive inland? I chose the latter option. An hour of high-stepping ensued, but I had to give up after a womanly effort, encountering impenetrable tall bracken and evil brambles, not to mention heather, willow and birch scrub and the odd mud chasm. More than once I went almost up to my knees in this black ooze – I blame the cows; but not one of these creatures was to be seen.

This walk nevertheless had its delightful moments. I saw a palm tree, a family of jellyfish snoozing on the high tide mark, a dazzling big rock entirely covered with yellow lichen, and a smaller stone with a green frill.

*

I drove back to the thin 'waist' of the island near the Giant's Tooth, and did a short walk onto both the east and the west coast of Gigha, at Tarbert. In earlier times, boats would be dragged over the isthmus from one side of the island to the other, so as to avoid a much longer route round the top or bottom. (I've met a few Tarberts in my travels.) While trying to explore the very obstacled path to Camas Nàireach, to the west, I encountered muddy and brambly terrain, but this time with the addition of a stout barbed-wire fence. These are not my favourite barriers, but I just about managed to climb over it, wobbling perilously.

The struggle was not in vain, as I was now able to see an old fish trap on the shore. I was beginning to recognise fish traps. There is usually a very low stone wall, or dyke, built across a small bay in shallow waters, with a gap in the wall to let fish swim in. These were caught on the ebbing tide in nets placed across the opening. The old walls were eventually broken up by gales, and the scattered stones often became covered with seaweed, hence the difficulty in recognising them.

Old fish trap on the west side of the isthmus

Oyster bags

Once back on the road, I crossed it and dropped down a friendly track towards the east-facing shore. I picked up the biggest scallop shell I'd ever seen, and noticed a line of oyster bags sitting in the shallow water.

So the walking day finished with oyster bags and blackberries. Two sightings of oyster bags in different locations in a matter of a day or two! And though I've described brambles as evil, I had never eaten so many blackberries straight from the plants as that late summer on Gigha.

One day while walking along a track south of Ardlamy near the shore, I passed an isolated cottage with an enclosed garden. Next to it was a small sheep pen, gated at each end. The track went through both gates. The hook

and eye on the first gate caught my attention, as the eye had been reinforced by a couple of layers of frayed string.

I was intrigued. After a short exploration of the coast beyond, including Cuddyport Bay, I returned the way I came, entered the sheep pen and noticed a woman busy gardening next to the house. An energetic

Fortified latch

woman in her forties, she greeted me in a very friendly way, told me her name, Marion, and we chatted for some time. I asked her about the string around the latch. Normally, she said, her car was parked in the pen. She had used a low-tech solution to stop a costly and annoying cow habit that I write about in the poem below.

Peigi's lament

Enticing new car parked in our pen,
so we unhooked the latch with our clever noses,
made for wing mirrors to scratch our itches;
me on the off-side,
Mairi on the on.
Our flanks need maintaining.
I was too rough, my mirror bit the dust.

It appears that Marion likes her mirrors,
tied fluffy string around the 'eye'
to stop us in our tracks.
We're in a huff, itching
like anything.

Marion and I discovered we had things in common, not least a penchant for collecting aluminium buoys. She gave me a tour of the garden where I admired the flowers, buoys of all colours, and other accoutrements, and she invited me in for a cup of tea. I told her of my inclination to find the Squirting Pit (Sloc an Leim), and she offered to take me there. It's a long subterranean passage next to the shore where, if you're lucky, a fountain of seawater will soak you.

Not all Gigha highlights are waymarked, let alone accessible, as you will have gathered. I'd never have found the cave by myself. On the day of our expedition we took a signposted track to the remote sandy beach, Gròb Bàgh, unintentionally startling a baby seal. There's a very obvious raised beach there and the erstwhile 'cliff' behind the raised beach is plain to see. From then on there were no waymarks, so there's a need for Tony Philpin's team here.

A rickety stile led us on to the pathless headland at Port Cùll, a maze of steep rocky outcrops and knolls. The 'pit' is not visible from even a few yards away, but you can hear the slurps, thuds and splashes that the sea makes as it is thrust up through a tight opening in the rocks, creating a thunderous fountain on blustery days. There was a narrow black-rock fissure that needed careful negotiating as we clambered down to experience it at close quarters. I was envious of Marion's agility, but I should have ditched my walking pole earlier on because I had to use both hands and shuffle on my bottom to get down to the action, and the pole kept getting in the way.

Sloc an Leim on a day when the squirts were less disappointing

Because the sea was calm, the squirts were underwhelming and my smartphone recording app didn't even pick up the sounds. I've heard that the fountain can rise as high as several metres in stormy weather. We climbed back up, retrieved my walking pole, and found an easier route to the stile, trying not to tread too heavily on plants such as grass of Parnassus, tormentil and cotton grass.

Marion and I completed our walk with a detour to the 'twin stones'. These are to be found near the four wind turbines that were humming loudly as we passed under them. We followed signs to the Cnoc a'Bhodaich (Hill of the Old Man), climbed over a couple of unopenable gates, and saw what we'd been looking for. On the top of the small hill where there are the remains of a fortification, we came across two curious stones, named locally as the Bodach and the Cailleach, the Old Man and the Hag, or Witch. They were less than a metre in height. These twin stones, regarded in the old days as 'terrifying creatures that walk the heath at night', apparently had mysterious powers. They also have been interpreted as fertility symbols because of their shape, which can be construed as genitalia. Glen Lyon in Perthshire is the only place on the mainland of Scotland where there are stones with very similar shapes, but those ones have their own little shelter, and some stone 'children' around them.

The Gigha Cailleach was firmly rooted in the soil, but the Bodach was loose, and was known to fall down regularly. He had a peculiar jug-shaped head and neck. We found him on his side, probably kicked over by cows. Or perhaps the Cara Brownie, of whom more later, had played a mean trick on him. Marion went to pick him up and replace him in the middle of a nest of stones – a low-tech solution for keeping him erect. She brushed aside my offer to help. 'I go to weightlifting classes,' she said. And so he was reinstated.

Later I was to meet another resident, Henri, who has a cafe-cum-gallery-cum-craft shop adjacent to the IGHT office, and a miniature pair of stones roughly in the shape of the Bodach and Cailleach stood outside the cafe door. She told me that her recent attempt to have the real ones 'scheduled' (officially protected) had been put on hold.

*

I was keen to visit two more fascinating ancient locations, one of which was the ruined Kilchattan church with its cemetery. This was easy to find, up from the unmade road past the Achamore Gardens car park. The sandstone church was built in the 12th or 13th century. A fine eastern gable with a lancet window survives, and about thirty interesting grave-stones within the church ruins, and more outside in the graveyard. Many were beautifully carved with patterns of foliage, animals, a warrior with a claymore, a mermaid with flowing hair – but the patterns were difficult to make out because of lichen, moss, weeds and soil.

Difficult to find, but temptingly visible from the churchyard, the tall Ogham Stone is one of a small number of pillars of its kind in the British Isles, carved with ancient Celtic writing. The word Ogham refers to the actual writing used, a kind of shorthand. (Coincidentally I'd come across an Ogham Stone in Killarney, Ireland, only a few weeks previously.) Without a guide this time, I had some trouble finding the stone, which is up a small hill surrounded by whin and trees. The little path to it was unmarked but I found it eventually.

The Ogham Stone

The stone is scheduled and has a wooden fence around it. An engraving on one side of the stone indicates the meaning of 'X, son of Y' in a Goidelic language – it is said that this might reflect the first wave of colonisation of Scotland in the 5th and 6th centuries, by Gaelic speakers from Ireland.

You can reach over the protecting fence and touch the stone if you so wish. Henri had told me that she got a tingle in her fingers when they were about an inch away from the stone. I didn't get any feeling – except that of relief that I'd finally found it.

*

On the walk the previous year, where I stood at the pier at the south end, I shivered in a brisk wind that was feeding an approaching rain shower. The restless sea was the colour of dust. To the south I could make out Gigalum, recently for sale. A bigger island, only about one kilometre away from the southernmost tip of Gigha, was Cara Island, uninhabited since the 1940s. I had better views of Cara while walking to the 'Sloc' with Marion near the tiny airstrip alongside Leim House where the land reaches the dizzying heights of almost 25 metres above sea level.

On Cara there is the recently renovated, but still uninhabited, Cara House. A large herd of wild goats wander about on the island; in summer they are hidden by tall bracken that smothers the island, but you could come across a horned skull or a rotting carcass. I wonder if their antecedents had 'come off a Spanish ship', like the goats on Colonsay I'd heard about. I made enquiries about a fishing boat trip to Cara, but no one was

64

*Cara lies between Gigha in the
foreground, and the Kintyre coast*

available to take me. Cara was on my mind, because I had heard and read
about the Brownie of Cara, and was curious to see his island. There are
many stories about Scottish brownies, but the following one is the most
compelling.

For centuries Cara was part of the MacDonald Estate of Largie on the
Kintyre peninsula. The MacDonalds of Largie claim direct descent from
the Lord of the Isles. But ownership of the island was in dispute for a
long time, the MacDonalds' main enemies being the Campbells and the
MacNeills, some of whose ancestors I have mentioned. Having recaptured Cara after several skirmishes, the heads of the Clans MacNeill and
Campbell had a celebratory dinner in Cara house, while enjoying the
fact that eight of the MacDonald clan were in the process of being hung
outside. These were then buried in the chapel. But their spirit lives on in

the attic of the house, in the form of the brownie.

Smuggling, as well as the brewing of spirits in stills, was common in Cara and in Gigha in the old days, and R. S. G. Anderson tells of caches of smuggled goods, and of twinkling lights from the windows of the attic of Cara

The Brownie's chair on Cara

House – where the Brownie was most likely playing his usual tricks.[11]

The Brownie is said to protect the island from any visiting Campbells and has the power to conjure storms. Near the southern tip of the island stands the Brownie's Chair – a massive piece of whinstone that may have been positioned so its occupant can see Ireland, the Kintyre coast and the hills of Knapdale; a good vantage point to sit and await rampaging Campbells.

Stories of the Brownie on Cara popped up regularly in my research and I have been fascinated by them, some of which seem to ring true. A brownie (pronounced broonie) is a very little man dressed in brown with a long beard. Opinions vary as to how he looked. He could be stout with long flowing hair, or with wrinkles and curly hair. He sometimes carried a switch. Brownies usually lived, or live, in the attics of rich people's houses. They demand respect, are usually loyal, but can get in a huff very easily. The best part of their character is their helpfulness, especially around the house. Most accounts relate how, if you meet the brownie, you must take off your hat and say, 'Good Morning, Mr Brownie.' He takes umbrage, and might play a trick on you, if you fail to do this.

Hamish Haswell-Smith tells of how he met a fisherman who told him that he and his son had pulled up their boat on Cara to get a drink of water from the Brownie's Well (which never runs dry). When they got back to their boat, a bench seat was missing. The next day they were in the same spot and noticed the plank stuck between two rocks on top of the hill.[12]

It seems some people still believe that the Cara Brownie exists. A reporter for the Glasgow Herald newspaper recounted, 'Some years ago, when staying on Gigha, I was negotiating in the hotel bar with a fisherman to take us to Cara. The deal was struck, but in subsequent conversation, Jean [the reporter's wife] happened to mention her mother was a Campbell. 'There is no way that I can take you to Cara,' said the fisherman, 'as the Brownie would be very upset.' Persuasion was absolutely useless and the trip had to be abandoned.'

And the same Herald reporter heard this from a Gigha resident: 'Angus McGougan had a big beard and fourteen children, who incidentally were all baptised at the same time. Angus was the last man to work on Cara Farm. After a family trip away from Cara, because of a massive storm, they weren't able to cross over from Gigha, and were concerned as the cows needed milking. When they finally got back to Cara, they found that the cows had all been milked – yet there was no one else on the island at that time.' *Glasgow Herald*, May 1998.[13]

To my knowledge there isn't a song about the Cara Brownie. I was so taken by the legend that I offered a workshop at the Gigha primary school, so as to teach a brownie song. I composed it after my first visit and held the workshop the following year. The head teacher was greatly supportive. The tune was relatively easy to compose (the same melody that I used for all five island songs), but I had to write it note by note on manuscript paper, the old way, with pencil and rubber, until I heard about Finale Notepad. I struggled long and hard to learn how to use this musical composition program, and was delighted to master it eventually. I envy younger students of music who have been brought up with these IT aids for composing.

Song of the Brownie of Gigha and Cara

Chorus
   A bearded wee man who's dressed all in brown
   Will he be kind or will he be mad?
   Just take off your hat!
   Say 'Good Day Mister Brownie' and give him a grin,
   his trust you must win!

1 Let's go to the pier and jump in a boat,
you take the oars and from Gigha we'll row!
The sea's nice and calm and Cara's not far,
we'll get there quite soon, we'll come to no harm.

2 As we wade through the bracken the rabbits and goats
will come to say hi, then off they will slope.
The canny wee man lives under the roof
of big Cara House, we'd best not intrude!

3 The brownie's big chair with only one arm
on the south of the isle, where the sea's never calm.
Your wish might come true if you make your voice clear,
but don't sit on his seat, you may disappear!

4 Come back to Gigha and he might help you
do your sums and your chores and mend your bike too!
Make sure that your speech is always polite,
he'll be by your side from morning till night.

(musical score in appendix)

I was looking forward to meeting the schoolchildren. We couldn't use the school for our 'lesson' because there was a meeting there that afternoon, so we had our session in the church. I was delighted in one respect.

The all-denominations parish church has a stained-glass window dedicated to Kenneth Macleod, minister of the Gigha church from 1923 to 1927. Macleod composed The Road to the Isles. 'It's the far Cuillins are putting love on me…' This was one of many folk songs I learnt as a child, but it was only recently that I read it had been written for 'the lads in France during the Great War'. Nor had I realised that Macleod also wrote a great deal of lyrics, prose and poems, including translations from the Gaelic. He collected some of these old songs to form the book *The Road to the Isles*. I was delighted to find a copy of this book in a charity shop in Oban. It's an astonishing collection of Scottish tales and poems of brownies, fairies, seal-folk; lore and legend galore.

The final paragraph of Macleod's preface goes towards justifying my own attitude towards composing songs for the islands, as well as echoing my favourite themes. 'An 'Islesman' is dominated to a large extent by the evening walk down to the creek, where lies the old wreck, now partly covered with sea-pinks. There he cannot but think of the many strange boats that have passed by; one steered by a woman singing far-away tunes; another by a little child who came and went like a tune, and is at the heart of all true song.'[14]

The expression 'child who came and went like a tune' strikes a chord in me; perhaps it's something to do with innocence and impermanence. The themes here are walk, boats, poems, songs, children, with subtle reference to lore and legend. This doesn't say it all, but almost!

I have another old book that I have already quoted from. This is by Alasdair Alpin MacGregor.[15]

And a surprise on reading the dedication, which is set out like this in his book.

To the Elusive
KENNETH MACLEOD
'The Most Distinguished Fairy of Modern Times'
In Recollection of His Esteem for
the Brownie dwelling on Cara,
and of the small hours spent over
the Manse fire
at Gigha
In the Kingdom of the Isles.

So Alasdair and Kenneth had good times over the Manse's peat fire, chewing over many a fairy 'story'. It would have been fascinating to join them and work out how they married Scottish folk tales with Bible stories. Or not. And I wonder in what way Kenneth was 'elusive'; perhaps he kept disappearing like the Brownie.

*

So there we were in the church, overlooked by 'the most distinguished fairy's' memorial window, with thirteen children and three helpers, including Tony Philpin who was wearing his teacher hat that day. Tony had arranged for us to make use of classroom percussion instruments, and had brought along paper and colouring pencils. I had the use of the church organ. We started by playing a game to concentrate their minds and to develop rhythm skills – a kind of Simon Says game. They clap after me, and I change the rhythm every time. If I clap the same rhythm twice, they aren't to repeat after me. Simple rules – they get the picture after a while, and hate to be the only one caught clapping.

The children seemed to like the story of the Brownie and not all had heard of it before. We discussed the intricacies of his personality, and they liked the fact that you had to bow to him when you met him. So when we came to sing, 'Just take off your hat,' there was an excellent mimic, one child with her head almost to the floor.

The teaching of the song became a little peripheral to the lesson. I thought that it was better to instil the chorus and first verse rather than to plough dutifully through the whole song. I asked for ideas; 'if you had a brownie living in your house, what would he get up to?' We tried out a brownie playlet in groups, and one group had the idea of their brownie laying down a tripwire. Another group made full use of the back of the altar, which seemed to be OK with the reverends looking down on us from their windows, but I wasn't sure.

I also told the children my favourite brownie story, based on the island of Berneray in the Western Isles, about two men playing backgammon which morphed into chess in my version. They listened well. I'd asked my two granddaughters to draw a picture about this story and showed the pupils the girls' artistic work. This led to their colouring a picture of the Cara Brownie that my friend Anita had sketched for me.

The Cara Brownie

The session ended with their taking away the words and music of the song. Will I ever get to Cara, I wondered. That day at the south end of Gigha, when I first saw the small island, I'd started to shiver. There had been no time to hang around as the rain was setting in good and hard, perhaps a precursor of a storm conjured by the Brownie himself, although I hadn't heard of him then. Something had made me hurry back up the road.

I left Gigha on a rainy morning with regret. There was so much more to see and discover. I'd love to master the undergrowth/jungle and see Càrn Bàn; to find the Great Well and ask for good weather, to revisit the Spouting Cave on a blustery day with a south-westerly swell and see and hear the thundering splashes in full splendour. And to be taken by small boat to Cara Island, find the Brownie and take my hat off to him.

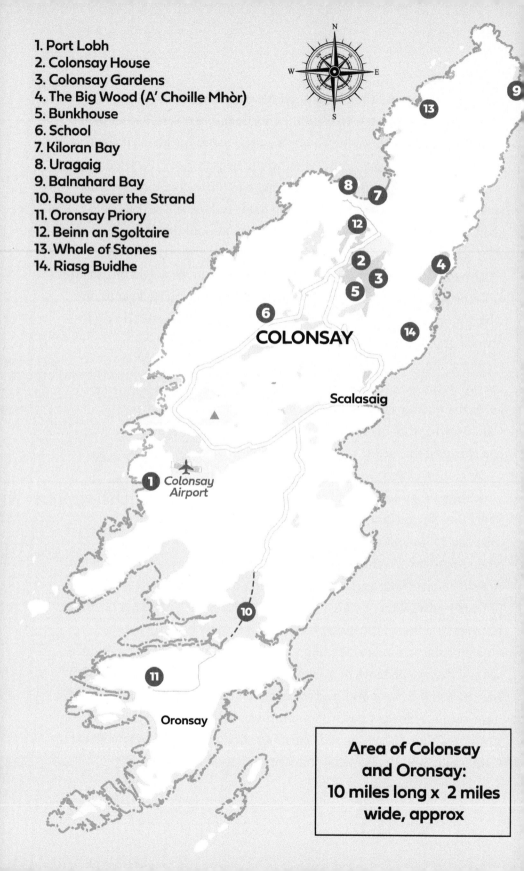

1. Port Lobh
2. Colonsay House
3. Colonsay Gardens
4. The Big Wood (A' Choille Mhòr)
5. Bunkhouse
6. School
7. Kiloran Bay
8. Uragaig
9. Balnahard Bay
10. Route over the Strand
11. Oronsay Priory
12. Beinn an Sgoltaire
13. Whale of Stones
14. Riasg Buidhe

COLONSAY

Colonsay
Airport

Scalasaig

Oronsay

Area of Colonsay
and Oronsay:
10 miles long x 2 miles
wide, approx

CHAPTER 3
COLONSAY

leant forwards, backwards, sideways; I sank to my knees, I stood on tiptoe; I tried to peer between the slats of lenses while turning in all directions. With each tiny movement I made, the colours changed; vertical and horizontal blue, green, yellow stripes and patterns; I'd never witnessed the Northern Lights, but I was reminded of the images I'd seen.

This was my reaction on coming across a lighthouse optic in Colonsay House Gardens. I was not being watched, of course.

The island is ten miles long and two miles wide and can be reached by ferry from Oban in about two and a half hours, and from Islay in about seventy minutes. There is a small airport, which I passed one day while musing over whether I'd just seen an eagle or not, but instead a small

Port Lobh

yellow plane landed discreetly to my left. Despite being another lozenge-shaped island, it has the luxury of a circular road, which makes exploring just that bit more exciting.

Colonsay has a population of about 120 people, roughly the same as Gigha, and I was lucky to be able to explore quite safely many of its beaches, hills, caves, ancient stones, and its twin island reachable at low tide, Oronsay.

*

Unlike Gigha, but like Muck, Colonsay is owned by a single person, in this case Alex Howard. His family have owned the island since 1905 when the first Lord of Strathcona, who was a Canadian Scot, bought it. Alex's title is 5th Baron Strathcona and Mount Royal. This is a title in the UK peerage. Soon after my arrival I drove to Colonsay House, where Alex Howard lives. This attractive stately home is just up the road from the bunkhouse where I was staying. Colonsay House (listed Category B) is a Georgian mansion house built as a rectangular block in 1722, then extended around 1830 with additional wings. It stands on the site of St Oran's Chapel, and it is said that stone from the chapel was used for building the house. The gardens are open to the public a few days a week, and are famous for a huge collection of rhododendrons, just like Achamore Gardens on Gigha.

Many exotic plants – azaleas, hydrangeas, escallonia, camellia – were sadly past their best flowering period at the time of my two recent visits, which were in late summer of 2017 and 2018. Further away from the house in a section of woodland I came across eucalypts, acers and acacia and magnolias – to name just a few.

Even this more 'natural' woodland reminded me of Achamore Gardens. I followed a path around a murky pond, and noticed gunnera, a plant with enormous rhubarb-type leaves like umbrellas that could shelter Lilliputians from any rain shower. As for shelter for Brobdingnagians, there was plenty of that on the lawns under three massive Monterey cypress trees (*Cupressus macrocarpa*). One of these was planted by King Edward VII

Bark on a Monterey cypress

in 1902. The bark of these trees was a picture of intricacy: stringy, twisty, multi-layered, and one of them has the largest girth in the UK. I quite fancied a go on the swing that was attached to an enormous thick branch.

Just a handful of people were around and it was towards closing time when I entered the old kitchen garden near the house. I was intrigued to see a lovely structure in the middle of an expanse of lawn. Dumping my rucksack, I dived into the dalek-shaped folly which I soon realised was an optic from a lighthouse.

I hadn't been prepared for this. Later, when I read up on it, I discovered that the optic, or lantern, belonged originally to the Rhuvaal (Rubh a' Mhàil) lighthouse at the northernmost tip of Islay, which I'd passed on the ferry from Port Askaig in Islay. In 1992 it was gifted to Lord Strathcona, Alex Howard's father, after the Islay lighthouse was automated. I've read that the Baron paid two bottles of whisky for it.

The lighthouse optic in Colonsay House Gardens

Each lens was individually shaped and angled to direct the light emissions to the horizon using prisms of special glass. Designed by the Fresnel Brothers of Paris, the lenses date from 1874 and were made by a Birmingham company that went on for many decades to be the worldwide supplier of lighthouse lenses.

A speeded-up video of the optic's kaleidoscopic images, as well as my peculiar actions and reactions, as detailed below, would have greatly embarrassed my grandchildren, I expect. I made sure no one was watching me.

Carousel
I flit like a dunnock
excited by a new feeder,
out and in.
A delight of beams
transforms me
into a shimmering hummingbird
poised for ambrosia
betweenbelowabove each Fresnel lens.

I would hang upside down if I could.
pop my head to left
and right,
preen and peck,
suck the nectar of the rainbow arcs.

Greensbluesyellows swirl me.
I cling for sheer life to the lenses
musicmovementlightcolour merging.
If there was a tune, it would be Bill Haley,
Rock around the Carousel.

On a later visit to Colonsay House Gardens I was determined to inspect St Oran's Well (Tobar Odhran) and St Oran's Cross. I found them in the gardens to the east of the house, in shade. St Oran is associated with Oronsay. The well itself, the water of which is said to have had magical powers, like many wells, has been there forever. The cross, a ninth-century carved early Christian cruciform stone, was originally sited at the ruined village of Riasg Buidhe, where it covered a well just outside a chapel. It was removed for safekeeping to the House Gardens in 1870. (The cross is in contrast to the Bodach stone on Gigha, which has no Christian connection.) These two photos show the front and rear of the cross.

Two sides of St Oran's cross

The cross, which is only seventeen inches tall, is skilfully carved from local stone, and has retained much detail of the face of the subject, which may be of a monk or a bearded cleric wearing robes. These are draped in such a way to denote the symbol of a fish, an early Christian symbol, although that isn't too apparent in my photo. The stone is locally known as Dealbh na Leisge, which means 'the sleepy figure'. The other side of the stone depicts a pagan fertility symbol, or in one islander's words, 'a whacking great phallus', some of whose features are modestly covered in moss. It suggests that the ninth-century Viking inhabitants of Colonsay wished to incorporate older, more traditional beliefs within their Christianity; a belt and braces approach. It's reported that when, on a visit to Colonsay, Edward Vll saw the stone cross, he said it was an excellent representation of the chief engineer of the Royal Yacht. Nobody knows which side he was looking at!

*

Behind Colonsay House Gardens there is a much wilder woodland that stretches to the east coast. Kevin Byrne, a resident, takes people on walks to look for fungi and ferns, which are two of his many passions. Early one morning we met at the old sawmill in the Colonsay House garden. An enthusiastic man, not in the first flush of youth and with boundless energy, he greeted me warmly; I was the only 'guest' on this excursion.

First he showed me skunk cabbage growing next to the gunnera I'd noticed the day before near the pond. I'd never heard of skunk cabbage. It grows in swamp-like conditions and when the leaves are crushed or bruised, it gives off a smell of skunk or rotting meat.

In spring there are large yellow petal-like bracts, or spathes (a little

Skunk cabbage in spring

like lords-and-ladies, or cuckoo pint); the plant develops huge glossy leathery leaves later on. In Canada, bears that have become constipated during hibernation look for skunk cabbage to devour in the spring, to clear their gut.

Humans may also benefit from the plant. It is said that the root is good for diabetes and pain relief, but I wouldn't eat it. In 2016 the EU prohibited the sale and exchange of the plant as it can be very invasive. I have since seen it growing in a controlled way in a Leeds park, and in an uncontrolled way in two other parks.

Kevin took me through the wilder parts of Colonsay House Gardens, until we were in a rarely visited area, through A' Choille Mhòr, The Big Wood, which is a magnificent example of ancient and mature woodland, rich in ferns, lichens and mosses. The gnarled oaks and other species of tree are a remnant of the groves that used to swathe the island. Every now and then Kevin takes people in the spring, but hardly ever in the summer when it is practically impenetrable. This was July. His dog Lola led the way, followed by her master; I had to trot to keep up with them, often half-stumbling down the many hidden ditches.

Quite soon we came across the remains of a pole farm where timber was produced for the island's needs by the coppicing of hazel (for creels and hurdles), birch (for faggots, scantlings and poles), and oak (for rafters and boat-building).

We took an old path that was uneven and overgrown, so we had to yank up bracken and rhododendron plantlets (escapees from the gardens) as we picked our way on the uneven ground. Kevin used his special hacksaw to saw off thicker obstacles. He had been trying to resurrect the path for many years; it would have been used by visitors to Colonsay House in its heyday, as the woodland was probably a pleasure garden in Victorian times. Occasionally we climbed up or down dilapidated steps or staircases, the route of which had been marked by Kevin on earlier visits with bits of string tied, Hansel and Gretel-style, in the tree branches. In one of his favourite 'dells' a lovely spread of hazel reminded us of The Lord of the Rings. There were old terraces hidden in the undergrowth, and a rickety narrow stone-built bridge where a bottomless chasm awaited us on the other side.

The path may even have led to the nearby east coast, where, marked on the OS map, are the remains of an old pier opposite which lies a tiny island called Eilean Olmsa. Its Viking name means 'a warm sheltered spot'. I was reminded of a quotation of John Muir: 'The clearest way into the Universe is through a forest wilderness.' I imagined the view of the island would be a little like arriving at 'the Universe'. We didn't get that far.

In the Big Wood

There are thirty-three varieties of ferns (of 13,000 in the world) in this patch of woodland. They have no seed and run through two quite distinct generations each time in their life cycle. The origin of ferns, 400 million years ago, predates flowers; they are regarded as special as they are found in fossils and allegedly have medicinal properties. Some legends state that ferns confer the gift of invisibility in humans!

I learnt about galls. I've heard them called 'witches' brooms' (not to be confused with witches' knickers which, in Yorkshire, are dead plastic bags caught in trees). Galls are plant growths, a little like tumours in humans, caused by the feeding or egg-laying activity of insects and mites. For example, the gall of a fly creeps up a leaf, creating a cluster of leaves bunched close together. I'd seen many witches' brooms before, but I didn't know how they were formed. 'Virtually every plant has a gall, and these are made by some parasitic creature, often a wasp, which lays its young in it and it creates a biological change of some sort,' Kevin explained.

The Big Wood is a Site of Special Scientific Interest (SSSI) and was as yet unmanaged. Kevin hoped naturalists or dendrologists would come and monitor the trees.

Lola stopped suddenly in her dog tracks. She had sniffed something. We stopped too. It was a feral goat, which jumped out of his hiding place and scampered away. Kevin recognised the goat; one with a badly deformed leg.

There are a number of these goats on Colonsay; they are wary of people, and have tall horns and a shaggy brown coat. There are at least two explanations of their presence on the island: one tells of the Spanish Armada boats pulling in on Colonsay, needing water and other supplies, and the Spanish paid for them with goats; and the other is that an Armada ship was wrecked off the coast and the animals escaped. In either case, the goats have been here ever since. Keeping goats and other animals for provisions on a long voyage was commonplace.

We came across ancient burial sites and other old ruins almost completely hidden by bracken. Kevin showed me a kerb cairn. This was a Bronze Age tomb, unrecorded, totally unknown, a low mound ringed by a prominent circle of stones that are often taller than the mound itself. He thought that 'our Victorian friends had been treasure hunting'. These tombs tend to be in a prominent position. On one side there was a slightly circular twisting entrance pathway. This would originally have been stones; the whole thing would be covered with soil, and perhaps an oak planted on top. When a new member of the family needed to be interred, the mourners knew the way in, and would pop their cremated remains in the middle.

We stopped at some other stones in a thickly wooded area. This site was our second Bronze Age tomb; a listed National Monument. There was a headstone and a footstone about six feet from each other, and evidence that the grave had been robbed. Someone must have died in the woods and the stones from the ancient tomb recycled.

As for orchids – as well as a huge twayblade, he showed me heath spotted orchids, pink and white ones, very varied in their colour. I mentioned a dark purple orchid I'd seen the day before – it might have been a late northern marsh orchid, or a fragrant orchid, which is the only one that has a scent. Other flowers we noticed, as we negotiated what he called 'the worst terrain of the day', included self-heal, butterwort, bog myrtle (which has a magical scent, said to work as a midge repellent), burnet rose, and bog asphodel. But to Kevin, ferns were of supreme importance.

On our way back he explained the origin of his fascination for ferns. It was a pragmatic decision of the head. Not many people know about ferns (as distinct from the millions of birders, for example), ferns can be studied all year round, they keep him out of doors and healthy. Enough good reasons!

I was full of admiration for this non-native man of Colonsay who has made it his life's project to discover, record and disseminate so much of his knowledge. We hadn't actually achieved 'the clearest way into the universe', but we'd made a few steps in that direction.

*

My walk to Balnahard Bay, or Tràigh Ban, at the northeast tip of the island, was another clear step into the universe. It was probably the most enjoyable of all the walks I've done in the islands – easy going, no map-reading problems, fabulous views and birds galore. The warm sunny weather helped a great deal.

One or two cars were parked in the field at the end of the road at Kiloran Bay, where a rough Land Rover track led behind the dunes. Two cows watched me as I parked and there was a lonely wheatear on the track. From its side this bird looked like a very small thrush, but when it flew off I could see the flash of white on its rump.

After a mile, I looked over a narrow rectangular cove called Port Sgibinis; I was drawn to it by a jagged rock formation behind it. The map showed that there was a raised beach there, but I wasn't able to make it out yet. I could hear singing seals in the distance, but couldn't see them.

On the pebbles in the cove a group of greylag geese were all facing the sea, perhaps watching the tide coming in. As I waited they started to move to the water's edge, quietly, just a few grunts. The first geese went into the water, and the others followed in single file. A couple of oystercatchers nearby disturbed the quiet with their shrieks.

Opposite me there was an obvious high tide mark on the shore; the rocks up to the mark were a dark grey-brown, covered with seaweed. Above the tide mark the rocks formed horizontal layers of limestone, some with yellow lichen on them; then another layer of greyish rock, and above this was a plain grassy slope leading up to the eye-catching promontory.

I continued along the track where a huge amount of beach stones had been thrown up by the waves over hundreds of years. A surprise awaited me – a massive outline of stones laid out in the shape of a whale, on a now obvious raised beach. I learnt later that Julian Meredith, a sculptor, started to create this 160 metre-long structure a few years ago, and that it is now classified as a 'hill-carving site' by the Ordnance Survey.

Passers-by are encouraged to add to the sculpture. When I reached it, much of the whale body was filled in with stones, but the tail fins were 'empty'. It was quite a sight, and I placed a stone between two that needed to be joined together. The whale's mouth was marked by a tyre filled up with more stones. I wasn't sure about the tyre; it seemed out of place.

Whale of stones

I looked for higher ground nearby to take a good photo and, climbing a little, I took a few, but the sculpture needed an observation point that was nearer and higher than nature allowed.

I walked on. Having passed the ruins of a nunnery, I took the sandy and grassy path towards Tràigh Ban (*tràigh* means beach, and *ban* means white). To my left and right there was the first obvious patch of machair that I had come across in Colonsay. Machair is sandy soil made of shell fragments that supports particular flowers. I took a picture of a very tiny pink-purple flower and couldn't actually see it through the camera lens. There were thistles sticking up to goad me into thinking it was inferior machair, yet around them was a feast of reddish-purple clover, daisies, buttercups, ragwort, scarlet pimpernel, harebell and silverweed. Legend has it that Roman soldiers put the cushiony leaves of silverweed into their boots for extra comfort. In more recent times of famine, Scots ate the roots baked, boiled, or roasted. A common blue butterfly tried to land on me while I was examining lady's bedstraw and white yarrow.

Near a wet patch was a spread of pink purslane. Yellow, purple and white were the colours of the day; white clover, daisies, and red bartsia (which is more purple than red), was about ten inches tall.

A pick-up truck came towards me, negotiating the few rocks on the track. I waved as it passed, trying to ignore the itching on my hand. I'd been bitten a few times, by insects bigger than midges. The beach was half hidden from my view by dunes. The plants in this part of the machair were shorter, and the area was more like grassland. More harebells; and tiny eyebright – smart, tidy flowers shaped like a lady orchid. Eyebright always reminds me of Swaledale where I took notice of it for the first time.

The track became featureless, but a rocky outcrop signalled the beginning of the dunes. In front of me was a little hillock of marram grass; sheep had been here, maybe the reason for the stunted plants in this area.

Up on a sandhill, wheatears were flurrying above dense mats of burnet rose, and – at last! – the sea was in full view. I was enthralled by the curve of the bay, the azure water and wonderful shadows and shapes from the few passing clouds. The sky was a lighter blue, and on the horizon was the subtle grey of the islands of the Garvellachs, Seil and Scarba, and the mountains and hills of Mull and Jura.

Balnahard Bay

A small group of people were messing about at the water's edge with a chugging boat, and a little sailing dinghy was anchored a little further out. A RIB (rigid inflatable boat) bobbed up and down further along the bay. Unusually I didn't approach the people for a chat, but was content to enjoy the day *toute seule*.

There was a wreck on the sand that I examined with interest. I learnt later that this was the wooden Swedish steamship Wassa which caught fire midway between the Dubh Artach rocks and the north end of Colonsay, in 1920. Four of the twenty-eight crew were lost but twenty-four survivors were picked up by a trawler that towed the burning Wassa to this lovely beach. The keel timbers of the steamship were still held together with rusting iron bolts. The Colonsay museum now displays a small amount of timber from the ship.

85

There is a famous splendid namesake (Vasa) in its own museum in Stockholm; a 17th-century warship I visited years ago. That capsized too, but was salvaged nearly intact having spent more than 300 years on the seabed. I looked up Vasa/Wassa on the internet: 'Vasa (ship), 17th-century Swedish warship, formerly spelled Wasa.' The name means 'to hiss' – an apt name for the wrecked steamship. Apart from these remains there was no litter anywhere to be found. I'd picked up a leaflet, funded by the Group for Recycling in Argyll and Bute, urging us all to drink tap water instead of bottled. It told us that Colonsay was the first island in the UK to be 98 percent litter-free after a continuing campaign to clear litter, especially from beaches.

Rather red from sunburn, I made my reluctant way back to the car by the same track, and pondered about how we can learn from these islanders committed to their beach-cleans.

*

On just as sunny a day as the Kiloran Bay walk, I explored Oronsay, the tidal island south of Colonsay, where there is a ruined priory of great archeological interest.

From the bunkhouse I drove to the road end of the B8085. At two and a quarter miles long, it must be the shortest B-road in the UK. My 1987 map marked it as the A869, so a downgrade had taken place. There was a small parking area, with about five cars, next to the slipway overlooking the strand – an almost land-locked expanse of sandy water, or watery sand – between Colonsay and Oronsay. I could have done with a notice informing us about the tide times, but I'd made a note beforehand. It goes without saying that the strand is completely under water at high tide.

The sand between the two islands looked too wet to walk over, and I chatted to two senior women in a Renault van, who were, like me, just 'chilling'. I was impressed by the van; with sliding doors, it was just right for the odd sleepover. They told me they were not intending to cross over, either with the van or by foot.

The route over the strand is interestingly the longest distance between the two islands. My map indicated a number of places where there's a mere snip of water between them; for example, between Rubha Bàgh nan Capull and Poll Gorm on the east side; but there seemed to be no paths or tracks on either island in that vicinity!

There were vehicle tracks over a wide area on the strand; each vehicle having taken its own path. I made a choice of boots rather than wellies, but wasn't sure if it was the right decision. It's about a mile to go over to Oronsay, and I took my own path too.

The low-key cries of a few gulls were almost obliterated by noisy oyster-catchers, but there were no other birds around. There were plenty of cockle-beds to crunch over, or avoid, and a rampaging torrent or two to wade across, but I managed to keep my boots dry.

Crossing over to Oronsay

At last on terra firma, the path to the priory was longer than I expected, but lovely, flanked with dark purple orchids. I examined patches of tormentil that I hadn't seen on my trip so far. On my way to the priory I was tempted to walk up Beinn Oronsay where choughs breed, but I decided not to digress.

Oronsay is the island where St Columba was believed to have first landed from Ireland. One source says he climbed a hill known as the Cùl Ri Èirinn, which means 'with its back to Erin', and saw Ireland. This hill is not named as such on the OS map, but I assume it is Beinn Oronsay. Columba had sworn not to see Ireland again until he'd saved more souls than had been killed in the battle of Cúl Dreimhne. So he told his men to sail on. He went to Iona instead of staying on Oronsay.

*

The island has two spellings: Oransay and Oronsay. The larger island is named Columba's Isle, but with two 'o's – Colonsay. In Gaelic they spell Saint Oron's name Odhran, so maybe some think the smaller island's name must follow the exact spelling of the saint in Gaelic, hence Oransay. However, others might think that it must be Oronsay, in order to follow the two 'o's as in Colonsay.

Perhaps it doesn't matter. I have already mentioned that the two saints, Oran and Columba, knew each other; one source says that they were brothers. Both play a part in Colonsay's folklore and history. St Oran's Well in the House Gardens was a catholicon like the Great Well in Gigha; the water had magical or healing powers.

As I have just mentioned, one source says that St Columba beat a retreat immediately after landing on Oronsay, but the two saints must have been together on Oronsay for a while to have had the following quarrel about what happened in the afterlife.

St Columba thought that there was perpetual punishment in Hell for the wicked, but St Oran didn't agree. They decided to test the theory and St Oran said he'd be happy to be buried alive for three days. After three days he popped up and proclaimed: 'The good are not eternally happy, neither are the evil eternally unhappy.'

St Columba was very angry. He probably couldn't cope with a nuanced approach to the afterlife and ordered St Oran to be buried for good. After the event, St Columba seems to have regretted his action; he might even have wondered if his own deed was wicked. He was upset and cried because, after all, he and St Oran had been good friends. Eventually a chapel was built on top of the burial site. That's how Oronsay got its name. However, one source says that St Oran died on Iona and the 'buried alive' tale has also been told as happening on Iona.

This is another example of folk tales as 'belonging' to numerous places; I quite like this, as it gives the storyteller permission to digress and improvise.

*

The lovely path from the end of the strand finally led me to the Augustinian priory. There's little doubt about the origin of the priory, which was built on the site of a monastery founded in 563 by St Oran. The priory is dedicated to St Columba, was founded around 1340, and functioned until the second half of the 16th century. It was possibly second only to Iona in importance with its late-medieval world of Celtic art, crosses, cloisters and carvings. One of the best examples is the tall 15th-century cross known as the Oronsay Cross, which stands west of the chapel. It is of the Iona school, with a crucifixion scene on one side and the other showing beautiful interlaced foliage designs.

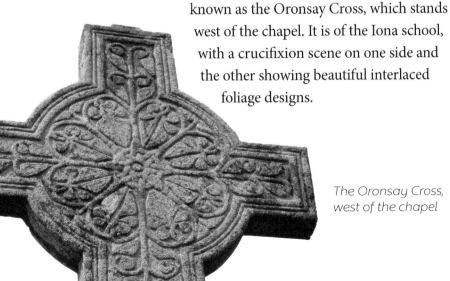

The Oronsay Cross, west of the chapel

I stepped into the Prior's House, where the inside walls were lined by about thirty up-ended grave slabs of warlords, knights and priests. There was no natural light here; some visitors had torches, including a French couple whom I spoke to. They were particularly impressed by the brilliant carvings, features of which include swords and leaf and animal patterns. Masons of the Oronsay School were still working there in the first half of the 16th century. Outside, on the east side of the chapel, I sat down to drink tea from my flask, next to a mound where there was another cross. This time it was an amalgamation of two separate pieces: a cross head that had been joined with a cross-shaft which was not its original shaft. This is seen in the photo on the right. It is thought that the main body of the cross is in its original place, and the 'head' had been taken from elsewhere. The figure on the cross head has been identified as St John the Evangelist.

The cross on the east side of the chapel

*

Oronsay has an American owner who bought it from the Strathconas in the 1970s. She has leased the island to the RSPB and keeps the farmhouse, which is next to the priory, in good shape. I was on the lookout for birds, so took a track south from the priory and found a small beach backed by sand dunes where I ate my picnic. In this area it was mostly green turf, but few birds, alas. I spent ages trying to catch sight of a corncrake that I could hear teasing me mercilessly in a scrubby walled field. Corncrakes are ventriloquists and their call is unmistakable – a rhythmic sore-throated double-croak. The rhythm is the same as a standard telephone ring. At least twenty of these birds breed here. Anyone watching me might have been concerned about my bizarre behaviour, as I ducked and dived and zigzagged, following just aural clues, desperate to catch sight of this elusive bird.

Colonsay's newsletter is called *The Corncrake*, but that's the only corncrake I saw this time on the island. There are also raucous gull and tern colonies on Oronsay in summer, while huge flocks of barnacle geese and other wildfowl can also be seen. Seal island (Eilean nan Ron), which I have mentioned already, lives up to its name and is the home of vast numbers of grey Atlantic seals who congregate there every autumn.

Showing my lack of trust of the tide times, I turned back on the path towards the strand. I would have loved to explore further south and east, but was conscious of the time. With hindsight I could have spent at least another hour on the smaller island.

Returning over the sands to the slipway on Colonsay, I could make out the mountains of Jura in the far distance to my right. I was aware of lovely patterns at my feet; of shells, sand eel hillocks, patches of seaweed. The slapping rhythmic sound of my boots paddling in two inches of water would have sent me to sleep if I hadn't been walking. A Land Rover came towards me very slowly, sounding like flapping wind from afar; I assumed that it was bound for the Oronsay farm. Going back over the strand was easier than on the outward walk and I almost missed the watery challenges I'd encountered then.

The two Renault van women were still near the slipway, but this time basking in the hot sun. I realised that they and other car occupants were waiting for the tide to come in. It was as if the water just gradually rose from beneath the sand to fill up the bay – there were no waves. I sat on the turf and watched with them for about an hour. It was one of the most peaceful moments of my trip; a beautiful setting, very quiet, no one talking loudly, just watching a wonderfully calm natural event. I didn't stay as long as my van friends. I met them again the next day and they told me that they'd waited until the water came right up to the slipway.

*

Among the smaller islands I've visited, I've encountered more folk tales from Colonsay than from any other island, so I am retelling a few, especially the ones that are island-specific. Other tales have been attributed to clans in various parts of Scotland and the islands.

In ancient times people's day-to-day world was often unpredictable, so the constant telling and retelling of familiar stories would serve as an anchor in their lives. Uncanny noises, premonitions, haunted houses, lights at sea, phantom ships, sacred wells, caves, black dogs, people with second sight, fairies, brownies and glaistigs, seal women; these were all subjects of folklore. Many a ceilidh would last until the small hours as these stories were retold. They developed from times when people sought to understand the reasons behind unexpected and often incomprehensible happenings, especially those events that were associated with the daily life of the people. If a cow died, for example, it could be the glaistig who made it happen because she was cross with the dairy maid.

MacPhee's dog

MacPhees have been the biggest clan in Colonsay. In their tales, there is often a black dog, famous but particularly useless at hunting. However, in the following tale, the dog has more to offer us than at first appears.

MacPhee, the laird of Colonsay, was a breeder of dogs. One pup grew up to be no use at all; it not only wouldn't hunt, it even failed to bark. The laird decided it had to be put down. But his cook came to him, and asked him not to harm the dog, saying that it might be wiser than was apparent. One evening MacPhee went out and his cook suggested he leave the dog in the kitchen. MacPhee agreed. On his way home alone he got lost. Suddenly a strange light appeared before him, and a breath of cold air blew past him. MacPhee realised that he was faced by the Evil Spectre of Colonsay. No one knew anything much about this spectre but they did know that none who met him ever survived.

In the deep dark, the moon behind lowering clouds, MacPhee couldn't see to run away. His knees were weak and his feet refused to obey him. He sensed that when the spectre's breath touched him, that would be the end.

The light came nearer and nearer. MacPhee stood glued to the spot. Suddenly something brushed past him – it was the black dog, which must have escaped from the kitchen. It sprang between him and the spectre, turning to face it and 'the cold breath of death'. As the dog fell dead, the spectre, having taken its one life, vanished as quietly as it had come. The moon broke through the clouds and MacPhee went home.

Fairies, or Little People

It is said that the fairies were the original inhabitants of the islands, driven underground or into hiding by their conquerors. In several places on Colonsay and Oronsay, in fact all over the islands along the lower lying parts, are mounds that appear to be of artificial origin. These are known as sithean and legend has made them the homes of the fairies.

In the Highlands fairies allegedly possessed many of the physical characteristics of the small, black-haired race who were the first known people of the Isles, Bronze Age or Stone Age. They stole goods and babies from their conquerors, and lived in subterranean recesses, or knolls. They were suspicious, peevish, easily annoyed, and were always on the lookout to snipe at the landowners – land was what they coveted the most. The Highland and Island fairies had 'the second sight' (the ability to tell the future). They wore green clothes and took offence when any ordinary humans wore their favourite colour. Their daughters were more beautiful than the mortals. If a mortal man or a woman communed with the fairies by eating or drinking the food they offered, or by cohabiting with the other sex, they died. However, there are tales that subvert this.

As well as second sight, tales of uncanny noises, haunted houses, lights at sea and phantom ships were notions that these fairies introduced into the Celtic brain. Sometimes they interfered with the dairy, like the glaistigs, or the water wells – all things that were associated with people's daily life. Wherever there were accidents, mysteries, or simply happenings with no obvious cause, people would be inclined to 'explain' them in tales or folklore. In a strange way, this could make unwanted life-events more palatable.

A glaistig (grey slinking one) and a gruagach (long-haired one) were originally human beings who had developed fairy characteristics. These fairies, witches, giants or hags loomed large in the tales and mythology of ancient Colonsay.

Fairy men and women played bagpipes, and there are many references to the bagpipe-playing expertise of the fairies, whose music is called pibroch. A. A. MacGregor gives us, in manuscript, eight bars of pibroch music with words, which he noted down on Barra.[1]

The playing of bagpipes is astonishing; bagpipes are very heavy instruments, loud and unwieldy. Almost the last instrument you'd think fairies would play, just as we don't expect fairies to steal human babies.

Tale of two cockerels

Another tale concerns a MacNeill from Barra who married a daughter of the Colonsay MacPhee chief, went to settle in Colonsay, and was granted a piece of land adjacent to that of his father-in-law.

But when MacPhee's cock began to crow, MacNeill's cock answered it. The wife of the chief saw this as a threat to her husband's authority and status, despite the probability of MacNeill having nothing to do with his cock's crowing habits. How dare another cock mimic the chief's cock! She resented this assertion of independence and equality. So she persuaded her husband to order MacNeill to move house to a place called Aird-an-Duin, where the land was much less fertile. We are not told how the MacNeills fared after their move.

The Flitting Well

Martin Martin, the first chronicler of the Islands, tells of a sacred spring, or well, with healing powers, called Toubir in Knahar. This can be translated as 'the well that sallied from one place to another'.[2] The story goes that a local woman had the insensitivity to wash her hands in it. The well being thus 'abused' immediately vanished from Colonsay to reappear in Islay where it stayed, the Islay folk being able to adhere to the sacredness. Stories associated with wells, sacred or not, are common throughout the islands; Gigha, Tiree and Lismore have wells with stories attached, as do so many wells in the UK. I have an interest in these stories because I was taken as a small child to well-dressing events in Derbyshire. One of the village wells was annually decorated with flowers and ribbons to give thanks to the gods for providing pure water.

A hunting trip that bore fruit

I particularly like this tale as it portrays a strong woman with attitude. A chief of Colonsay, an enormous man with renowned strength, was hunting in Lochaber. This is a long way from Colonsay, so it's a mystery why he went all that way to hunt. I've decided to imagine the scene in the Fort William area, it being a place I've often passed through.

After a day's hunting, this MacPhee found a bothy towards nightfall, walked in without knocking, and an older lady, whom I shall call Granny, appeared and said, 'There's no shelter here, go away!'

MacPhee replied, 'I'm a chief, I *will* stay the night in your bothy.'

Granny said, 'You just wait until my daughter Mòr comes back. She will be a match for you.'

So they waited until Mòr came home. She was a huge young woman with plenty of muscle. She picked up MacPhee by the scruff of his neck and placed him outside the bothy door. MacPhee retaliated at once, swept Mòr up with his huge hands, and heaved her back to the fireside. Mòr was an Amazon, MacPhee a Hercules, and this was a stand-off. Mòr was impressed, and said, 'You're the first person to have ever done this to me!'

And she invited him to stay the night.

MacPhee left the bothy the next day to return to Colonsay. After nine months, Mòr gave birth to a son, who grew up with Granny and Mòr. Granny planted a tree in front of the bothy to celebrate the baby's birth. Every seven years the boy was asked to pull out the tree so as to test if he had inherited the strength of his parents. At seven and fourteen, he couldn't. At twenty-one he pulled out the tree with his bare hands and no spade. Mòr decided to tell the young man who his father was.

'You can go to Colonsay if you like, and tell your father who you are!'

The young man followed his mother's advice, went to Colonsay, and told the MacPhee chief that he was his son. He was welcomed with great joy. It's not explained how he proved that he was his son, but I would guess that he performed a gargantuan feat of strength.

The young man must have eventually returned to his mother, because legend has it 'that's how the first MacPhee got a foothold in Lochaber.'[3]

Seal women or selkies

Seal tales are found in similar form in Ireland, the Hebrides, the Orkneys, Shetland, Norway and Iceland. Legends state that seals are reincarnated humans, mostly women, who, either by punishment or by witchcraft, or simply by being shipwrecked, have been transformed into seals.

Many of the legends see the human male in dominant mode. But I really like the tale of a seal woman who captured one of the Colonsay MacPhees and kept him in her cave. When the lady left her cave for a while, MacPhee escaped to his home and the protection of his black dog, who might by that time have learnt how to bark. The lady gave pursuit and would have recaptured her beloved, but the dog defended him, and the contest between the seal and the dog continued until each had killed the other! Another case here of the diversity of character in not only 'humans' but also dogs, in different tales.

*

More folk tales are connected with the area around Kiloran Bay. Natural sea-caves, favourite haunts of sea birds, penetrate into the rocks at both ends (west and east) of the bay, for considerable distances.

One sunny day in September 2018 I followed a signposted track from the road near Uragaig, wondering where it would lead me. After passing a small wood I came across a meadow, newly scythed, very near the shore, which was invisible at that point. What was visible were the mouths of tall thin caves facing the sea. In one of these caves – the Uamh Uir, the Cave of the Grave – flint tools and the bones of domestic animals of a Neolithic people have been found. There are a number of legends associated with these particular caves, telling of fugitives being trapped there by their enemies. One story concerns the last of the MacPhee lairds of Colonsay who had been defeated by his enemies, the MacNeills. He took refuge, with his three dogs, from an approaching gang of MacNeills, in the Slochd-dubh-Mhic-a-Phi (MacPhee's Dark Cave, or Pit).

This had an entrance from the sea and another from the land. At the sea end MacPhee placed his three dogs. He stood in the cave at a point where anyone trying to get in from the land entrance would have to get down on all fours to pass through. MacPhee cut the head off each MacNeill in turn as he crawled through. Eventually the MacNeills, who waited outside, suspected trouble and started to dig an entrance through the roof, where-upon MacPhee went out by the sea entrance and swam across the bay to a rock still known as the Black Skerry of the MacPhee.

I climbed over some broken rocks, stumps of bracken and natural debris partly blocking the mouth of an open-ended cave, which I hoped was MacPhee's Dark Cave, and as my eyes adjusted to the dark, managed to see one or two unusual features.

The entrance to one of the Uragaig caves

Whether the cave I explored was the Dark Cave or not, there were colourful patterns on the walls to admire, and on the ground I noticed some startling circular patterns in water which at the time I thought was a puddle. The photo below shows the cave 'puddle' with circular patterns. There wasn't anything dripping from the roof of the cave, so this might have been a well.

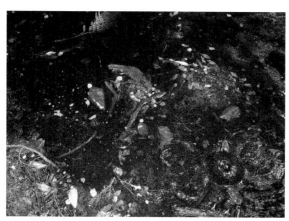

Bubbles in a cave puddle

It was time to move on. I dropped down to Kiloran beach via a good stile, and enjoyed the brisk walk along the empty beach which was backed by sand-dunes and flanked by rocks and reefs. Even at low tide there was nothing but sand – no seaweed, no pebbles, no shells. A few showers threatened but didn't add up to much. The rollers would have been good for surfing with a strong westerly wind, but no one was out today. Where a dyke of igneous rock appeared just above the low water mark there was a tiny bay called Port Easdail. There I came across a decomposing fin whale, which caused a diversion to the natural flow of the burn running into the sea.

Carcass of a fin whale

The carcass was a bit smelly but still in good shape. Apparently fin whales aren't that common, but this was not the first time one had paid a visit to the island. If their food source in the ocean changes course due to currents, this can force whales to drift off course, swim into shallow waters and possibly end up being beached. There was no way of knowing what happened to this one.

I climbed up on to some rocks at the end of the bay to the Endless Cave (Uamh Shiorruidh) which, it is said, housed people of the Azilian culture (7000-5000 BC), and then round a corner to the higher Lady's Cave (Uamh na Bantighearna), from where I had a wondrous view back along Kiloran Bay. A kitchen midden was found here during excavations. A midden is an ancient rubbish dump, often of bones and shell remains, which can reveal the type of food people ate.

I had heard of another nearby excavation at Cnoc Coig on Oronsay. This revealed another shell midden. In addition to shells, a few human bones were also discovered, all of them either fingers or toes! This may hint at some kind of burial rite – and the shape of the finger bones suggested strong muscular attachments, indicating that the people had a firm grip. Perhaps they were Herculean MacPhees! Later, I would find more Scottish folklore about cut-off fingers or toes, and I would wonder if the stories had some grisly basis in reality.

I didn't linger too long as the caves can get cut off by the tide.

*

I didn't see any references to folklore in the Heritage Centre, but I wasn't looking for any when I first visited it. Some small islands have long-established heritage centres, including those of Tiree and Lismore. The one on Colonsay was relatively new and was housed in an old Baptist church, open all the time, and displayed a growing collection of artefacts, books and photographs. I was keen to see an exhibition of Jean McAllister's artworks. Jean was a native of Colonsay and her artworks included lovely collages. A typical example was a picture of a hen made up of strips of crepe bandages that the local doctor had used to bind up Jean's leg after a fall. She presented the picture to the doctor after her leg healed!

*

At the exhibition I met Izzy, aged five, and her grandmother, and we fell into conversation. The older lady said she was happy for me to record my chat with Izzy. Actually, the youngster didn't need any persuasion. She was shortly to go into Primary 1 at the Kilchattan Primary School, which happens to be next door to the Heritage Centre.

She told me that there was just one child, herself, in pre-school that year. There were no other children her age to play with, but her one-year-old brother would be coming into preschool later on. She was looking forward to Primary 1 as she would be able to see her friends because they would all be in the same class. Izzy was keen to tell me what she'd learnt in pre-school, and danced and performed as she talked to me.

She had already gained some arithmetic knowledge in preparation for school:

Maths is absolutely simple!
I can show you my elevens if you like.
One times 11 equals 11; 2 times 11 equals 22; 3 times 11…
Izzy did a swirl and a twirl as she completed her 11 times table.
And I can do one more… 13 times 11 equals 143! My pre-school taught me it!
She paused, with a proud smile on her face.
I'm really a fan of breakdancing!
Izzy broke into a fine performance of breakdancing.

I went to teach the older kids about space.
Izzy demonstrated a slow spacewalk.
In Google years the universe will be a death which is one followed by a hundred zeros.
If we went to Pluto we would freeze to an ice cube, and if we went on Venus, we would get a fire!
She smiled triumphantly and I told her how impressed I was.

A year after my first encounter with Izzy, I met her as one of the pupils at the school.

The primary school just visible behind the van

After my chat with Izzy, I went in search of an older person to talk to about their school memories, and a helpful person suggested I talk to Netta, who had also been a pupil at Kilchattan school, but quite a few years before Izzy. I knocked on Netta's door, cold-calling, and she invited me in for a chat – another example of the kindness and trust I encountered all through the islands.

Netta was born in Glencoe during the Second World War, and came to Colonsay as a small child with her family for what she thought would be a short time. She spoke of her memories of Kilchattan school. She was roughly the same age as Alasdair on Gigha, but their school experiences were very different. When she started school in 1947 there were forty-nine children and two teachers, one for the little ones and one for the older ones. Two classrooms were at either side of the schoolhouse. She realised very soon that she and the teacher 'didn't get on'. For a start, Netta couldn't speak Gaelic, unlike everybody else apart from her family. She had only just started to learn it as a second language in Glencoe. But also she was left-handed and the teacher tried to make her write with her right hand. She had been allowed to use her left hand in her Glencoe school and still thought of Glencoe as home.

'I went home after school one day and packed my wee suitcase and sat down with my coat on, waiting for someone to take me back home to Glencoe,' she told me. They didn't have Gaelic as a subject in school because 'everybody had Gaelic'.

But she was lucky in finding someone other than the teacher to help her with the language. 'I was pally with a wee boy that stayed across the road from us. He was three years younger than me, and he didn't have any English. Gaelic was his first language, and we played together from square one, and taught each other. I taught him English and he taught me Gaelic.'

Netta and her school mates had some freedom, which she remembered with satisfaction. When they were let out at playtime, they didn't stay in the playground, but were allowed to wander up the hill behind the school. They fished for minnows in a big stream that ran down from the hill and put them in jam jars. 'At the end of the day we let them go again.' She smiled at the memory.

*

Netta spoke about the past and present socio-economic situation on Colonsay.

There were 300 residents in the 1950s. When the daily ferry began in the 1960s tourists were few because the island's houses were all occupied. Relatives and friends would come for a short visit, but there were no holiday houses.

At that time there was plenty of work on the estate for youngsters who could go to work straight after leaving school. Most people had a croft and ways and means of doing work, and the estate employed everybody.

Netta told me: 'Some of us had work on a Saturday because there were plenty of people who needed help and were quite willing to employ you for about two shillings. I had two Saturday jobs; I worked on the farm and then I helped an aunt of my husband. She 'took in' a few people, like vets, who came to the island, so I had a cleaning job.'

She thought that the biggest difference in island life between then and now was that young folk don't stay; they leave and go over to the mainland to school or university and they don't come back.

'There's no work or housing for them; you need one to have the other.' At present there were one or two young crofting families but Netta believed the situation was getting desperate. Some social housing had been decided upon but no building had happened yet, unlike in Gigha where a few houses were available to let.

Lord Strathcona was the fourth generation of owners that Netta knew of, but 'as they come down the line, the money gets less'. She added that it was cheaper now to employ folk from other countries than to employ people from the island. 'If a job does come up, the local people won't go for that job,' she told me.

*

I managed to talk to one of these 'folk from other countries'. One morning while I was in the main bunkhouse kitchen, Agnes the cleaner walked in. I said how spotless I found it. She told me she looked after thirteen houses and seven flats on the estate; she saw her cleaning job, which she found on the internet, as temporary.

She was from Hungary, and she had been waiting for four years for her PIN so that she could work as a nurse in the UK. She had a son and daughter living in England, and was looking forward to sharing a house with her grown children in the London area. Her mother chose to remain in Hungary and wasn't in the best of health; she sent money to her every month. She looked wistful and sad when talking about her.

The following year I learnt that Agnes was still on Colonsay, but had another job.

*

As on Gigha, I composed a song for the school children. When it came to devising one based on a Colonsay legend, I was at first tempted to choose a complex story about a MacPhee. That tale involves MacPhee and his hunting party of sixteen men who went on a boat to Jura; a dark cave, the 'useless' black dog, the men's sixteen sweethearts, and a strange hand or arm belonging to a monster who massacred them all except MacPhee. The black dog managed to kill the monster rather late in the day.

But there were too many deaths in this story, and I was intrigued by the fact that there are so many seal stories based on Colonsay. There is an island called Eilean Nan Ron – Seal Island – at the south-western tip of Oronsay, but I couldn't find a tale connected with it. So in the end I chose the tale of a handsome MacPhee who went to the mainland for hunting. While he was there, he met a lovely young woman and became engaged to her. He returned to Colonsay full of anticipation, to prepare for the wedding, while she took a few days to pack her things. She then boarded a boat in order to join her fiancé, but the weather was dire, and the boat became shipwrecked halfway to Colonsay. She jumped into the sea, immediately turned into a seal, swam for a while and landed on a Colonsay beach – and the song tells the rest of the story.[4]

Seal Lady

Johnny MacPhee and his Seal Bride
Chorus
   Under the rocks and next to the sea
   on the Colonsay coast searched Johnny MacPhee.
   Look out for your bride!
   She was drowned in a shipwreck, turned into a seal,
   and swam through the tide.

Verse 1 When people are lost in storms and gales
they live a good life as seals in the waves.
The King lets them turn back to human form
but just for one night, they must leave before dawn!
(chorus)

Verse 2 Once on the shore, Molly took off her skin.
Now a human girl, looked for Johnny MacPhee

but he was hiding inside a wee cave
and watched where she placed her skin in the shade.
(chorus)

Verse 3 Johnny sneaked up, grabbed the skin with both hands
and ran to the furthest place on the isle,
hid it for good where it couldn't be found,
then rushed back to Moll, and they danced all around.
(chorus)

Verse 4 The King was cross, Molly's skin disappeared;
without her skin she was human again.
The couple got married the very same day
and had lots of kids, who with seals liked to play.
(chorus)

(musical score in appendix)

Another version of the story states that Molly was obliged by the King to keep on searching for her skin. One day she found it, which resulted in her having to go back to join the seals. It is said, though, that Johnny MacPhee and the children were always provided with fish from the sea, but they never saw who brought them.

*

There were only four children in the school classroom when I visited (two were poorly), and I was delighted that Izzy, whom I'd recorded a year before, was there in P1. She didn't remember me – I was a touch disappointed – but it's unusual for a five or six-year-old to recall such a fleeting encounter. One or two pupils were very musical, and they all sang the song with gusto.

They had a big dressing-up box that they dived into when I suggested acting out the story, pulling out suitable garments, shawls and hats. Friendly and fun to teach, they allocated the roles between themselves paying no heed to gender-matching. I enjoyed the teaching and hoped that they would remember the song.

*

A few days later, after shamefully getting lost on a walk trying to follow a path next to Loch Fada in the middle of the island, I happened upon the school again, completely by chance. I decided to ask if anyone was driving to Kiloran, where the bunkhouse was. The children were playing in the garden in front of the school and they greeted me like an old friend. In the event I had no luck with the request, but once back on the road, I hitched a lift back to the bunkhouse with a kind van driver.

Here I digress a little. I do not see myself as a regular hitch-hiker. But small islands have virtually no crime, and so I feel very safe. I occasionally do it if I attempt a linear rather than a circular walk where there is no suitable public transport. This was the case on Gigha, for example. On the mainland, hitch-hiking is something I'd definitely not do. However, once I thumbed a lift because I wanted to be taken to the far end of the Crinan Canal in Argyll and Bute (there was no bus service), so that I could walk the length of the canal back to my car. I just had a whiff of anxiety at first, until I was pretty certain the male driver was trustworthy.

*

The bunkhouse, where I stayed on two separate occasions, was the location of a number of unexpected encounters. It was managed by the Colonsay estate, and unlike the bunkhouse on Muck, there wasn't a warden who dropped in from time to time. The main house had a small kitchen and living room, but good-sized bedrooms and washing facilities; I stayed there happily my first time. A year later I was placed in the annexe opposite the main house. This was a long building housing a large kitchen/dining/living room and four small two-person bunk rooms each with their own door to the outside (I had one of these to myself). A multi-sex washroom with a clear glass window was in the same block. Anyone looking in from the outside could see you cleaning your teeth, and any night visit from your bunkroom to the washroom/toilets involved dashing out and then back in, to brave the elements. Outside toilet facilities are unusual in hostels – I've only come across this three times in twenty years.

Bunkhouse on Colonsay

I wasn't too happy during my second stay in the bunkhouse, because of the outdoor facilities. Perhaps it was the cold, rainy, windy weather, or I felt too old and fussy, but it was worse than I thought. A very early morning loo visit resulted in my coming face to face with a naked man drying himself flamboyantly, arms outstretched, in the communal area, having eschewed his shower cubicle. He was intent on looking out of the clear-glass window at the pouring rain. He did apologise, saying that he didn't expect anyone to come in so early in the morning. I said nothing and went into a toilet cubicle. He disappeared after our meeting and I never saw him again.

I resolved to talk to the manager about this, which involved searching for him in the Colonsay hotel, but it wasn't clear if the man I spoke to was the one who could get things done. I explained to him, in my patient teacher voice that, for a start, and at a small price, they could easily make the washroom window opaque by sticking on frosted-glass film. I should have added that none of the doors of the loo cubicles had proper locks, and that the cubicles had a tendency to open by themselves, resulting in the occupant vulnerable to being seen by comers-in or even passers-by. I mentioned that children would be extra-vulnerable, thinking of my grand-daughters. In fact, this unisex washroom issue, and multi-gender dorms, are two of my pet hates about independent hostels and bunkhouses. The Youth Hostels Association hostels keep the sexes separate, unless couples take a dedicated room.

*

However, in the annexe kitchen the atmosphere was lively. I happened upon a small friendly group of new people trying to chase good-hu-mouredly the resident kitchen mouse that ran around the shelves at person-height for some minutes, then disappeared. These friends were full of stories and fun, and had arrived on the island to attend Ceol Cholasa, the island's folk festival held yearly in September. One of these was Tim, who had a surname related to the MacPhees, and who had come to Colon-say with his wife to chase his ancestors. We talked about mouth music, or *puirt-à-beul*. I told him how I'd first come across this Gaelic musical tradition at a ceilidh in Skye.

Tim, a larger-than-life character, was a past president of the Lothian Gaelic choir, and his favourite Gaelic music was *puirt-à-beul*. *Puirt* is the Gaelic word for 'little ditties'. In his opinion, Scottish mouth music is a great contribution to European music, but it was sometimes regarded as trivial and not to be treated seriously. I asked him to sing a bit for me to record, but he declined; I understood from his explanation that in his choir, it was only the soprano voices who sang the 'melody' – the other parts would be like an accompaniment, so he might not be used to singing all the twiddly bits.

Mouth music developed at the times when the fiddle was banned by the Presbyterian church elders and yet people still wanted to dance. In all cultures (according to Tim), first came the human voice, then came the dance, then came the instrumentation.

He talked about mòds – festivals of Gaelic song, arts and culture. They largely take the form of formal competitions. Solos and choral events in Gaelic, and traditional music dominates, including fiddle, bagpipe and folk groups. He explained that the first mòd was introduced in Scotland in 1892. That's when it was finalised that choirs could sing four-part harmony mouth music. I was surprised hearing about four-part mouth music, as up to then I'd only heard solo singers.

Tim expanded on his theme. 'Even in a beginners' Gaelic class the teacher will try to get the students involved in singing *puirt-à-beul*. The whole point of it is that although it's nonsense words, 99 percent of the time they do mean something, but they are funny little phrases. One phrase is not always related to the next in meaning, and it's often repeated. It's the vocables, the 'percussion', that keeps the beat so that you can dance to it.' This reminded me that singing in a foreign language gives the learner extra pronunciation practice. I had discovered this as a pupil when learning French and German.

Tim was proud of the success of his own choir, and said the reason why it was particularly good was that their singing was 'danceable'. The year they won the mòd competition, they had got a professional Highland dancer to practise with them. She was very fit, but they exhausted her!

Although Tim didn't want me to record his singing, I met someone who was happy enough to. Innes Watson was also staying at the hostel, and he was going to play at the Colonsay music festival. He and his friend Hamish Napier form a duo, and both are singers who play multiple instruments. He had been taught *puirt-à-beul* at the Scottish Academy of Music and Dance, now known as the RCS, the Royal Conservatoire of Scotland. He recorded two small pieces of himself singing two different mouth music songs for me, which I was delighted with, but I was sad that I wasn't able to hear him perform on stage.

It was bad timing on my part – it was the first full day of the festival, which I'd happened on by chance. But it was my last day on the island and I was due to catch the ferry later that evening. At breakfast in the bunkhouse, festival goers spoke of their favourite folk bands, and I felt as if I could have easily been a band-follower.

A guided walk was on the festival schedule that morning, and about fifteen of us, visitors and islanders, congregated quite near the bunkhouse, to walk to Beinn an Sgoltaire. It was led by Dave of the Heritage Trust.

We were not following any footpath, but went up a steep field and had to scramble over a fence or two. Dave was carrying a piece of carpet to lay over a barbed-wire fence, ingenious! An inland loch, Loch an Scoltaire, could soon be seen in the distance. This is where Colonsay gets its water from – a concrete dam was built in 1982. An island in the loch houses a medieval castle that can be reached by a hired boat.

While on the summit of the hill, many of us were taking photographs, but somewhere on the way back to the starting point, I lost my camera. I was stupid to have failed to zip up the case, and the camera must have dropped out while I was either climbing over a fence, or bending down for some other reason.

I was relieved that I had transferred my photos onto my computer only the night before, so I didn't lose much, but it was a wake-up call. On this trip I had already lost my gilet and my Fitbit. Was I falling into the sinking mud of decrepitude? Or is it common for anyone of any age to lose things in unfamiliar places? I tried to forget the lack of camera; I still had my smartphone after all.

*

In the early afternoon I went to an open mic event at the hotel, another event of the Colonsay Festival. The atmosphere was easy-going, but very few visitors were willing to sing or play. The two Colonsay stalwarts who were heading up the event had to scrape their barrels deeply to fill in gaps, and I was amused that they kept on running away from the action, to the bar, I think. I stepped forward to do one of my party pieces. It's a song I wrote to the tune of *Wildwood Flower*, a traditional ballad that I'd come across in my Joan Baez days. The lyrics of my song are a spiteful dig at another woman who steals the affections of the singer's partner, and then swans off.

Another, better, singer was a visitor from Leicester. I'd met him and his wife on a quest to find the well at Riasg Buidhe (where the fertility stone originally came from). Shamefully I had misread the map and hadn't walked far enough eastwards towards the coast, so missed the well and the ruined houses. But it was good to talk to fellow well-searchers.

We'd chatted, and I'd recognised his accent, which I hardly ever hear these days. It turned out that he had lived only about a mile away from where I was born and brought up in Leicester. He had known the family of my first 'pash', as we used to call them, a choirboy who always had his hair in his eyes, which annoyed me. This was one of many island encounters with people who know or knew people I know or knew.

After the open mic event, it was time to drive back in the pouring rain to the bunkhouse and pack the car.

*

Later that evening I took the three-hour ferry to Oban, and stayed overnight in the Oban SYHA hostel. It was a very hot night, and although I rated this hostel one of the most comfortable of all, my top bunk in a female dorm needed a great deal of ingenuity to climb up to, owing to a mysterious lack of ladder.

CHAPTER 4
TIREE

How do you discover that a man is from Tiree? He stoops, head into the wind.

And he must park his car into the wind, too.

The weather is often sunny in summer, but Tiree is one of the windiest places in the UK, largely because there are no proper hills and it is fully exposed to the south-westerlies. There are long sandy beaches with heavy swells and big waves, so it isn't surprising that it is well-known among the surfing community.

On Tiree there are no rabbits, no deer and no foxes, but plenty of hares. One came to the bunkhouse car park and stood for a couple of minutes, staring at me staring at him. He lolloped off after a while. Later I followed one in the car for half a mile on a road – he kept to the middle to make sure I wouldn't overtake him.

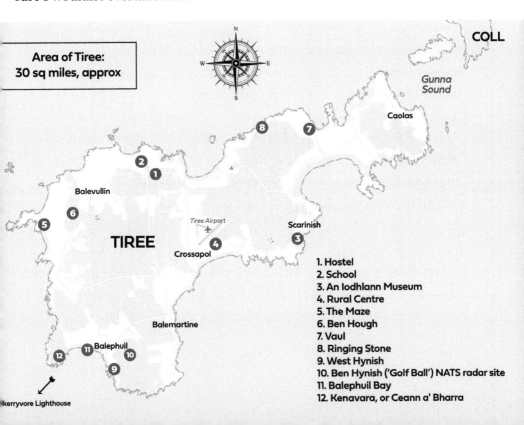

Area of Tiree:
30 sq miles, approx

COLL

Gunna Sound

Caolas

Balevullin

Tiree Airport

Scarinish

TIREE

Crossapol

Balemartine

Balephuil

kerryvore Lighthouse

1. Hostel
2. School
3. An Iodhlann Museum
4. Rural Centre
5. The Maze
6. Ben Hough
7. Vaul
8. Ringing Stone
9. West Hynish
10. Ben Hynish ('Golf Ball') NATS radar site
11. Balephuil Bay
12. Kenavara, or Ceann a' Bharra

Beach at Uvaig

In Islay a pub punter had told me there was no haggis on Tiree 'because there are no hills'. I understood the reference – it is said that haggises are short four-legged animals that run round the contours of a hill, and therefore on one side of the body the legs are longer than on the other side. I didn't let on that in another life as a special needs teacher, I had come across a super reading scheme called *The Fuzzbuzzes*. And learnt about a certain MacHaggis who had legs fit for purpose.

*

Tiree is thirty square miles in area, and unlike Muck, Gigha and Colonsay, it has a network of roads linking the scattered townships. You can get to Tiree with the CalMac ferry from Oban in just under four hours, and it calls first at Coll, which is Tiree's nearest neighbour. Once a week you can go from Tiree to Barra in the Western Isles, but only after deep scrutiny of the CalMac timetable.

One visual memory that will always stick with me is the view from the ferry of 'The Land beneath the Waves'. The land between three small hills sinks, or gets 'lost', in the sea, so you see just three bumps rising above the waters. Two of these 'bumps' are: Ben Hynish (141 metres), where there is a 'golf ball' – radar station – and Ben Hough (119 metres). There is a great deal of machair, which I've described in the Colonsay chapter, and which has given rise to another name for Tiree: the Land of the Corn.

Tourism, alongside crofting and fishing, are the main sources of employment for the islanders. Cattle and sheep are grazed. Gaelic is still spoken in Tiree, with almost 38 per cent of residents speaking Gaelic in 2011, the highest percentage of speakers in the Inner Hebrides.

*

Martin Martin was the first person to write a comprehensive account of the Hebridean islands. He was a native Gaelic speaker from Skye who, in the 1690s, became convinced of the need for a first-hand account of the society, culture and the natural history of other islands to the west of Scotland's mainland.

His book includes some interesting observations about Tiree and its people. Some of my favourite quotes are below:

The natives... live on barley-bread, butter, milk, cheese, fish, and some eat the roots of silverweed; there are but few that eat any flesh... Some years ago, about one hundred and sixty little whales ran themselves ashore in this isle, very seasonably, in time of scarcity, for the natives did eat them all, and told me that the sea-pork, i.e., the whale, is both wholesome and very nourishing meat.

The isle is unwholesome, and makes the natives subject to the ague. The inhabitants living in the south-east parts are for the most part bald, and have but very thin hair on their heads.

The inhabitants are all Protestants. They speak the Irish tongue, and wear the Highland dress.

The cows and horses are of a very low size in this isle, being in the winter and spring-time often reduced to eat sea-ware (seaweed).

The water of the well called Toubir an Dòmhnaich is by the natives drunk as a catholicon for diseases.[1]

For me the compelling facts are that the natives were susceptible to fever and thin hair, and the cattle and horses were small. The healing well mentioned by Martin lies east of Sandaig and north of Balephuil Bay. Supposedly the water did you good only if you drank it on a Sunday. Both Johnson and Boswell read Martin's book and took a copy of it along with them on their own famous tour in 1773. Johnson felt Martin had failed to record the more interesting aspects of Tiree life at the time, and suggested that this was because Martin was unaware of just how different the social structure of the isles was, in comparison with life elsewhere. Was Johnson implying that only 'outsiders', like himself and Boswell, could give the best account of Tiree life? Perhaps he was envious of Martin, who could not only speak Gaelic (at that time called Irish), but also actually visited Tiree, whereas the Boswell duo didn't.

*

Soon after my arrival on Tiree I visited An Iodhlann, the excellent heritage centre at Scarinish. Staff on duty were friendly and informative and I spent a long time looking at some of the exhibits, including the model of a Tiree house.

Model of a typical Tiree house – in An Iodhlann, the heritage centre

I was to discover many of these houses for real. One of the first things I noticed when driving around the island were renovated thatched houses. Mostly they were croft houses, standing alone. Many faced east, 'back to the wind, face to the sun'. They were modernised, with dry-stone walls, rounded corners and roofs that sat within the outer walls, almost the opposite of traditional Alpine houses whose roofs dangle almost to the ground.

Neat finishes

In earlier times the Tiree house had double walls, up to eight feet thick and six feet wide, made of uncemented stones, with rounded corners. The two layers of walls were separated by a layer of sand and rubble, called the 'heartings'. This 'damp blanket' was supposed to create good insulation and a channel for the rain to discharge from the wall top, and drain through until it percolated to the soil, as well as preventing the wind from getting through. However, it didn't always work.

Chimneys lacked the support of a gable and were relatively unstable, so they were built at a slight angle outwards in case they collapsed. Roofs were thatched with marram grass placed on top of turves cut from the moorland, and laid upside down over the roof timbers. As is shown in the following photo, turf often covered the wall tops where grass and flowers grew – and dogs, sheep and sometimes cows got up there for tasty morsels. Sometimes the woman of the house would sit up there and sew, weave or knit.

This dwelling is waiting to be modernised; the indents in the walls are windows, not at first apparent!

Hebridean Island Life

Roofless houses huddle
against a stubborn wind,
hopeful sheep seek shelter.
Stone upon stone in barren fields,
yellow with ragwort, prickly with thistles.

Cardigans ill-fastened,
old men stumble
along the sheep tracks
to greet the brash supply boat
cutting through the dark grey swell.
They talk to Angus, of Celtic, Rangers,
the price of gin and whisky.
The stone seat near the jetty has heard it all before.

Since Martin Martin's visit there have been many other important visitors and incomers, some in considerable numbers, who have made an impact on Tiree and its culture.

*

After admiring the Tiree House model, and many other artefacts in the heritage centre, I spoke with one of the volunteers working there. He was John Fletcher, and we fell into conversation. He told me that in the 1930s, like most island and highland communities, ordinary crofters were struggling to make ends meet. Farming meant hard physical work for the whole family, so an extra hand or two, or an extra child to grow up and help with the croft, was always welcome. Into this scenario, before and during the early war years, came an influx of small children from Glasgow needing to be fostered. They swelled the school population significantly.

John was one of these children. Now in his eighties, he recalled his early life, and showed me a photo of himself, his sister and the others in his primary school in Balemartine, in 1945-6. 'I came here as a one-year-old baby,' he told me. 'A lot of these children came from Glasgow Corporation because they weren't looked after in their own place. They were called boarded-outs – their mothers had died or taken to drink.'

According to John, officials from the Corporation came to the islands twice a year, with no forewarning, in a big black car, and tried to 'drop children off' at croft houses. Many crofters were happy to have an extra pair of hands to be of use in the future when the child was older, and the parents received some remuneration. The Corporation remained responsible for the children, and an inspector came regularly to check that the children were being looked after. Parcels of clothes and sweets were sent twice a year until the child was in work for a year. 'Once you got to work they kept you in control for a year, kept you in clothing until you got on your feet,' John said.

John's wife was also one of these children, and the couple are two of the very few boarded-out children left now on Tiree. 'Most of these children scattered after they reached sixteen, and never came back.'

I asked John if he had any strong memories of his school time. 'Some pleasant, some not,' he said. 'Some of the foster children weren't accepted as easily as the local, more privileged children... We were led to believe that...' He spoke too softly for me to hear.

'I had no English when I went to school,' he continued.

'I've heard that some children, in various Gaelic communities, got punished when they spoke Gaelic in school,' I said. I hoped that I wasn't leading him to say something he'd regret later on.

'That's what you're saying,' he replied; so we changed the subject.

John's foster parents were good to him. But this wasn't the case with many of these children. I sensed a reluctance to speak of this, not only from John, and I was told that some of the very numerous records of that time are considered too sensitive for people like me to read.

*

Another group of incomers, who came to Tiree for a very different purpose from the 'boarded-outs', were the Second World War airmen. My own knowledge of the airmen began on my first day on Tiree. I arrived early at the independent Millhouse hostel, as I'd caught the very early ferry from Oban. After a spot of lunch I walked west along the road for some time, making for Ben Hough. An uphill path ended at one or two dilapidated buildings and a communications mast. A road going downhill on the other side led to a grassy area to my right, where I was hoping to arrive at Tràigh Hough, a likely looking beach, according to the map.

I never made it to the beach. This was the 'Maze' area. Breeze-block bunkers and buildings were semi-hidden in the enormous grassy sand dunes. I found the going difficult as there were barbed-wire fences to climb over and the vegetation was thigh-high. There were no signs, no one was around to ask for explanations or directions, the area seemed huge, and it was easy to become disorientated, as the beach was hidden from view. I had no idea of the history at that point, but discovered later that the buildings are concrete relics of the early 1940s when RAF Tiree used the island as a front-line base, due to its strategic location on the edge of the Atlantic, the most westerly Inner Hebridean island.

The war was a great turning point in Tiree's history. Although more than 200 islanders left Tiree to serve in the forces, up to 2,000 airmen, including Poles, Englishmen and Canadians, were stationed on Tiree. The island population shot up. Interestingly, the 'invasion' of the airmen had been predicted by a certain John MacLean (Iain mac Eachainn Bhàin), Tiree's most celebrated seer in the 19th century. He had foreseen that 'many armed men would come to the island living in strange houses, and large birds steered by people with noses like pigs, would rise up and lie down on the Reef.'[2]

At least three squadrons had their base there, including 518 Squadron who regularly flew into the Atlantic to make weather measurements. During 1944 the squadron flew every single day but two. Often icing on the planes' exteriors and enormous waves made this extremely dangerous and they lost twelve aircraft during their spell on Tiree. In 1944 two Halifaxes collided in low cloud over Island House.

Socially the huge RAF base and the NAAFI made a tremendous impact. There was a lot going on; dances, films, concerts, shows, and the inevitable romances. Before the arrival of the airmen, Gaelic had been the predominant language, but quite swiftly it became English because it was the lingua franca of the airmen, used by different language groups.

Tiree's Reef is unimpeded by natural barriers and therefore ideal for an air base. This area was requisitioned by the Ministry of War in 1940, and labourers were brought in from Ireland and several Scottish jails. They built many of the island's roads and a large airstrip, which is now Tiree's airport.

*

An eighty-four-year-old Tiree woman is quoted as saying she was too young for the airmen during the war, and now she was too old for the surfers! Tiree has forty-six miles of coastline, with plenty of safe sandy beaches facing in all directions, so there are excellent opportunities for sports related to surfing.

Most surfers who come to Tiree are visitors, so strictly speaking they cannot be called incomers. But some of them stay a long time on the island in the summer, and some Tiree residents have become firm aficionados of the sport. For about twenty years, Tiree has attracted surfers of all ages and abilities. Kite surfing, kayaking, stand-up paddle boarding and trail running are all on offer. There is a national competition every October.

One day I strolled down the road from the hostel to the inland Loch Bhasapol where there is a surfing school. I loved the fact that there were a number of quite small children having fun in the water. The loch was shallow, so an ideal place for learners. I stood watching them and their families for some time.

The Millhouse hostel, a converted barn next to the restored watermill at Cornaig, was warm and comfortable. The warden, David Naylor, was patient with me and my old-lady requests such as not to be put in a mixed-gender dorm. He allocated me a small room to myself, temporarily, that had a three-quarter bed with a bunk on top. A young woman came and took the top bunk for two nights, otherwise I was on my own for four.

Other guests were a doctor and his daughter who both took pity on me as I was having computer issues. They spent quite a time with my laptop and sorted me out; I was really grateful. A group of ex-public school surfers were also staying. Their boards and wetsuits were hanging out at the back on purpose-built racks. They were a friendly lot but took over all the airspace in the kitchen-cum-living room. One of them was amenable enough to turn off his radio (we could all hear it) when I asked him to. His friend offered to show me the speed with which he could wash a coffee pot. I was impressed. They left some mess on the kitchen surfaces after their meal, but I was in a good mood and didn't complain.

Later during my stay, David the warden took a picture of my car in the hostel car park, and sent it to my phone, labelled 'Crime Scene'.

I had thought that the headrest was a good place to dry out my hat and scarf

A suspiciously placed hat and scarf is probably the closest Tiree gets to a grisly crime. The island with its 650 inhabitants has a police station but hardly any crime, and no recorded murders. On the nearby island of Coll, with 220 people and no police presence, a public convenience was vandalised in 2011; the constable on Tiree had to wait two days for a ferry to get to Coll to investigate, but didn't find the culprit. Later I discovered that cybercrime is the main crime on these islands – perpetrators and victims can live anywhere – and Tiree has its fair share of victims.

*

I went in search of Tiree residents to chat to and asked around for people willing to give me their time. I found Louise, a friendly young woman in her twenties, in the Tiree Trust Office. She had been recommended to me as someone who would be happy to be interviewed. We spoke about her work for the North Argyll Carers. The majority of people in Tiree are over fifty, and a few older or infirm ones, some with dementia, need help that her organisation can give. Louise goes to people's homes to visit. Often these visits can just be social, but she helps with things like form-filling, too. The carers organise group sessions, where people draw or paint pictures, tell stories and reminisce in Gaelic. Many clients grew up in Tiree, so they were more comfortable speaking that language.

Recently, Louise told me, a lady from Barra came to Tiree to teach the clients how to 'waulk' the tweed, and introduced the traditional Gaelic waulking songs – these are great songs with actions. Waulking isn't traditional in Tiree, and you will read more about it in my chapter on Barra.

The North Argyll Carers had eight carers on its books. 'It's quite a new service, and it will get busier as time goes on,' Louise told me.

Louise also volunteers for Cùram – Care in the Community, so her paid work is similar to her voluntary work. Cùram was set up to explore and take forward integrated progressive care services for the island's elderly residents, including a lunch club, various social activities, respite care, meals on wheels, and a minibus to take the elderly to events and appointments. The volunteers who run Cùram arrange a series of events to raise money locally and there is a good network of helpers.

We also spoke about Gaelic, and I was fascinated with her explanations. 'There are a lot of people on Tiree who don't have Gaelic as a first language, but who can speak it,' she said. 'At first, you might mistake such a person as a native Gaelic speaker, as long as they get the sounds right. It's a harsh-sounding language.'

She spoke English at school, but learning Gaelic was compulsory until S3 (third year of secondary school). At that point in school the first-language-Gaelic speakers and the Gaelic learners like herself were taught together for the first time. Among themselves they usually spoke English, but they had certain phrases and colloquialisms they uttered in Gaelic because it sounded better. One of these phrases was, 'O mo creach,' which would be a response if you heard something unpleasant or were sad about someone or something.

A first-language-Gaelic person is always able to tell the difference between learner-speakers and birth-Gaelic speakers, because the former tend to be more formal in the structure of their sentences, whereas fluent speakers who've spoken it from childhood speak in a more informal way.

I asked if a learner-speaker would have an accent. Louise said that formality/informality in language use was more of a 'telling' difference than accented/non-accented. And a learner would say, 'I've got learners' Gaelic.'

*

Another willing interviewee was Rou. I had managed to contact him by phone, and he invited me to his parents' house for a cup of tea one rainy evening. He edits the Tiree newspaper *An Tirisdeach*, and told me about his background.

Born on the island, he is digitally very literate, self-taught. 'At school I was alone in not being interested in sport, fashion and pop bands like my school mates. I was into anime and manga.' I didn't know what these were, typically for my age, but I didn't let on. I looked it up on Google. They are hand-drawn and computer animations, created in Japan.

'I'm nerdy,' he added, grinning.

Rou went to university in Derby (where his parents are from) to study animation.

'A lot of my writing at university was based on, or influenced by Tiree,' he said. Unlike some of the young people brought up on the island, he wanted to make Tiree his home. When he came back to Tiree after university, he told me that there was not much demand for an artist, so when the position as the *An Tirisdeach* editor came up, he said, 'I can do that!' and jumped straight in at this great opportunity.

The paper comes out fortnightly, and there is a digital version too. When I met Rou he had been doing the job for only a few months. He writes articles, and also looks around for local newsworthy stories.

The newspaper appeals to residents and visitors alike. In one edition, I read about the Tiree Music Festival, a community archaeological dig asking for volunteers, the Tiree Art Enterprises annual summer exhibition and RSPB information.

Rou was looking forward to conducting more interviews with islanders and writing pieces for the newspaper based on the interviews. But he still has time for non-newspaper work; for example writing adventure stories and drawing comics, and would like to devise his own computer game.

'Writing and pictures go together,' he said. He has joined an online community, collaborating on stories with friends across the world. He paints as a hobby, and is a freelance artist, designer and illustrator, offering personalised CVs and gift art. His own small business is called Gromity.

Being fascinated by language, I asked Rou if he spoke Gaelic. 'Recently I've been out of the habit of using it, yet I think I could pick it up again,' he said. Did he think there was any tension or rivalry on Tiree between first-language speakers and Gaelic learners? My question was based on my own experience, many years ago, of being 'shut out' by a bilingual group who habitually chose to speak, in my presence, their 'other' language which I didn't understand. He replied that he had never noticed any tension, as people are very polite to each other. 'I think that people keep their manners in check in a small community; it's safer to do so. If they don't like each other they would be polite and just avoid them,' he said.

When he was a child there were about 1,000 people on the island and now the population is down to 650. But people are beginning to come in again. He acknowledged that there was a little tension 'at the beginning, with new people coming to the island,' but said it had done the island good because 'without people moving to the island, we'd be dying out.'

There's a contemplative side to Rou. He loves the safety of Tiree, and thinks he will always return there. He made me envious as he described how he could go out in the dark alone and see auroras, shooting stars, and even a moonbow – a rainbow over the moon; 'weird but cool!' He used to spend a lot of time on the beaches, and got inspiration for stories there – especially the sunsets – that's why he prefers the west coast to the east; and from his house he can often hear the sea, listening to the storms, wind and rain.

As we were finishing our chat, he said that he would send me a link to an animated piece he'd created for his degree. It's called *Isle of Tiree* – it couldn't be anywhere else. As I watched it I realised the colours of the shallow coastal waters were just right. I loved the recurring 'action' of waves and tides going in and out, and continuous movement of an old man and his non-laying chicken (which ended up on a dinner plate).

Finally, we discovered that we were both fascinated by the Skerry-vore lighthouse and the Hynish shore station. He would love to go to the lighthouse itself, he told me, despite the possible risks involved. I told him about the 2016 film *The Lighthouse* – a dark story that made a big impression on me as it captured the loneliness and hazards that lighthouse keepers and their families used to endure before lighthouses became automatic. (There is a 2019 film of the same name.) I wondered if a computer game based on the Skerryvore lighthouse could be a money-spinner for him.

*

Rachel was another friendly resident who was willing to chat with me. One day I came across a small poster about a yoga nidra session. It was to be held near the Cobbled Cow cafe in a big circular tent such as the ones that Scouts and Guides used to use, with a central pole. I peeped in and looked at the array of rugs, wonderful Indian-made rounded cushions, and other colourful soft furnishings. And it was warm inside.

The session was due to start at 10am the next day. At the appointed hour, I climbed inside the tent to join a couple of early arrivals. Rachel, the yoga teacher, came in and introduced herself; she wouldn't look out of place in a Wagner opera, I thought, strong and handsome. Three more participants besides me lay down on the tent floor with a strong cold wind and heavy drizzle outside.

I knew nothing about yoga nidra so was curious to experience it, especially as I'd been alerted to the fact that you have to lie down without moving at all for an hour. There is no stretching, for example, like in hatha yoga, which I've done a lot of. I couldn't help thinking that I'd only just got up and had breakfast, so I'd been prone for a long time in bed up until two hours beforehand!

My lie-down was pleasant and relaxing, and Rachel read from a text. It was soothing to listen to her soft, clear voice with my eyes shut. But outside the tent was a noise that couldn't be avoided – the howling gale. We were all wrapped up in the many blankets and shawls and cushions scattered around. Twice I thought that someone had touched me on the knee, but that turned out to be the wind buffeting the tent strongly against me, unexpected as I was well away from the tent's side.

After the session, Rachel told me that she had been interested in meditation and spiritual well-being for a long time. 'There's not much opportunity to express spirituality on Tiree outside of the churches,' she said, but there is a Baptist and a Church of Scotland church. She was engaged with both of these places of worship, but is trying to create a space for those who are interested in what she calls a 'quieter spirituality'. I told her I'd meditated before in a Buddhist context, and had also been taught self-hypnosis which is very useful for relaxation purposes.

She nodded – she'd trained as a children's nurse in Great Ormond Street and had been really impressed by the work of the psychologists and psychotherapists who were teaching children self-hypnosis. Here in Tiree she was doing yoga nidra with various children, enabling them to 'find that centre' – so that whatever life throws at them, they've still got that 'centre'. I needed more explanation about what the 'centre' was, but let it be. She engages children with storytelling. 'It's partly entertainment and fun, but it's also aimed at transformation through inspiration and imagination,' she said.

Rachel home-schools her own children. I asked her if there was a philosophy behind this. 'There's wisdom in childhood and if you give them free rein they are able to 'unfold' – follow their own spiritual path.' This is in contrast to the constraints inherent in regular schooling that shape them very early. Personally I have my doubts about home-schooling. There may be a lot wrong with state and private schools, and to quote Rachel, 'many constraints', but to my mind nothing can make up for the social learning that takes place naturally in school. At the time of writing, during the Covid-19 crisis, home-schooling has put these issues into the limelight and I expect that unlike so many parents Rachel and her family were in their element.

We went on to discuss provision for mental health needs for Tiree residents. The GP can often take care of the mental as well as the physical health of patients, as they usually have more time than the average city GP. There is also a mental health nurse. Otherwise, services based in Argyll can be accessed by phone or by Skype.

*

It turned out that I had already met Rachel a year before in a knitting group that had been held just next door to the tent. The penny dropped when she mentioned the names of her children! I'd been a little thirsty so had made for the Cobbled Cow cafe in the Rural Centre, but the cafe itself was shut. However, my curiosity was aroused by some friendly-sounding voices coming from down the corridor. In the back room I happened upon a group of residents. One of these was Rachel. Nine women and one man were knitting, sewing, weaving and chatting. I said hello and smiled.

'Come and join us,' said one woman. I suspect that if I had not been alone, I wouldn't have been invited – a real perk of exploring on your own as an older woman. They were all Tiree residents, I the outsider.

'But I haven't got needles or wool!' I said. This was not a problem; they lent me needles and wool and I dredged up my knitting knowledge, casting on twenty stitches. From then on it was garter stitch.

I learnt that this group met weekly, bringing their own knitting, sewing and weaving. After half an hour they stopped for a small break for tea and biscuits, and again I was urged to partake. They were really friendly in a quiet way. Rachel had mentioned her daughters, and I talked a little about Isabelle, one of my granddaughters, who might well have been interested in a child's weaving set for Christmas. (Having grandchildren makes you think laterally.) They told me they'd once knitted tiny bottle-hats for charity.

My knitting

Unravelling
In the windowless hall
round the table,
through stitch and pin we cast
off our shyness.

Nine women, one man
knitting, sewing, weaving.
Join us, they said,
lent me wool and needles.

In, round, through, off.
My mother would wind the yarn;
I held the skein in both hands,
my thumbs moving in nimble rhythm.

Just a whisper or two
of quilts, fabric, ribbons, felt,
weft and warp, hem and thread,
of bottle-hats for charity.

In, round, through, off.
My mother made a perfect ball;
I wanted to play cat's cradle.

I gabbled about family, garden,
Leeds and Yorkshire,
Could someone take me up?

And left behind a square of garter stitch,
hoping someone would take it up
In, round, through, off.

On driving west from Scarinish I had parked the car on the roadside and wandered around the reef for a short while listening to the buzzing of bees and inspecting the wonderful variety of flowers, but started to feel guilty as it was like treading on someone's carefully tended huge flower bed. I'd come across machair on Colonsay near Balnahard Bay, and wanted to find out more about this habitat.

Janet Bowler, another dedicated woman of Tiree, was the person to ask about machair. She was often to be found at An Iodhlann, the island heritage centre, which I mention at the beginning of this chapter. When I asked her about the Tiree machair, she was in her element.

Tiree is the most fertile of all the Hebridean islands. Janet explained that the Reef, in the middle of the island, where I'd had a wander, is a massive grassy plain, the soil being made up of sand and shell fragments where wild flowers grow in abundance. Machair is a rare habitat usually restricted to the Atlantic seaboard of Scotland, and provides rich foraging for sheep and cattle. The Tiree machair has been managed for generations by careful grazing and improvement with seaweed as a fertiliser. Otherwise the soil is undisturbed, rabbits being absent from the island.

I'd picked up a postcard: 'Have you seen this Bee?' and read of the great yellow bumblebee project on the island. This is a rare bee that feeds, in particular, on red clover, vetches and knapweed (all flowers that grow on the machair) and can be identified by its yellowish-brown colouring and a thick band of black hairs between the wings. A hundred years ago, this bee could be found throughout the British Isles, but it has declined by 80 per cent in the past century.

Other bees also feed on machair flowers, including the northern colletes mining bee, which is rare too, but feeds on a greater variety of plants (they are polylectic).

Janet was very keen to preserve the great yellow bumblebee by extending machair habitat on the island, and raising awareness about its importance. She started Tiree's Great Yellow Bumblebee Project and she and her team have been working with volunteers – some of whom are pupils at the school – and gardeners, to monitor the bee.

The project's objectives include finding out more about the status of this bee population, and seeing how many of the right kinds of flowers are available throughout its colony cycle, which starts in June and ends at the beginning of September. Sometimes the bee is first noticed only at the very end of June; so just two months of frantic feeding.

One tentative conclusion was that Tiree bee numbers were down because of the lack of forage when the queens first come out of hibernation in early spring. So Janet and her team have sown and planted wild flowers such as knapweed, kidney vetch, birds-foot trefoil and red clover to create new areas of suitable forage.

The project has been successful in its bid for funding and has recently been awarded £2,000 from Tesco Bags of Help.

I showed Janet a poem I'd written about the machair and the bee, asking her for feedback on the facts. I was very glad I did this, as I hadn't understood that the bee doesn't feed on all the machair flowers – so I had to erase references to orchids, lousewort, ox-eye daisies and hogweed! The great yellow bumblebee is a long-tongued species which means they like flowers with a long tube such as clovers and vetches – the pea family. The bee can reach nectar that other bees can't. Janet used the word 'use' to mean 'take nectar from'. The bees' favourites are white and red clover, meadow vetchling, yellow rattle and knapweed which they feast on late in the season. All these flowers have a long tube down which the bee pokes his tongue, or proboscis. I was reminded of the Aesop fable of the Fox and the Stork, and the differently shaped receptacle each needed to feed from.

The bee and the machair
Snug in the lee of the lowest dunes
a fragile garden tends itself
in scrawny soil and shell sand
blown inland by westerlies.

Here the great yellow bumblebee
pays her respects and seeks her nectar,
flowers bright with spring-like fever
anticipate their visitor.

Meadow vetchling scrambles tall,
tendrils spurt from leaflet pairs,
bee lands soft at florets' entrance,
pollen catching on her hairs.

Bolder, brasher than the vetchling,
yellow rattle stands erect,
brown pods clinking tiny seeds,
wills the bee to reconnect.

Purple knapweed bold and stalwart,
florets frilly, welcoming,
long tongue of the busy insect
lingers with her much-loved bloom,
last one of this long day's quest.

Her pollen-heavy body tiring,
flies back to her queen and nest.

Machair flowers

As well as bees, the machair provides food for a variety of other insects. Butterflies such as common blue and meadow brown are found, as well as a range of day-flying moths, hoverflies and beetles, including a particular machair beetle that can bite. Ground-nesting birds also thrive on machair.

Janet talked about the common grazing in sections of Tiree. It's not obvious on the OS map where these areas are, but there's a fascinating map called the Turnbull map, drawn in 1768, which I'd admired in the heritage centre. The map shows the island before it was partitioned into crofts around 1800. Tiree is still divided up; thirty-one crofting townships are controlled by a grazing committee.

Each township has a common area of machair and a moorland share that is not necessarily adjoining the croft house. The Isle of Tiree website explains: 'Roughly speaking, Tiree has an outer ring of machair, a middle section of dark, rich, cultivatable earth, and a centre of wet, peaty ground called *sliabh* (pronounced 'slieve'). Most crofting townships are divided so as to have a 'slice' of each type of ground. The hill grazing and *sliabh* which keep their moisture are for summer grazing, the field land is cropped and the machair provides grazing for sheep and cattle at the wetter times of the year.'[3]

*

For me as a walker and explorer, fences can be a nuisance. I told Janet that on one of my walks I tried to get to the shore but was put off by a stout barbed-wire fence just above the beach at the edge of a field. In the old days on the common grazing lands, there was a shepherd who kept the cattle separate, so crofters didn't need to partition their 'share' of common grazing. Now they are allowed to put up fences.

Janet's husband John is the RSPB manager of Tiree, and has written a book about the island's birds. He writes a monthly bird information column on the Tiree website and encourages islanders and visitors alike to keep him posted on unusual sightings of birds and other wildlife. Corncrakes are as elusive on Tiree as on Colonsay! But there's an annual night-time census of corncrakes every June, and recently around 300 calling males were counted. This healthy population makes up about a third of all corncrakes in Britain, a result of the careful management of the bird's natural habitat by crofters and famers over the years.

I heard about the recent sighting of three rose-coloured starlings, a very rare non-resident bird, which were hanging around a flock of ordinary starlings. They are like small hooded crows, but with pink 'hoods'. And a crofter I spoke to said she'd just seen a peregrine falcon – there is just one pair on the island.

*

One day I was on my way to explore the south-west headland called Ceann a'Bharra, or Kennavara, which meant driving past Island House to the west of Crossapol. This house has a history and folklore associated with it. Peeping through its gates I could make out the small freshwater loch called Loch an Eilein, where the remains of a castle stand on an island (crannog) on the loch's east side. The original drystone dyke that surrounded the castle is still in existence, but this is all that remains of the castle. I wondered about its history. The basis of the present building was erected in 1748 by the 3rd Duke of Argyll to house his factor, and it has been altered and extended over the years. At one time Island House had a courtroom and a prison cell. It is now owned by the present Duke of Argyll, and has been upgraded to superior self-catering accommodation.

I'd heard about a brownie, like the one in Cara in the Gigha chapter, who was said to have lived in the castle, which was once the seat of the MacLeans. The brownie of the castle liked to go about his nightly business – without any clothes on – of keeping the cattle away from the crops. On one occasion he was discovered by a passing couple, who offered him shoes and 'breeks' (trousers). But this was a typical brownie who didn't like people taking pity on him and he was annoyed. He was too proud to accept the clothes and stomped off. He revealed his name in a chant (a bit like Rumpelstiltskin); 'Shoes and breeks on Gunna/ And Gunna at the herding;/ But may Gunna enjoy neither shoes nor breeks,/ if he should herd the cattle any more.' He was never seen again. (A. A. MacGregor[4]) I recognised Gunna as being the name of the narrow stretch of water between Tiree and Coll called Gunna Sound. Perhaps the brownie jumped over to Coll after disappearing.

I'd also heard about a glaistig who used to 'live' in the castle. Glaistigs are the brownies' female counterparts. They are thin, green-skinned women, dressed in green, and with very long grey hair. They often lived in dairy farms, hated dogs, loved cows and milk, and would demand it from the crofters who had to give willingly. Like the brownies, they expected respect and gratitude. The glaistigs were very good at yelling, especially at the cattle or in the dairy. Interestingly they were known to take care of 'persons of weak intellect'.

They also liked to spin and use tools that they found lying around; this attribute might have encouraged people to be tidy. If you left your spinning wheel out on a Saturday night, and were very religious, you would be ashamed on the Sunday morning as the glaistig might have indulged herself spinning all night. Work had been done on the Sabbath, shame! Devout people would remove the band of the spinning wheel every Saturday evening to prevent any Sunday early morning meddling by the glaistig!

This particular glaistig, with long yellow hair, lived in the attic of the Island House, so she must have transferred herself from the castle. People called her the Sea Gruagach; *gruagach* means 'the hairy one'. She worked extra hard at housekeeping before visitors were expected. She was hardly ever seen by the genteel folk, but servants must have seen or heard her more often, because she supervised them and gave them a 'doing' when they slackened.

After lingering at the Island House gates, I drove south

Glaistig with jug and pail

136

and parked in a car park among cars laden with surfboards in the dunes behind Balephuil Bay. These were at the south-facing beach called Tràigh Bhi, a lovely spot. Walking west on the sand with the sea on my left, busy with surfers, my destination was clear enough – I wanted to reach the highest point of the headland in front of me, called Beinn Ceann a' Mhara. At the end of the beach I expected a path going uphill, but there were just sheep tracks going in all directions. I headed due west, high-stepping the rough ground, but soon came across a stout fence. With some difficulty I skirted it and other obstacles, taking care not to land in sloughs of cow-muck. I finally reached a cairn that I took to be the highest point of the headland. The views were terrific, especially looking north to Tràigh na Gilean, a beach not frequented by surfers, at least on that day.

View north from Beinn Ceann a' Mhara

Under my feet but not in view were caves, about which there are more folk tales, including one about the disappearance of a man entering a cave but not exiting it, and whose dog survived. (I'd come across a version of this tale on Gigha.) Natural arches, an ancient fort, and dramatic rocks and skerries completed the picture.

As I turned south there was relatively easy, flattish terrain that led to another 'cairn'. This was part of the scant medieval remains of St Patrick's Chapel, or Temple, with its enclosure and monastery walls. They possibly replaced an earlier, less substantial chapel. In the centre of the east gable wall were the traces of a square altar base. There was also a 'vat' that is believed to have been a well, Dabhach Phàraig, the vat of St Patrick. The water came from a big round opening in a rock that is now filled with stones after a lamb drowned in it. But if you took the stones out and baled it dry, it would fill up again. It is one of the many wells that had healing properties, catholicons. There are two stones carved with Latin crosses on both faces, but sadly I didn't see them, as I had had no prior knowledge of what to look out for. It was only when looking up on the Canmore website that I discovered their existence.[5]

I found out that Erskine Beveridge, the archaeologist and photographer, had visited the site in 1898 and had taken a couple of photographs – one of the two stones, and the other of the temple itself. I was excited to see these on my laptop screen, particularly the photograph of the two stones, which so reminded me of the Bodach and Cailleach stones on Gigha (which in contrast had no crosses carved on them). I write more about Beveridge's archaeological and photographic career in my chapter on North Uist.

But I knew nothing then about the Tiree connection to Beveridge – if I had, I would have stayed longer. The Temple commanded a wonderful but very isolated position, and it was already late afternoon so I was in a hurry to get down to the car.

As is often the case, the descent to the beach was rather quicker than the ascent, and I made my way through the sand dunes with the sun behind me and flocks of starlings leading the way.

*

Looking east from St Patrick's Temple I had been able to see Balephuil Bay and Ben Hynish. This was the destination of another memorable exploration. About fifteen of us assembled for a guided archaeological walk – mainly visitors but a few residents joined the group. We assembled just above the beach that I had walked along a couple of days before. We negotiated car-sharing for the short ride up to an area very near the radar station. A flock of twite circled around us.

We arrived at the south-west face of Ben Hynish, and stepped out of the cars. The ground sloping south towards the sea had wonderful ocean views; there was nothing between us and the Antrim coast due south of us, except for the Skerryvore lighthouse glinting on its rocks about fourteen miles away to the south-west. There was a wonderful blue sky and sea; a glorious day.

John Holliday from the Tiree Ranger Service was our guide. He was the island's GP for many years, and since retirement he has devoted his time to studying and writing about the history, heritage, culture and archaeology of the island. We were warned beforehand of the wet, boggy, uneven ground. John called it 'poached' – a new word, in this context, for me, but I have since heard it even in England. It means muddy ground churned up by cattle. We clambered around the huge site, quite steep in places. It was like a minefield; big stones, small stones, uneven tufty banks of turf and heather often disguising a hole or two, and large pockets of mud in unexpected spots. I was glad of my walking boots and stick. Many tiny pyramidal hillocks made the going even rougher. I expect that there is a name for these natural Hebridean grassland features (I've not seen them anywhere else in such abundance). If there is a name, I expect Robert Macfarlane would know it, as he has studied and collected names in English and Scottish dialects, and in Gaelic, for tiny (and big) natural features of a landscape.[4]

Uneven ground at West Hynish

Among many structures in this complex hillside, John showed us a Bronze Age hut circle, field boundaries, some on top of each other; medieval sheep folds, and a possible Viking boat memorial. Archaeologists believe these may have been built to commemorate sailors lost at sea; they consist of a boat-shaped structure with a large stone as a prow.

We saw the remains of medieval buildings higher up on the hill that would have been shielings, which are small huts or houses only occupied in summer by shepherdesses, for example. This was when

Viking boat memorial

140

the climate was colder and the area used for summer grazing only. But when it was warmer and drier, the buildings would have been farms, and the area used for year-round farming. 'Half a degree difference in the mean temperature can transform a landscape,' John said.

Lower down the hill were 'rigs' – ridges and furrows in the land nearer the sea for barley and oats; and lazybeds – patches of ground where potatoes were cultivated by laying them on the surface and covering them with kelp and soil from parallel trenches.

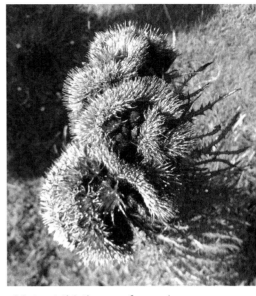

Mutant thistle seen from above

There were two surprise 'finds' on the walk, neither of them archaeological. A recently dead buzzard sprawled on the grass enabled us to examine its powerful wingspan; and a mutant thistle whose dark blue flowerhead had gone berserk in a pattern of what the knitting group might call cable stitch. We all marvelled at this.

*

I was intrigued by the few place names of this area: Dìobadal, Tràigh Bhalbaig, Dùn Shiadair, Dùn na Clèite – both duns on the shore – and Happy Valley, which is a newer name, dating from the Second World War airmen.

At the end of the walk, John summarised what we had seen around the south-west face of Ben Hynish. 'We can deduce that it's been used by people at least since the Bronze Age, 4,500 years ago. It looks very poor grazing land now, the weather has been warmer and colder at different times, and the vegetation's changed.'

He explained that the land was once forested, then it was deforested,

141

with the result that the soil changed from being fertile to its present state of being acidic and wet. 'You can see when you look down the hillside the hundreds of meandering walls and enclosures. We know that one side of the hill alone had over 150 structures, so we can tell that the landscape has been intensively managed since prehistoric times,' he explained. According to John, this area is a part of Tiree people don't often visit, ' it's a tucked-away secret', yet he believed that once it was managed by at least fifty people. But it's a very intensively used and interesting part of the island that has only recently been discovered.

'Reusing the stones by new communities produces what is called a palimpsest landscape,' he explained. 'You've got fields that criss-cross each other, buildings which have been built on other buildings, and that Viking rectangular building which we've just looked at – that's probably four different levels of buildings from a Bronze Age foundation to a medieval farm. It's wonderful to see, but it makes it very difficult to interpret. Once you start to disentangle the different layers it does seem to make a little more sense.'

I had nothing but admiration for John's enthusiasm, energy and passion for archaeology. I wished him all the best for many further resources and academic interest from outside the island, so that this fascinating area can be more extensively studied. His zest for new knowledge reminded me of Kevin Byrne on Colonsay and his passion for ferns.

*

I'd glimpsed Skerryvore lighthouse far in the distance from Ben Hynish, but not paid particular attention to it, possibly because I was deep into archaeology.

Lighthouses symbolise the way forward and help in navigating our life through rough waters. Nothing else speaks of safety and security in the face of adversity and challenge quite the way a lighthouse does. And nothing prepared me for the awe I experienced when visiting the Skerry-vore shore station museum at the visitor centre in Hynish.

I have visited, or passed by, many lighthouses around the British Isles, and all of them have been on the coast. On learning about the location of Skerryvore, I knew I wouldn't be able to visit the lighthouse itself – although there is the occasional boat trip for tourists. I was determined to catch sight of it, at least. This I managed to do by walking a short distance on a track behind the museum on a grey day, and fiddling with my binoculars (I couldn't see it without them). There it was on the horizon!

Skerryvore lighthouse

The Lighthouse

In the Hynish gloom –
a glimmer, is it there?
screw-eyed
I stay rooted,
straining.

A glint flickers
once, then vanishes.
It teases, feels and fuels
my frustration.
Again, again.

As darkness deepens,
the rays sharpen and shine.
My journey enters
the possibility
of resolution.

The lighthouse lies on a patch of dangerous and gale-blown rock fourteen miles from the Tiree coast. It is reachable by helicopter and RIB, but the seas are tricky to say the least, so it's always touch and go if you find yourself booked on a trip. The boat trip people will tell you many facts – here are a few.

1. It's the tallest lighthouse – 48 metres – in Scotland, twice as tall as Eddystone.
2. The light shone for more than 100 years, from 1844, and was automated in 1994.
3. A wooden barrack erected on the rocks in 1838 to house workers was destroyed by a gale. Four months' hard work had disappeared, but Alan Stevenson immediately started building a new one similar in design, but stronger, which lasted.
4. The first three courses of blocks for the base of the tower are of hard Hynish gneiss.
5. The remainder of the blocks are granite from the Ross of Mull.
6. Stonemasons at Hynish could take 320 man hours to complete a single block.
7. Work on the lighthouse often had to be abandoned because of bad weather – once no landings were possible for seven weeks.
8. A keeper who fell asleep on duty faced instant dismissal.
9. In heavy storms, the tower would sway.
10. A sailor survived a shipwreck to the west of the lighthouse, and he swam to the lighthouse pulling his wounded companion by holding his jacket in his teeth; both survived. One can only imagine the keepers' surprise when the sailor knocked on the door!
11. No life was lost during the construction.

Lighthouse keepers and families lived in these four houses at Hynish

Rant of the Wind

Whoever thought of building
that stupid lighthouse
they call Skerryvore.
Why, that bird-brained Stevenson
and his kin.
Drown them all!

Hundreds of masons,
thousands of blocks of stone,
useless, pointless!
That puny construction,
those flimsy rocks it stands on,
destroy, destroy!

I whip the waves,
create my most ferocious blasts
to smash that crazy pinnacle
with its poncy light.

I'll do it in the end, you'll see.
I'm elemental, a demolisher
of all things made by man
to hinder my passage over the sea.

Just as I was determined to catch a glimpse of the lighthouse, I also wanted to find the Ringing Stone of Tiree. This is an erratic granite boulder, possibly dating back to the Ice Age, the same age as the Mull granite that formed most of the stones which were chiselled for building Skerryvore. An 'erratic' is a boulder that has been moved by natural means such as a glacier, so the geology is usually different from that of the surrounding rocks.

One morning I took a walk that was described in my booklet of walks. Parking at the western end of Gott beach, I walked along the road, turned north to Vaul, or Bhalla, on the north shore. From here I hoped to see the Isle of Muck in the far distance, but wasn't sure the blob on the horizon was Muck.

I made my boggy way to a broch, Dùn Mòr Bhalla. A broch is a circular Iron Age stone-built fortified home, with an inner and an outer wall. This is fascinating in itself, but I was bent on finding the Ringing Stone, which from my map looked about a mile to the south-west of Vaul, somewhere on the coast, so I only nodded to the broch this time.

The path kept on disappearing but I trudged on in my welly boots, with no one else around. I found the Ringing Stone close to the shore, although there was no marker post or explanatory information board nearby.

Its Gaelic name is Clach a' Choire, the 'rock of the hollow', and it stands five feet high near the shore opposite Saltaig lochan. It is pock-marked with more than fifty Bronze Age cup marks,

which were probably used in religious rituals. Legend has it that if the stone breaks, so will Tiree. People have helpfully left small stones in the cup marks, so all you do is pick one up and strike the boulder. Have these people had a wish to break Tiree? Probably not. They've

The Ringing Stone

wanted to make it ring, which it is supposed to do when you hit it.

I've always been fascinated to discover a pitched note in any noise. For example, on a windy day walking past an electricity pylon, I try to guess the sound pitch – such as E in the octave above middle C.

I picked up a pebble and struck the stone, but I was disappointed to

146

begin with – the noise was just that, a noise; but when I knocked gently at the edge of some of the cup marks I heard a faint difference – not a noise, but a sound, a musical note. I recorded the knocks and sounds on my smartphone, with me singing the same note. I guessed it was about G sharp. When I got back to the hostel, I listened to the recording – my voice was loud and clear, but the microphone hadn't picked up the pitched note. All I heard was pitch-less knocking. I was glad to have sung and recorded the note, so I was able to confirm my guess on the piano later. It was indeed G merging into G sharp.

The local newspaper, *An Tirisdeach*, featured another 'Ringing Stone' that a Coll archaeologist discovered in North Korea. From the photograph it looked very similar to the Tiree stone, with cup marks. He notified local Korean archaeologists, and the stone is now in the grounds of Kaesong Museum. Whether this one rings was not reported. Back in Yorkshire, I have long been fascinated by the many Neolithic carved stones on Ilkley Moor and Rombalds Moor, but to my knowledge, none of them 'ring'.

I googled 'why do some rocks ring?' After reading the explanations, it was my head that rang, with confusion. However, a year after my visit to the Tiree Stone, on a trip northwards to Oban through Kilmartin Glen in mid-Argyll, I stopped for a time at the museum and cafe. Kilmartin is a huge area of archaeological interest covering 9,000 years with standing stones, stone circles and rock art scattered over many acres of the valley. A CD on sale in the museum featured sounds that our ancestors might have heard daily, including a cow-bone flute, eagle and swan-bone flutes, a Bronze Age horn and pottery drums. And I was delighted to discover that there was a recording of the Tiree Ringing Stone. I had to wait until I was back home before I listened to the CD, because my newish car didn't have a CD player in it. I was thrilled to discover that the Kilmartin museum recording was similar to mine, except that the musical pitch is audible, and is around G. It isn't a pure tinkly or musical sound, but definitely pitched.

*

I had decided that composing a song about the Ringing Stone and teaching it to school children was a good idea. So which school? I wondered. Ann Langley, a retired teacher, kindly sent me a handwritten letter about Tiree's schools' history. I was also helped by John Fletcher's recollections. In the 1950s, with a bigger population than now, there were five primary schools at Ruaig, Scarinish, Balemartine, Heylipol, and Cornaigmore. This latter school was attached to the only secondary school on the island which catered for pupils up to the third year (S3). After this, pupils could continue their education in Oban High School or go to colleges on the mainland, or go to work either on Tiree or the mainland.

In later years Cornaigmore High School became known and registered as Tiree High School, Ard-Sgoil Thiriodh, and accommodated pupils throughout primary to sixth year secondary, and that is how it is at present.

'At the beginning of the 1950s there was only one teacher covering each primary school – primary one to primary seven. This was hard work for teachers but all the primaries were very fortunate to have competent staff. The curriculum was up to scratch – the three Rs were very important then!' Ann wrote.

Pupils walked to school if they lived less than two miles away. Otherwise transport was provided. When pupils transferred to Cornaigmore Secondary, transport was provided by two contractors – east and west of the island. 'Those that walked were often given lifts by drivers (cars were then a luxury) who were travelling their way.'

Numbers of pupils started to dwindle in the late 1960s, and one by one the primary schools joined forces or closed. By 1974 Cornaigmore was the only school on the

Decoration on wall of Tiree school – talented pupils and teacher!

island. Ann believed pupils adapted well to this transition and reminded me that there were no specialist teachers in those days. 'Teachers had to be multi-talented,' she wrote. They still do.

*

I was keen to work albeit briefly with at least one of these multi-talented teachers. The main reason for me to choose the Ringing Stone as subject matter for my song was because I was fascinated by it. But also, I felt that I could play around musically with the words and perhaps end the song itself on the note G (see musical score in appendix).

The present school is very close to the hostel. I looked forward to meeting a group of Primary 4 and 5 pupils and I'd asked for there to be access to classroom percussion instruments such as triangles, tambours and chime bars.

I parked next to the school, walked in and signed in as a visitor, and a teacher led me to the music room with all these instruments at hand.

I had picked up a handful of pebbles, took them into the classroom and gave out one for each child. My idea was to demonstrate the difference between a noise and a note. This might just have been a mistake, but I had enough confidence that these children would be like saints compared with one or two of my classes in an inner-city middle school in the 1980s. I was right. At first they knocked their pebble vigorously on their table, and elsewhere, and I hoped they would hear the noise as noise, rather than notes. As the knocking continued, I said that I'd take away any pebble that was knocking at the wrong time. That worked! Then I demonstrated how playing chime bars and xylophones produced pitched notes rather than noise. Most were more interested in banging or making sounds with whatever they had with them, but they never got out of hand.

The 'lesson' was a success in that they were able to 'do' the rhythm, but a bit disappointing for me in that we only managed to get through the first verse and the chorus. However, it made me more realistic about expectations for the next schools' song-teaching.

Song of the Ringing Stone

Chorus
Pick up a pebble and give me a tap!
Is it a noise, or is it a note?
Keep striking the stone!
Put your ear to the cup marks and pull down your hood,
you'll hear a dull thud.

1 I sailed on the ice from the island of Mull,
I landed near Vaul on the Isle of Tiree.
Ten thousand years I've been lying alone,
they've come and they've gone and they've all had a go!
Chorus (as above)

2 Come put on your wellies, the going is rough
and boggy and squelchy with rocks underfoot.
The footpath is faint but you won't lose your way,
if you keep to the shore, your eyes on the bay.
Chorus (as above)

3 I'm next to a beach where you hear the gulls cry
I'm covered with cup marks, and two metres high.
I stand out from the crowd, I'm a massive big rock,
give me a tap and you'll just hear a knock.
Chorus (as above)

4 But don't give up hope, keep striking the stone,
Is it a knock or is it a note?
Try tapping around the rim of each cup,
be patient and calm, and you'll soon be in luck.

Last Chorus
Pick up a pebble and give me a tap
Is it a noise, or is it a note?
Keep striking the stone!
Put your ear to the cup marks and listen to me
you'll hear the note G!

(musical score in appendix, in the key of Eb major)

Note for musicians: I transposed the song into E*b* major. We ended the last chorus by singing 'G' on G, the children being invited to play G several times on tuned percussion. In other words, not B*b* as in the other choruses.

After I'd returned to Leeds, Rou sent me an e-copy of *An Tirisdeach*. The teacher had written about my visit to the school and taken a photograph. I had no part to play in what was written and was delighted to be included in the paper.

'A Song for the Ringing Stone' – from *An Tirisdeach*

Margaret Greenwood visited the school on Wednesday 29th August to work with the Primary 4 and 5 pupils to work on the composition 'Song of the Ringing Stone'. She was inspired by the Ringing Stone on her visit to the island last summer. She is a retired music teacher and a writer who is travelling solo through the Scottish Isles. She collects words and images, composing songs and writing a blog that chronicles her experiences. The children learned the song and joined with percussion. She was an inspiration to us all.

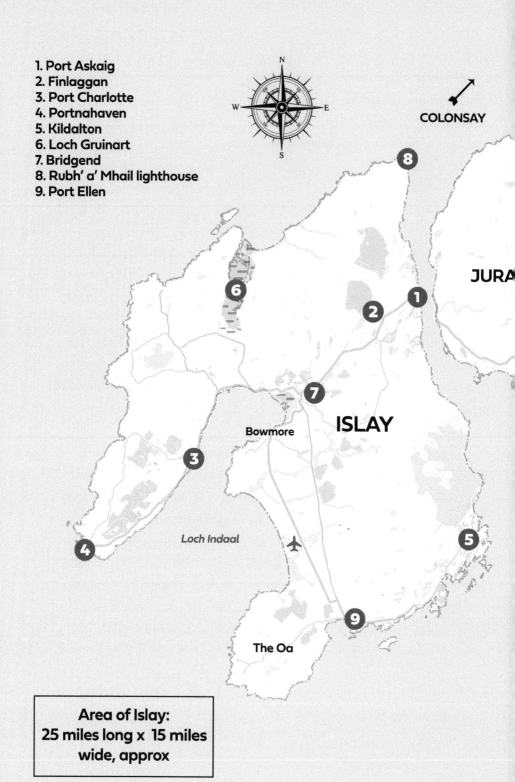

1. Port Askaig
2. Finlaggan
3. Port Charlotte
4. Portnahaven
5. Kildalton
6. Loch Gruinart
7. Bridgend
8. Rubh' a' Mhail lighthouse
9. Port Ellen

COLONSAY

JURA

ISLAY

Bowmore

Loch Indaal

The Oa

Area of Islay:
25 miles long x 15 miles
wide, approx

CHAPTER 5
ISLAY, KNOYDART AND LISMORE: STOPS ON THE WAY TO OTHER ISLANDS

Islay is a much bigger island than those I've mentioned so far; around 3,000 people live there. I was on my way to Colonsay and thought it a good plan to stop on Islay for a few days.

The ferry that sails between Kennacraig on the Kintyre peninsula and Islay is the only ferry I've taken that thinks it's a cruise ship. It was the hand sanitisers, dozens of them, and this was long before the Covid-19 outbreak. I had the feeling that this feature alone was catering for the serious whisky travellers.

Many people associate Islay with whisky. This island has eight distilleries, the greatest concentration of distilleries in the world. Using pure spring water and rain-soaked barley, the taste depends, among other factors, on the shape of the still and the wood of the cask.

Display boards on the ferry telling us about the Finlaggan story caught my attention, and I decided to find out more. So as soon as we landed at Port Askaig I drove to the site, a little detour from the road to Bridgend.

Community Gardens, Islay

Situated around a pair of small islands in Loch Finlaggan, near Ballygrant, Finlaggan was the ancient seat of the Lords of the Isles in medieval times, and independent of the Scottish crown. New Lords of the Isles were crowned here.

For three centuries, these lords, descended from a 12th-century prince called Somerled, ruled the islands and most of the west coast of Scotland. Their power depended on their mastery of the sea.

There are two small islands in the freshwater loch. Starting at the information centre at the car park, I walked along the boardwalk leading to Eilean Mòr (Big Island) on the loch. Few other visitors were around on this glorious, sparkling day, and on the water full-blown white lilies were so thickly intertwined beneath the walkway that the water was invisible. I've noticed many little islands near loch shores in Scotland and even in Wales – they are usually called crannogs. A crannog is a man-made island, often built in a lake, on which stood an important unfortified building such as a mansion. 'The surrounding water was no substitute for stout walls since a horse could trot through its shallows in a matter of minutes.'[1]

On this tiny, 'big' island there used to be more than twenty buildings, some of wood, turf and clay, but now you can see only stone remains of the chapel, some walls, and the Great Hall which was used for feasting and entertaining.

Finlaggan also served as the administrative centre for the Lords of the Isles and Clan Donald from the 13th century until the lordship was taken over by James IV of Scotland in 1493.

An even smaller island lies about fifty metres from the southern tip of Eilean Mòr. This is Eilean na Comhairle (Council Island), so called because it was where the lords built their council house, where the parliament met to adjudicate on matters of law. These two islands are connected to each other by a stone causeway, substantial remains of which can be traced under the surface of the loch. I didn't get my feet wet, but instead inspected the flora of the main island.

Remains of the Great Hall, Finlaggan

Finlaggan was a just a short detour on my way to one of the best youth hostels in Scotland. This is housed beside the sea in Port Charlotte, in the upper floor of an old warehouse. It is clean, business-like, friendly and kind to oldies. To my delight I was allocated an unroofed bed with quiet female roommates. I was happy to see a recent edition of the Scottish YHA magazine in the reception area, and able to show the warden an article I'd written in it about another warden who is based at a hostel on the Scottish mainland.

Quite soon after I had settled into the hostel, I heard about the nearby Toothache Stone. How it was described to me made me think it was about the same size as the Ringing Stone of Tiree; and instead of cup marks from eons ago, it has small holes with nails, including rusty ones, copper and iron ones, and even a few old pennies stuck in slots. I was told by a resident that the area around the stone had been a playground for local children and that if you had toothache in the night, you went up there and hammered a nail in it. The act of hammering took the toothache away. Apparently it had to be done in the dark, which meant that the whole experience was somewhat frightening and painful.

The stone is described as 'not unlike a human molar' by the Royal Commission on the Ancient and Historical Monuments of Scotland, although some see it as more like a canine. I also discovered that there is a toothache stone in Ireland. On the rock of Cashel in the county of Tipperary, the granite pedestal of St Patrick's cross, which was once used as a coronation stone, is known for its healing properties. Anyone who suffers from toothache could place their head at the south-east corner of the stone and be cured. No need for a hammer there.

Sadly I was not able to go and see the Islay Toothache Stone but it is on my list.

*

During my time on Islay I was able to talk to a retired primary school teacher – she lived not far from the hostel. When I knocked on Effie's door she invited me in for a cup of tea. With my teaching background in inner city schools, and my own experience of being a pupil at a girls' grammar school in the 1950s, I am always keen to hear of others' memories, particularly those of people my age, like Alasdair on Gigha, and Netta on Colonsay. Effie, a softly spoken lady with a quick smile, explained that both she and her parents were pupils at the same school in Port Charlotte. She went to teach there for 35 years, from 1960 to 1995. The school was housed in an imposing white building built in 1830 as a church. It is no longer used as a school, or a village hall, but survives as upmarket holiday apartments.

'Numbers were low in the days when I was a pupil,' she said. In the Infants, there was one room with twelve children, and two teachers in the school who taught all subjects. She remembered a big boiler that had to be stoked with anthracite to keep it going; and a high desk for the teacher which is now in the local museum. 'We used slates, I remember that, but we didn't take the peat to school!' This was a reference to the fact that in many highland and island areas, including during her parents' time, children were expected to take peat regularly to school to help heat the building. 'We were always taught in English. In my day, we didn't speak much Gaelic even outside – it was just the language of the home. But you had more freedom, as a teacher. I was able to do a lot of project work; it was really different. The children were allowed to express their own opinions. We did more out in the community. Trips, local projects, wildlife, you had the freedom to do it. The children enjoyed local history, and they taught the other kids.'

One memorable school trip was to Kildalton, which is a wooded area in the east of the island. 'There were lots of wee coves, a broken coastline, a huge cave which people used to camp in.' They had horrible weather, and stayed in the old school house. She remembered the fusty blankets they used. She and the head teacher had a room partitioned off from the children's, but they could hear every word the children said as they nattered away into the night. She laughed as she remembered this. 'I also took them to some of the old villages around here – there are lots of little settlements.'

A laird, Walter Frederick Campbell, planned and built the village in the 1820s to house workers for the distillery. The crofters weren't 'cleared', they were given a building plot and enough lime to build a house site and a garden site. Effie was the only islander I met who mentioned the clearances. 'The laird wanted the land for the sheep but the people didn't think of it as clearances; the conditions in the settlements were not good and the new houses were much more preferable.' There is a local estate record of people 'having been cleared' from Kilchoman on the west side of the peninsula not far from Port Charlotte. This came as a surprise to a later generation, because it had always been thought they had left willingly as they were going to better conditions.

I was reminded of the dreadful story of crofters in the far north-east of Scotland whose crofts were burned by the Duke of Sutherland and who were driven to the coast to make a new life as fisher people in Helmsdale.

I asked, 'Were they nudged into fishing?'

Effie paused a little to think. 'Perhaps. Some people went to Ireland to sell fish from Portnahaven. There was some commercial fishing, and also a distillery, but it closed in the 1940s. My grandfather worked there.'

Port Charlotte, which nowadays has a population of around 300, was named after the laird's mother – Lady Charlotte of Campbell. In this area the people had been very, very poor, Effie said. 'We have a croft and there's a ruined village on it. Somebody has put together an Islay cultural database, and the database team got hold of information from all sorts of sources, and put it together. The museum has access to the database, and that's where I got the information about the settlement which is partly on our croft. It was amazing to discover that it was such a big place – it had an inn, so many horses and cattle, and there were schools there

Still open for business! On my way back to the hostel from Effie's, I had to take this photo of the sign above the post office – which possibly dates from Effie's and my youth

too. The database sources went back several generations.'

Effie and I chatted for a while longer, and then I took my leave, wishing I'd experienced Islay when both Effie and I were a lot younger.

*

One day, I drove from Port Charlotte along the east coast of the Rhinns peninsula, and took a left turn at the head of Loch Indaal, towards Gruinart. I was very keen to revisit the RSPB reserve at Loch Gruinart. My claim to fame is that it was here, many years ago on the sea shore at the north of the loch, that an otter swam quite close to me and didn't go away for quite a time – I like to think he was intrigued by my scarlet raincoat. So much for birders and the like wearing camouflage! (A friend tells me that otters are colourblind, though.) It was my first sighting of an otter, and ever since I have been searching for them, usually in vain. It just goes to show that when you are not looking for something, it finds you.

That day, sadly, the weather was nothing like that first time. After a few minutes of sheltering from the downpour in the visitor centre at Bushmill Cottage, I put on my wet weather gear and walked into the rain, making for the first bird hide. It was empty of bird watchers.

Islay is the best place in the UK to see barnacle geese and on that earlier visit I'd seen thousands of them picking over the marshy land, a marvellous sight. This time I peered out of the opened shutters. Absolutely nothing. No geese or any wading birds. However, I was captivated by the posters pinned to the wooden wall behind me. There was the poem by Norman McCaig about a ringed plover, which I mention in Chapter 1. 'They sprint eight feet and stop. Like that. They sprintayard (like that) and stop.' There was also a poster depicting a goose barnacle tree.

So what was this goose barnacle tree? In 1597 Gerard's *Herbal* mentions barnacle geese. 'They are found in the north parts of Scotland and the adjacent islands, whereon do grow shells of a white colour tending to russet, whereon are contained little living creatures. Out of them grow

little living things which falling into the water do become fowles, which we call Barnacles.'[2] As long ago as 1188 a Welshman called Gerald of Wales (not to be confused with Gerard) wrote *Topographia Hibernica*. He wrote in Latin. 'Of Barnacles that grow from fir timber' (Chapter XI).[3] The following poem attempts to describe a discovery I made in the bird hide that made me forget my disappointment in not seeing any birds that day.

Goose barnacle tree poster in the Islay bird hide

159

Barnacle Geese

Wrong time of the year at Loch Gruinart
where the Iceland geese come to rest.
I sheltered from Islay drizzle
inside an RSPB hut,
peered through the flaps.
Not one bird of any kind
but on the wall of the hide,
a poster of a barnacle tree.

Before they knew that some birds migrate
and nest in far-off places,
they believed barnacle geese
were born from barnacles
stuck to driftwood swept ashore.
Somehow the driftwood became a 'tree',
and grew five branches; at the end of each
was a large barnacle,
shaped like a fruit, or a tulip; open-ended.
And when the baby geese were ready to be born
they poked their fully formed heads out of the fruit
and took their first dive
into the sea.

Goose Barnacles on a
rope seen on Muck

On Muck the previous year, I'd seen and photographed a curious find. It was a section of a very thick rope with what looked like smartly designed mussels attached to it. Studying the poster in the Islay hide, the penny dropped. My photograph of the 'mussels' on Muck didn't depict mussels at all. They were goose barnacles! I was over-the-top delighted with this revelation.

*

160

There are a lot of places still to visit on Islay and I mean to return one day. I'd like, for example, to visit the Oa, another RSPB reserve, which Effie had spoken about. It is in the far south of the island, where a monument commemorates two American troop ships sunk off Islay during the First World War. From this vantage point it is possible to see Ireland, about twenty-five miles away. I like to be reminded of the proximity of other lands and islands – my car radio picked up Radio Ulster once or twice; a childish surprise.

*

On my final day on Islay, before the ferry to Colonsay was due to leave, I had just enough time for one short visit – the Islay House Community Garden. The garden was tidy with its four acres of paths and terraces, some of the area surrounded by trees and partially walled. I liked the fact that this lovely garden has aims 'to provide fruit and vegetables for locals and visitors, to educate, particularly young people, in the principles of healthy eating, and to provide volunteering opportunities for work experience for young people and those with special needs.' I came away with a kilo of broad beans and a punnet of blackberries; and I ate every one. But not straight away.

The ferry leaves Port Askaig and goes past the northern tip of Islay where the Rhuvaal (or Rubh' a' Mhàil) lighthouse still stands. This is the lighthouse where the optic was dismantled before finding its way to Colonsay House Gardens.

There are so many links between islands that are not at first apparent.

KNOYDART, AN ALMOST ISLAND

Most people I speak to about my travels haven't heard of Knoydart. It's a peninsula, though an island in all but name. Trying to reach it by foot involves twenty miles of serious hiking across wild territory, from Kinloch Hourne, Finiskaig or Barrisdale; all tiny settlements. There is no road, so

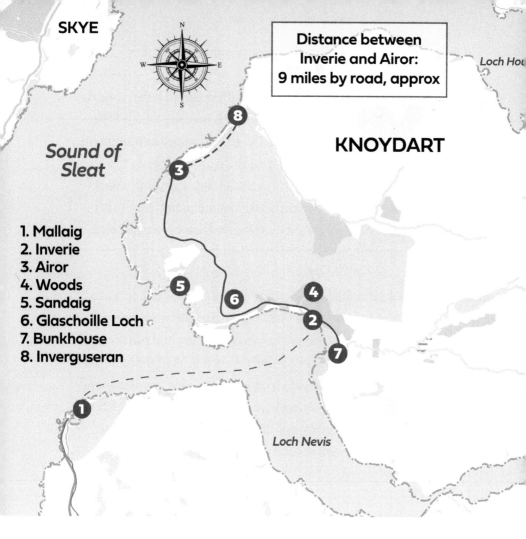

SKYE

Sound of
Sleat

KNOYDART

Distance between
Inverie and Airor:
9 miles by road, approx

Loch Ho

1. Mallaig
2. Inverie
3. Airor
4. Woods
5. Sandaig
6. Glaschoille Loch
7. Bunkhouse
8. Inverguseran

Loch Nevis

it might as well be an island. It has been known as Scotland's Last True Wilderness.

In 2017 I took myself on a 'coastal' journey starting from Edinburgh around the east coast of Scotland, through the Black Isle, along the north coast, then south from Durness, not missing an opportunity to visit Handa Island, a tiny uninhabited bird reserve. I eventually arrived in Mallaig. I was on my way to Muck, but first a trip to Knoydart by boat was in order. The passenger-only ferry trip from Mallaig to Inverie, the main settlement in Knoydart, is across Loch Nevis. The name of this sea loch is a little odd, I thought, as it is nowhere near Ben Nevis.

The boat landed at the small jetty at Inverie and I jumped out, and asked directions to the bunkhouse.

On the way, I called in at the Knoydart Foundation office and information centre, and discovered a little about the recent history of the settlement. I read there that in 1999 the foundation bought the Knoydart Estate, thus taking control of the inhabitants' destiny after '850 years of answering to a succession of landlords'. Quite a phrase. The population of the area had been 1,000 in the 18th century but towards the end of the 1800s around 400 people had been 'cleared' or emigrated. These days the population is roughly 100 people.

A particularly unpopular owner was Lord Brocket who had been a Nazi sympathiser in the 1930s. After the Second World War, returning Knoydart servicemen had the right to take over some of the estate land that was under-used, and farm it as their own. Seven men marked out sixty-five acres of arable land and 10,000 acres of hill land upon which to settle. Brocket obtained a court order to remove them, won the battle for the land, and became even more unpopular.

Near Inverie

He also refused to allow a road link across the peninsula to the rest of the mainland. Whether this has turned out to be a blessing or a mistake, I don't know, but I'd veer towards this being a mistake. However, a road link could still be built – possibly.

*

I am all for community gardens, especially if they are situated near hostels where I'm staying, which was the case in Knoydart. One of the first things I did after I arrived was to have a good look around. The small population of Knoydart may have something to do with my finding their garden somewhat straggly compared with Islay's. Islay with its bigger population means a greater pool of garden-users. I wasn't always sure if the Knoydart plants were growing of their own accord or not, but that really didn't matter.

It had two polytunnels, and beds labelled with people's names. Outside the tunnels the villagers had taken great care with their vegetable plots. An invitation to pick your own blackcurrants was good news for me.

Polytunnel in Knoydart community garden

The bushes were laden with overripe fruit – I would go back and pick some later. There was a money box in one of the polytunnels, with a notice of the price of a punnet.

From the pier, the bunkhouse was about a mile away to the east. On my way to the bunkhouse I had been helped with my bags by a couple of women who walked with me for about half a mile. On arrival the warden allocated me a large room on my own for the first night, and I was thrilled to discover that there were separate men's/women's facilities. There was even another room full of fridges next to the kitchen; the purpose of these remained a mystery.

I silently rated this bunkhouse nine out of ten. The warden was pleasant but the next day she asked me if I minded a dog in the room for the following night. She knew the dog – it would behave itself. I was in a good mood yet struggled to say that that would be OK. But I wondered what would have happened if I'd said no. In the event, the dog and its owner took a bunk a couple of metres away from mine, and the night passed uneventfully. The dog didn't even raise an ear when I had to creep past it on my nightly loo visit. Another example of my oft-quoted saying: 'It doesn't matter who you sleep with as long as you sleep soundly.'

In the bunkhouse kitchen two bored students were preparing their evening meal. One opened a tin of baked beans, and the other a tin of spaghetti. They had been studying woodland flora and fungi on the peninsula for several weeks, and could only go out when it wasn't raining, for some reason. One of them, Dave, was reading a textbook on fungi while he ate his beans. I prepared my own vegetable and lentil soup, and felt sorry for them. I offered them some of my blackcurrants, but James declined gracefully saying he'd never eaten them, so didn't want to 'risk it'. Dave accepted reluctantly.

*

My first full day in Knoydart was drizzly, very warm and muggy, and my cagoule sleeves were clinging to my bare arms. I walked in the mist in the forest above Inverie. This wood is managed by the Knoydart Forest Trust which aims to restructure 800 hectares of woodland with a healthy variety of trees. Since the community buyout in 1999, the wood is being partially replanted with native deciduous woodland. They will leave some of the older conifers including Scots pine, which is one of my favourite trees. I discovered later that a trading subsidiary of the trust, called Wood Knoydart, is developing a range of small products available to sell, as well as milled timber and firewood. Their methods and management enhance biodiversity, habitat resilience and mitigate against climate change, and at the same time sustain local employment.

As I climbed uphill I noticed some recently felled trees among older trees that had been left standing. Other trees had succumbed to the wind and fallen on top of each other. The track was steep and I had to jump over a few rushing streams. It got mistier – the cloud level had gradually come down to meet me. The floor of the forest was mostly covered with bracken or moss and the colours were amazing. The greenness of the moss brightened up the air.

I came to a place where a large tree had been uprooted by the wind, its roots showing a mini-ecosystem of mosses, lichens and foxgloves. Noticing a patch of wood sorrel a few metres from the path I came across a couple of *Amanita phalloides*: death cap fungi. These are highly poisonous and are responsible for nine out of ten fungi-related deaths, but look innocuous. I wondered if the two fungi students at the bunkhouse had seen them.

I trudged upwards. Foresters had laid out paths that formed a series of routes through the forest, and I was amused to see signs saying 'Knoydart in a Knutshell.' These fingerposts were most likely aimed at people who come over from Mallaig for a four-hour visit between ferries. As well as walking paths, I came across mountain bike tracks but not one mountain biker. Perhaps it was too misty for them.

But on my way back I noticed, in a large clearing, a couple of loggers, and blatantly watched and videoed the action as it was rare for me to see such a sight. A Wood-Mizer was attached to a trailer. One man was working the machine, guiding the saw along a log which had been carefully placed on the 'bed' of the trailer. I'll call him Grey Legs on account of the colour of his trousers.

His mate, Yellow Legs, was taking the newly fashioned planks from the top of the log on the machine and putting them into various piles away from the action. Yellow Legs' tasks also included preparing the logs for the machine. When he had finished adding the latest plank to the plank pile, he went back to the log pile, used a broom to brush off debris and a hand-scraper to shave off what he could from the bark. He made use of his sense of hearing – he had his back to the machine – when he needed to get back to the trailer to remove the latest plank. He could hear by the sound of the machine when Grey Legs had finished. Yellow Legs came across in my video as always on the move, never wasting one split-second of his available time between each plank-lifting, which often amounted to only about twenty seconds. I was impressed and wondered what they thought of my videoing them. I was at a distance from them and not intruding, I hoped, but regret that I didn't even greet them. They paid no heed to me.

*

The weather was warm and sunny the next day when I decided to explore the north-west coast of the peninsula about eight miles away. First I had to get there, but there was no public transport. My destination was Airor which is opposite Armadale in Skye. So I started walking through Inverie,

Near the wood

a cluster of a few houses with lovely views south across the loch, and every now and again looked backwards to see if a likely means of transport was approaching.

I needed to hitch-hike, yet again – this was beginning to be a common occurrence in the islands! An older woman asking for a lift on her own could be seen by a malevolent driver as easy prey. Similarities to my Gigha experience were there – a hot day, no public transport, only one road, about seven miles to go, and a dearth of traffic.

The single-track road away from the village led up a steep hill away from the mirror-calm sea. Struggling (only because of the heat, of course) up a steeper section, I passed a reed-covered lochan. Hitch-hiking in Knoydart is a matter of faith, I thought. No car appeared in either direction. After an hour and a half of road-trudging I was roughly a third of the way to my destination. I was about to fall by the wayside, (an uncomfortable ditch, as it happened), because I was convinced the fifty cars altogether in Knoydart – my estimate – were all lying low.

Just in time, a Land Rover pulled up beside me and gave me a lift to Airor, which turned out to be a tiny coastal settlement of five houses. Feeling peckish I went into a small cafe at the road end. Knick-knacks, some in very good taste, were strewn around the sills of windows that had spectacular views of Skye. The fruit scones and tray bakes looked scrumptious. After a cup of tea and a scone, I tried to make conversation with the cafe lady, an attractive young woman with an eastern European accent. 'Where are you from?' I said. 'The scones seem very Scottish!'

It may have been a bad day for her. 'That's what everybody asks me, where I'm from, and I'm tired of it.' After a moment of hesitation I told her that I was usually happy to let people know I'm from Leicester, or Leeds. It's an ice-breaker. She did melt a bit and offered me a fill-up.

I took my leave of her, and wandered along a couple of tracks parallel to the shore towards Inverguseran, and after a mile or two, turned back onto the shore and pottered in the sand, seaweed, rock-pools and mud. I even paddled, with my boots on, to a tiny island that was just reachable, as it was low tide, by a spit of sand. Here I ate my sandwiches, but I almost got cut off by the rising water. I decided it was time to return to the village. Back on the road for only about three minutes, a roomy car pulled up, driven by a man and his family on holiday. They told me that people who rented holiday houses in Knoydart were often provided with a car by the owner of the property. Great idea, even though there can't be much more than twenty miles of tarmac in the whole area. So I was lucky and thankful that I got back to Inverie with plenty of daylight in front of me and time to wander not far from the bunkhouse to look for otters.

Knoydart road and Loch Nevis

Otter spotting

Loch Nevis smooth and sultry
at the corner of the otter river
where the collapsed bank's mirror image
is reflected in the water.
Silent save for a squirt
and plop of a leaping fish.

I come across a hide called 'Duck'
and round the side you really have to,
Duck, that is. Crawl would be a better word –
and lie on your front for several hours
to watch for otters, unwatched by otters.

On leaving Knoydart I was struck that this was perhaps the only island I'd visited where I did not make any meaningful connection with any of the residents. Perhaps I didn't try hard enough, or didn't stay long enough. The most amazing coincidence happened about three weeks later. I was walking on the mainland, on the north coast of Ardnamurchan near the famous lighthouse, and about forty miles south of Knoydart as the crow flies. I chatted to two young boys who were bounding ahead of their adults. One of the boys recognised me. 'We gave you a lift in Knoydart!' he pronounced with glee. I was stunned. It seemed I wasn't invisible after all.

Looking for otters, Loch Nevis

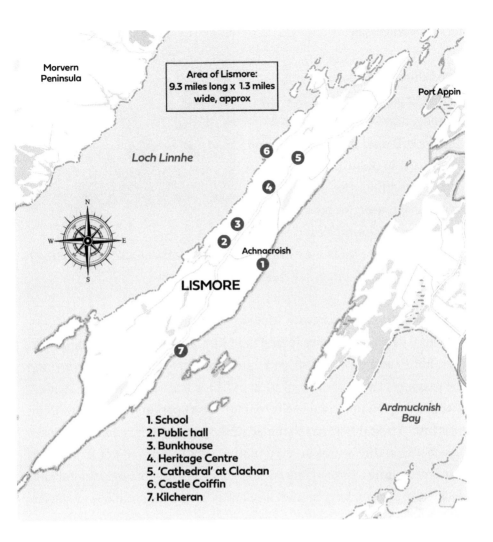

Morvern
Peninsula

Port Appin

Area of Lismore:
9.3 miles long x 1.3 miles
wide, approx

Loch Linnhe

Achnacroish

LISMORE

Ardmucknish
Bay

1. School
2. Public hall
3. Bunkhouse
4. Heritage Centre
5. 'Cathedral' at Clachan
6. Castle Coiffin
7. Kilcheran

LISMORE

I had a short but very busy time in Lismore, a thriving island that you get to easily by car ferry from Oban. The ferry docks at Achnacroish, which is the main settlement. There is a passenger ferry too which goes to the top of the island from Port Appin, a small village north-east of Oban. If I'd been a cyclist, that's the route I would have taken. Distances between places on Lismore are very short; the island being nine miles long by one and a half miles wide.

Lettuce on the roadside

Two saints used curraghs, not ferries, to get to Lismore. Curraghs are long, narrow seaworthy boats that are still used today. These boats are also named currachs, or coracles, but the latter were round in shape and used for river fishing. The tale of St Columba's and St Moluag's arrival on Lismore has been told many times and I am adding to the list of versions, but first here's a little background.

*

You can't miss references to St Moluag when on Lismore. The church, or cathedral as it is known, is dedicated to him. Moluag was born in Ireland around 510 and was bent on leading a missionary life, having his eye on the pagans of the west coast of Scotland. One tale says that the rock he was standing on detached itself from the Irish coast and became a raft to bear him across the waters to the Scottish west coast. His nickname was 'Teacher from the Sea', as he lived in his curragh, moored not far from the coast, preaching and teaching among the Isles. He came to Lismore and decided to stay, making himself a cell near where the church now stands. In 562 he founded his great community on the island but he was determined to travel further afield.

St Moluag and his disciples had a major influence on the spread of Christianity in Scotland, and it is likely he founded monasteries elsewhere in Scotland. The number of dedications to Moluag across western Scotland make him one of the most travelled and popular saints in Scotland. We can tell this by the number of settlements called Kilmoluag (Moluag's cell, or church) in places as far apart as Kintyre, Mull, Tiree, and Harris and Lewis. There is no surviving 'Life of Moluag' to parallel the 'Life of Columba' written by Adamnán in 692 AD. But we do know that Moluag lived to extreme old age, and died at Rosemarkie in 592 AD on the

Moray Firth, on the east coast of Scotland, a 'tame' place, most unlike the sea-swept shores and hills of the west coast. Some say he was buried there, but if so, his relics were afterwards brought to Lismore by twenty-four strong Lismore men who brought his body (or his bones) back from Rosemarkie. Twenty-four sounds to me an excessive number of men.. It is said that his final resting place is in front of the high altar of the church, or cathedral, which was built on the site of St Moluag's original seventh-century church.

I have mentioned St Columba already in tales from Colonsay and Oronsay. He seems to have travelled around a number of the western islands. St Columba, like St Moluag, was born in Ireland, and had a particular motive for his own missionary pursuits. He had been a chieftain in his native land, but had become embroiled in a copyright dispute over the Cathach of Columba, a psalter written in Latin. It is said that he made a secret copy of the book which had been loaned to him. This dispute eventually led to the deaths of thousands of soldiers at the battle of Cúl Dreimhne. Nowadays copyright disputes don't usually end in such slaughter, fortunately. Overwhelmed by remorse, Columba left Ireland in a curragh to atone for these killings, in order to win as many souls for Christ as had been lost in battle.

So here were two saints, Moluag and Columba, bent on making Lismore the centre of their missionary pursuits. They were heading for Lismore, both at the same time, in their respective boats, competing to reach it first. I wonder if they had been egging each other on from Ireland. Both appear to have chosen the same small bay as their landing spot. As they were nearing land, Moluag took up an axe, cutting off the little finger of his left hand and casting it on to the Lismore shore. He announced: 'in the name of the holy Godhead of the blessed Trinity, my flesh and blood are on the land.' So Columba had to agree that Moluag should be the one to Christianise the Lismore population.[2]

Columba was displeased to lose Lismore. Before he left the island there took place an altercation that sounds like a duel between rival magicians. In this version of events, Columba wishes the island ill, and Moluag counters his efforts by turning the curse:

Columba: The edge of its (Lismore's) rock be upwards!

Moluag: Be its venom under!

Columba: Alder be their fuel!

Moluag: May it kindle like the candle!

(translated by Alexander Carmichael relating the story of Lord Archibald)[3]

The curse and counter-blessing are explained by the islanders' conviction that, though the limestone rocks of Lismore are sharp, their edges never injured man nor beast, and that though the alder generally makes poor firewood, it is said that on the island it burns very well, a statement endorsed by Lord Archibald in a footnote: 'This is a fact.'

*

I jump now in time, from the middle of the first century BC when St Moluag was preaching on Lismore, to two centuries later when the Vikings, in this case from Norway, built a castle on the north shore. I'd seen photographs of Castle Coeffin, about which there is a splendid Viking folk tale dating from the thirteenth century, and was keen to go there as soon as I arrived and take some pictures.

Castle Coeffin covered with ivy

The castle was built, probably by the MacDougal clan, on the site of an earlier fortified building. A footpath from the church led to these startling ruins on the north-western shore. I clambered around them and took fancy ivy-framed photographs of the views.

The tale concerns Beothail, a princess with lovely golden hair, who haunted the castle. Beothail lived there in the days when Coeffin was a Norse stronghold. She was the sister of the king and was very much in love with a young Viking warrior from Lochlann (Norway) who happened to be on Lismore. But he was called back home to fight and was killed. When she heard of his death, Beothail grew pale with grief, faded away and died.

In the howling wind that swirled among the walls of Coeffin, Beothail's ghostly voice wailed too; the dead maiden was begging her brother to carry her bones over the seas to Lochlann, so that she could rest alongside her lover. The king finally relented as he had had enough of the wailing, but first her bones needed to be washed in the sacred spring of St Moluag at Clachan. Thus blessed, the bones were carried to where Beothail's lover lay buried in Norway.

But that wasn't the end of the ghostly wailing in the castle. It continued. Then word got around that while packing up her bones, the skeleton-washers had left one behind. A search was made, and Beothail's toe-bone was found at the bottom of the well. It too was carried to Lochlann, and reunited with the rest of her skeleton.

At last the wailing ceased, though the restless winds often sound like a maiden's sigh around the walls of Coeffin. I didn't hear them on my visit, possibly because there was a restful breeze on that sunny day.

*

Soon after I'd arrived on the island I'd gone to the primary school at Achnacroish to teach my song about the Beothail legend, the melody being the same for all the other island songs.

I said hello to all the children (about twelve of them) who were congregated in a corner of the school room. I was blessed with the presence of the pre-five group as there was no nursery school on the island. These tiny ones were only about three, and their favourite position was lying down on a floor mat. I wondered how they'd manage with the percussion instruments, but I used the technique of 'you only are allowed an instrument if you sit up'.

We discussed the story. One boy who had heard of the tale said that it was Beothail's finger, not her toe, which was found in the well. I was delighted with this comment. At least he had been following the story. He was not to know that I had come across a number of Celtic tales where digits from hands or feet had been separated from the rest of bodies.

Beothail of Lismore Song

Chorus
Here in Lismore I'm restless and sad.
My prince is wounded far, far away,
just send me to him! Just send me to him!
It's lonely inside our castle Coeffin,
send me to Lochlann!

Beothail

Verse 1
My prince and I used to wander the shore
he loved my face, 'just like sunbeams,' he swore,
and my steps were like songs, so loud we would sing
past Sgeir nan Uan and Sloc a Mhuilinn!
Chorus

Verse 2
On this ancient knoll it's windy and cold
but orchids and violets grow tall and bold.
I pick them to soothe my sad aching heart
and he's crying for me, so soon I'll depart.
Chorus

Verse 3
I'll wash my feet in Clachan's holy well
I'll have to make sure that my toe will not swell! (some may want to sing
'smell')
Then my brother's ships will take me to Lochlann
and my prince will revive and our wedding we'll plan.
Chorus

Verse 4 (slower…)
But our legend says the prince died of his wounds
and Beothail died one full moon in Lismore.
She haunted the coast in the wind and the mist
till her bones ('including her toe!' said by one pupil) were sent to lie next to
his.
Chorus

(musical score in appendix)

The teachers warned me that on Friday afternoons 'the children can't take much more'. And I was not to worry that the small handful of wrigglers may not have taken much in. Not for the first time, I wondered about the selection of words for my songs, and whether children of primary age could manage them. However, when I was at primary school we learnt quantities of intricate lyrics of British folk songs. Perhaps I just needed a Monday morning with the Lismore children.

*

Arriving at the bunkhouse I was met by the warden who told me I'd happened on a very important weekend which was just about to begin. I was amazed as this was the second time I'd stumbled upon a festival in the islands, the first one being on Colonsay.

At first the hostel was quiet – then all of a sudden people started to arrive from off the later ferry, all of them speaking Gaelic. Some of them came from places such as Canada and Australia, some knew each other, most were from the Scottish mainland and strangers to each other. I was the only non-Gaelic speaker. What struck me about the group in the hostel was that although most wanted desperately to practise speaking Gaelic, when I was in the room they switched to English so as not to appear rude, and to include me in their chats.

This was the annual Gaelic weekend (Fèis an Fhoghair), held for the most part in the Lismore Gaelic Heritage Centre which is a splendid newish eco-friendly building incorporating a cafe, museum and cultural centre about a mile from the hostel. One of the aims of the centre is to promote the Gaelic language and culture, of which Gaelic song has always been a strong part, with Gaelic sung at ceilidhs, church services and choir recitals. There are a number of Gaelic speakers on the island, old and young, and some older ones grew up on Lismore with Gaelic as their first language. There has been a resurgence of interest in the language in recent years which has resulted in a growing number of younger people learning Gaelic to a high level.

On the Saturday I attended the first workshop. This was housed in a small cottage museum close to the heritage centre. The cottage was a reconstruction of one that stood on that spot until the early twentieth century. Mary Ann Kennedy was teaching Gaelic songs to a group of about twelve of us. She used no instrument but her voice to teach us (a croaky one, as she had a bad cold). We were handed the words of the songs but not the music (by which I mean the dots on the staves). Many of us struggled but I had the most difficulty and the fact that I am a classically trained musician hindered rather than helped with catching the tunes, let alone the pronunciation. Over the years I have relied too much on reading sheet music. Also, my short-term auditory memory is not what it was.

A great deal of fun was had by all. Among many other songs, we sang one called 'Togaibh na drochaidean,' which Mary Ann had composed with Donald Meek from Tiree, another very well-known and inspiring poet, and Gaelic song specialist. (I wished I'd met him in Tiree.) The theme is bridge-building between nations, and lifting the poor from the 'shallows'. The song is inspired in part by the sight of the road and rail bridges across the Firth of Forth, and in particular the new Queensferry road bridge. However, the lyrics are a protest against Donald Trump's plans for a wall between the US and Mexico, and to the ongoing Mediterranean refugee crisis. 'It's a Donald Trump special,' she told us.

After the workshop Mary Ann explained to me the peculiarity of rhythm in Gaelic songs. 'In Gaelic song, the natural word rhythm governs everything,' she said. 'So you sing it like you say it. Even if people write out the dots, you adjust the dots to fit the rhythms of each verse. You'd not have exactly the same rhythm for each verse because of the different words in each verse. You let the words speak for themselves.'

However, an exception occurs in the rhythm of songs with a dual purpose, for example waulking songs which I mentioned in my Tiree chapter (and which I learnt about long ago in Barra), and song music for dancing, for example *puirt-à-beul*. 'In the dance songs,' Mary Ann explained, 'if you have the rhythms of the words going against the rhythms of the tune, the dance rhythm is paramount; it gives the 'lift' or the extra excitement. That means you would sing the words in a different rhythm from how you would say them; you would put the stress on the unexpected, normally unstressed, part of the word.' I asked if this happens in English folk songs – is it specific to Gaelic songs? She said, 'It's a particular aspect of Gaelic song.' While not having the same depth of knowledge of English song traditions, she said that stress in Gaelic language rhythm drove the music. 'In Gaelic, the rhythm is all, even in speech,' she added.

I was reminded of my conversation on Colonsay with Tim who'd told me about his Lothian Gaelic choir singing *puirt-à-beul* songs while the dancer was dancing, ensuring she had control of the speed and rhythm of the song.

179

Interior of museum cottage where we sang Gaelic songs

I was desperate to hear again one of these songs, and a kind student recorded, on my phone, a small section of the famous mouth music song, Brochan Lom, which is about watery porridge (made from the chaff).

'Brochan lom, tana lom, brochan lom na sùghain: Brochan lom, tana lom…'

The translation is roughly, 'Thin porridge, watery porridge… let's give it to that young man and girl…' The tune plus words is like a fiddle playing a Highland fling, and you can't stop yourself tapping your feet to the rhythm. In the old film of *Whisky Galore*, the men sing this tune in the pub after they've rescued countless cases of whisky from a shipwreck. I learnt later that brochan also means soft, squelchy ground. As a walker, from now on I will refer to wet weather as walking in porridge, especially on the West Pennine moors.

*

In the bunkhouse I talked to Kate and Lewis, keen Gaelic scholars. Kate worked part-time in the Digital Archive of Scottish Gaelic (DASG) – a resource for all students and others interested in Gaelic lore and language. Lewis was from Perth and worked as a translator for a company that produces books, dictionaries and courses for Gaelic medium schools. He was at that time working on short stories for children. Translating from English to Gaelic often poses challenges. He explained to me that some sentence structure in English cannot be translated word-for-word into Gaelic, so he has to 'redesign' the whole sentence. Gaelic has cases, like Latin. He gave an example of the word 'knife' (*sgian*) which changes

180

spelling according to the case. So you can get *sgeine* and *sgthinne* – both the same word. This would be a nightmare for a Gaelic learner coming across one of these variants on a page, and not making the connection with the nominative case they knew already. 'The genitive case is used a lot more than you would think,' he told me. In the present continuous case, for example, as in 'I am making the dinner,' the 'dinner' is in the genitive case (not the accusative) and the article 'the' changes as well.

Lewis told me there used to be a traditional conservative grammar, but through natural changes, including a decline of usage, Gaelic grammar has changed somewhat. 'There's a new pattern of rules – for example, the word for window, *uinneag*, is feminine, but when it's in the dative case you are supposed to 'slenderise' the end of it. The two final letters of that word are *ag* in the nominative, but in the dative you change it to *ig*.' I loved his use of his word slenderise.

Both Kate and Lewis were at the song workshop too, and I asked them how they'd found it. Lewis liked the song about building bridges. The fact that it was recently composed – 'a song that wasn't too Gàidhealtachd-centric.' Possibly implying that many Gaelic songs might be traditionally inclined and inward-looking? Lewis also rated a particular song with imitations of pipes using grace notes. Kate mentioned the way Mary Ann taught and talked. Her voice was 'fluffy and silky', and she was fascinated by her description of the *puirt-à-beul* songs 'functioning to move the rhythm on'. I am ashamed to say I didn't find out if Kate's and Lewis's first language was Gaelic, but they taught me 'Tha i brèagha', pronounced Ha ee bria (it's beautiful), which is true for how the Gaelic language sounds to me.

Many people reading this section wouldn't be as fascinated as I was, but with my background in linguistics, language-teaching and music, I was, for once, in my element, despite not being able to speak one word of the language. Also, I still have no idea how Gaelic is taught in my great-nephew's Gaelic school. He lives in Edinburgh and is the child I mention in the preface who asked me why I travel to the Scottish Isles every year.

Another event on the Gaelic weekend timetable was a walk to a fish trap just below Castle Coeffin, so this was a second visit there for me. We were to look at, and learn about, the Gaelic names of shore flowers and seaweed, and listen to 'a story or two'. The name of Lismore comes from Lios Mòr which is Gaelic for 'Great Garden', and we encountered a few of the many species of plants that flourish wonderfully on its limestone soil.

Our leaders were Roddy Maclean and his wife Kerrie. Roddy, or Ruairidh, is an expert on flowers, trees and seaweed and was a fount of knowledge. He had prepared a sheet listing at least twenty-five varieties of seaweed, with notes in Gaelic of their names and uses, but I was more interested in what he had to say about flowering plants.

As well as telling us the Gaelic names of plants, Roddy explained their traditional uses. Water mint makes fantastic tea, hazelnuts are good for knowledge, and grass of Parnassus was St Moluag's favourite, it seems. It's one of my favourites, too. In Gaelic it's called fionnan geal, and its uses included mouthwash and eye-lotion. It has a five-petalled flower and a tall stem, often growing on its own, not always in clumps.

Grass of Parnassus, above, and silverweed, below

Roddy also showed us the bright yellow silverweed that I've seen all over the islands, the soft, furry leaves of which were used by Roman soldiers in their shoes, as I mentioned in my Colonsay chapter. The roots of this plant are small (in the sandy machair they grow a bit bigger), but edible. They were mostly eaten in times of famine, but were crucial to the diet of people in the highlands and islands of Scotland before potatoes became common in the mid-eighteenth century. I had no idea of silverweed's importance during famine times. Roots were baked, boiled or roasted and apparently they taste a bit like parsnips. Roddy told us that the Gaelic names included *brisgean, briosglan* or *brislean,* meaning 'brittle' (to do with the roots).

Silverweed roots were also dried and ground into a coarse flour for bread or porridge. The plant is known as the 'Blessed silverweed of the Spring, the seventh bread of the Gaels'. Barley, bere (another type of old grain), wheat, oats, rye and peas were the other six ways of making bread. When times were really bad, especially during the clearances, the people would make for the shore and all they had to eat were the silverweed roots and shellfish, including limpets.

We came across a clump of meadowsweet, and Roddy had a tale for this too. Cú Chulainn was an ancient warrior who came from Ulster to Skye as a young man, where he was well-known for his bad temper and fight-picking tendencies. He honed his warring skills at a castle on the Sleat peninsula. The story goes that he was once getting into a life-threatening fit of apoplexy which was witnessed by a posse of maidens who convinced him to step into a bath of meadowsweet. This soothed him and saved his life, and from then on he would always carry a sprig of the plant tucked into his belt. As far as Roddy knows, this warrior's story isn't half as significant in Ulster folklore as it is in Scottish folklore.

More plants on the foreshore included greater plantain, named in Gaelic after St Patrick, Cuach Phàdraig. Cuach has evolved into the English 'quaich', meaning a double-handed drinking vessel, although I remain unconvinced that the plant looks like one. Roddy had seen the plant in Nova Scotia and had discovered that the Gaelic-speakers there used the same name. The leaves can be used as a poultice for stopping blood flow. As children we used to gently pull up the leaves from the base of the plant, and enjoy the making of ever-lengthening threads, the 'veins'.

As we walked towards the castle, I started to make out the fish trap on the beach. This type of fish trap is called *cairidh* in Gaelic. I was delighted, because I'd come across references to fish traps especially on Muck, and had seen one on Gigha, but still had some difficulty recognising one. If the tide is in, you can't spot them easily and if it is out, what you notice is usually lumps of stones, a bit of a small wall (dyke in Scots), often covered with seaweed, which you can easily mistake as natural phenomena. Here in the bay under the castle, you could, and we did, walk on the low dykes of the fish trap, which were covered with weeds of many varieties. It was all I could do to keep from slipping on the weeds and muddy sand in between. My stick was essential.

There was an obvious gap, facing the sea, in the dyke of the fish trap. At high tide fish would swim into the trap. At a falling tide, the fish would attempt to swim back into the open sea, but fishermen would have placed sticks in between the rocks around the gap, with nets attached, to catch the fish. Another method was to block up the gap at a critical point

Negotiating the dyke of the fish trap

and then scoop up fish trapped in the shallows.

Experiencing this fish trap by walking precariously on its dykes I would be forever able to recognise them much more easily, I hoped.

*

I had tried hard that Saturday to absorb as much new information and as many experiences as possible, and could have done with a quiet evening at the bunkhouse, but there was one more event I was not going to miss. A ceilidh was held in the evening in the village hall. I walked there with other hostellers, not forgetting my torch for coming back in the dark.

I had an immense surprise in discovering that Arthur Cormack was the compere. I remembered him from a few years before. I'd been staying at a hostel in Flodigarry in Skye and attended a ceilidh held nearby, where, among other singers, there were young instrumentalists who were attending a holiday music school in that area. There had been a lively atmosphere, with a mixture of soloists, dancers, small groups of musicians and plenty of opportunity to get up and dance. Then a man stood up and sang a fast, highly intricate song, and I was bowled over by his ability to sing the Gaelic syllables so quickly and precisely, keeping to a metronomic rhythm. Someone next to me in the audience told me it was mouth music, which I'd never heard of before. This singer was Arthur Cormack – he is one of the greats.

Arthur's name stayed in my memory, and here he was again at the Lismore ceilidh! I went up to him at the interval, spoke to him and later he sang a duet with Mary Ann Kennedy. They have been singing together for more than thirty years.

There were quite a number of local Gaelic-singing soloists, mostly from the older generation, which was good to see, but I was too overwhelmed with all this day's stimuli to get up and dance, and left the ceilidh earlier than the others to walk back alone. The empty road back to the bunkhouse was pitch-black, the trees not showing the clearest way to the universe, but I had my head torch and my anxiety level was only about ten per cent. I was much more in danger of tripping over a pothole in the road than of being mugged.

*

Exploring these three islands, albeit briefly, has added greatly to my enjoyment and island knowledge. A few years ago I would never have dreamt that I could become fascinated by mouth music, Gaelic grammar, wood cutting, goose barnacles, toothache stones and stories involving toes and fingers. And to have had at least two amazing coincidences involving chance encounters reminds me how we are all connected somehow or other with life outside of ourselves.

N
W E
S

Berneray

HARRIS

18

16

15

NORTH UIST

17

14

Monach Isles

Grimsay

12

11

10

13

BENBECULA

1. Barra Airport
2. Castlebay
3. Community garden
4. Aird Mhòr
5. Kildonan Museum
6. Lochboisdale
7. Howmore
8. Loch Sgiopoirt
9. Aird na Mhachair cemetery
10. Nunton House
11. Kallin (Ceallan)
12. Benbecula airfield
13. Ruabhal
14. Lochmaddy
15. Balranald Nature Reserve
16. Vallay
17. Camera obscura
18. Berneray Gatliff hostel

9

8

7

SOUTH UIST

5

6

Eriskay

1

4

3

Barra

2

Distance from
Castlebay to Berneray:
80 miles, approx

CHAPTER 6
BARRA, SOUTH UIST, BENBECULA AND NORTH UIST

Many people have heard of Barra's airport, as it's the only one in the world where scheduled flights from Glasgow land and take off from a tidal beach. This beach, at the north of the island, is set out with three runways in a triangle, marked by wooden poles at their ends, allowing the Twin Otter planes that serve the island to land into the wind from most directions. At high tide these runways are under the sea, so flight times vary with the tide. Cockle pickers and other beach enthusiasts are asked to take note of the windsock to see if the airport is in operation.

I have never come in by air, but my daughters and granddaughters took the plane and joined me in Castlebay where we rented a house for a week a few years ago. So I watched the plane land and later take off. Landing was a bumpy experience.

On the road, slowly

On my first solo trip to Barra I'd arrived by bike. It was in the last century when I thought I was a cyclist. I'd arrived in Stornoway on Lewis via Ullapool, with the intention of gradually making my way down the islands. I'd negotiated cheekily with various bus drivers, from Stornoway southwards, to bring my bike on their buses. I'd travelled all down the Spine Road, getting ferries where necessary, and only cycling on the side roads, in a pottering sort of way, when I arrived in Barra. I learnt the hard way that cyclists usually do this trip in the other direction, south to north, the reason being that the prevailing wind is from the south-west.

*

This time I didn't come to Barra by bike or by air; I took my car on the ferry. You need a degree in CalMac timetable reading to discover that it's possible not only to get to Barra (Castlebay) from Oban, but also there's a sneaky boat that goes once a week from Tiree. I'd made a pal in the hostel in Tiree, and he had booked in at the Castlebay hostel too. We sailed on the ferry together, and arrived at the hostel overlooking the harbour. The dorms were mixed, and because I'd struck up a comradeship with this young man, I didn't want to be in the same dorm. We found ourselves booked into different dorms. Which leads me to ponder about the fact that it is more comfortable for me to sleep next to a strange man in a dorm, than to sleep next to a familiar man (with the exception of my partner). I went to bed that night in a six-bed dorm and there were just two other women with me – great! It was going to be an undisturbed night and I felt relaxed.

I woke up in the early hours and crept downstairs to wonder at the amazing quietness of the morning – I was captivated by the light on the sea and took several photos, including the one on the facing page.

After this eye-feast, I went back upstairs and amazingly fell asleep again. I woke up later, hearing several loud snores from the bed next to mine. Eventually the sleeper, who must have crept in when I was asleep, awoke and threw off his covers to reveal bare torso and Y-fronts – somewhat less of an eye-feast – and said, 'Good Morning' with a cheeky grin. I failed to reply.

View from the Barra hostel door at 6.30am

Barra was the home of the 'Coddy', one of the island's famous characters. Alias John MacPherson, he was also known as the 'uncrowned king of Barra', and died in 1947. He was a great character and learnt and passed on many a folk tale. That first time in Barra in 1999, I had found myself at a B&B, in a house on the east of the island, my host being Niall MacPherson, the son of the Coddy, and his wife Chrissie.

That first evening Niall told me a great deal about his father. The Coddy was able to hold the attention of an audience no matter where his listeners came from, and attracted many a passer-by and tourist who came knocking at the post office house in Northbay where he lived. They wanted to hear his stories and folk tales which he told in either Gaelic or English, as he was fluent in both languages.

I will be forever grateful to Niall who had certainly inherited his father's storytelling abilities. It was from him that I learnt that his father knew John Lorne Campbell. Campbell was a great scholar and collector of folk tales and was instrumental in the publication of a book entitled *Tales from Barra: told by the Coddy*.[1] In fact, Campbell wrote the introduction and notes, and the actual stories in the book were mostly transcribed, in 1951, from the Coddy's speech, by a certain Miss Lockett, who took it all down in shorthand! The foreword of the book was written by Compton Mackenzie, another friend of the Coddy. Mackenzie was the author of *Whisky Galore*, which he first wrote as a book, and later, with Angus MacPhail, the screenplay for the 1949 film which became very popular. In fact, I have read that the Coddy was the inspiration for *Whisky Galore*.[2]

The three men – the Coddy, Compton Mackenzie and John Campbell – must have enjoyed many a long evening by a cottage fire, inspired by each other's versions of folk tales, and sustained by a tot or two of whisky. Rather like the Reverend Kenneth Macleod and Alasdair Alpin MacGregor on the island of Gigha. Grown men telling each other folk tales is quite unusual. Or is it?

At some point in this three-way friendship on Barra, the Coddy told Campbell of the Isle of Canna (one of the Small Isles) being for sale. Campbell later bought Canna and went to live in Canna House with his wife. By this time, Campbell had married an American woman called Margaret Fay Shaw. She was a photographer and took many remarkable photographs of life in South Uist.[3] Both husband and wife were gifted people, prolific collectors of Gaelic culture.

I hadn't heard of Margaret Fay Shaw but I almost met her when on a visit to the Isle of Canna in 2003. John Campbell had died by then. A friend and I rented a caravan for a week, and during one of my solo wanderings I met Margaret's friend and carer – the old lady was infirm and housebound, and she sadly died the following year. Margaret's carer, Magda, later became the archivist of Canna House, and we had a long conversation in the garden of the house, but she felt that Margaret couldn't manage a strange visitor. If I'd been able to talk to her, I'd have asked her about waulking – the subject of which I have briefly mentioned in my Tiree chapter.

*

That evening on Barra, I told Niall that I was interested in music, so he recommended that I read Margaret Fay Shaw's book *From the Alleghenies to the Hebrides*[4]. He told me about waulking (luaidh) songs, which were sung by women sitting at the two long sides of an oblong table, pounding a length of freshly woven wet tweed, pushing and pulling the cloth. On his recommendation I bought a CD of waulking songs.[5]

With the decline of traditional methods of cloth-making, there has been no genuine luaidh since the end of the Second World War, but the songs survive and the CD is of recordings made in the mid-1960s, with older female singers who remembered the process and the songs. They even reproduced the conditions of waulking for the recording, by pushing and pulling a blanket on a table!

Normally, during the luaidh, there's a leader who sings a phrase, then the rest join in a refrain. This is repeated again and again, sometimes getting faster, and often with variations. The songs are lyrical with some strong erotic and tragic themes, including laments for men who were lost at sea.

Margaret relates in her book that she had been taken to hear waulking singers. She mentions one song about the rivalry of a Barra woman and a Uist woman – and writes that she, Margaret, could sense this rivalry as they sang. At that time Barra was more prosperous than the Uists. I wonder if they vied with each other as to which group sang louder.

Mention of waulking songs is also made in *A Life of Song* by Marjory Kennedy-Fraser.[6] She gives a detailed description of how the songs progress musically, and get faster. There is a 'strangely exhilarating effect of socially performed, continued repetition of bodily movements accompanied by song,' she writes. She describes the scene: 'Normally there are just the women, working and singing… the young men take no active part, they look on from a respectful distance by the open door or skylight window of the barn where the women, young and old, are seated at work. It's the custom to leave the door open and to welcome anyone who cares to enter… No doubt the lads make note of the particular maiden they hope to see home after the function.'

My favourite quote from this book is a footnote. 'We left the island (Barra) next day, but heard that one of these waulking ladies, a very frail little old woman, had to be kept in bed for three weeks to recover.'

Listening to the women on the CD, pounding the cloth and singing, reminds me of watching a process of work aided by singing when I lived in Sierra Leone in the late 1960s. Two women would stand outside their dwelling place behind the house where I lived and, armed with a pestle each, they took turns to pound the 'mealie-meal' in a large mortar, singing rhythmical songs to help with the monotony of the work.

*

Community garden, Barra

At the end of my stay on Barra in this century, I was heading for the ferry to Eriskay. On my way I passed by the community garden on Barra, grandly named Gàradh a' Bhàgh a' Tuath. Here I met Jamie who told me that about twenty volunteers, some of whom were people with disabilities, worked there on a part-time basis. Some required more support than others, but all had a great enthusiasm for plants.

They grew, in two Keder tunnels and in one polytunnel, a range of beans, tomatoes and strawberries. He went on to mention all my favourites, so I stocked up on broad beans and tomatoes. There is a limit to buying a lot of fresh stuff when you are catering just for yourself, of course. It goes off.

*

You can't travel straight from Barra to South Uist by ferry or causeway. You catch the ferry from Barra at Aird Mhòr, just south of the airfield, which takes you to the small island of Eriskay, lying between the two larger islands. Long ago I stayed overnight there and discovered some of the rare breed of good-natured wild ponies, as well as the Prince's Beach where Bonnie Prince Charlie first stepped on to Scottish soil. But this time in pouring rain, I drove straight to the north of Eriskay where there's a causeway across to South Uist. This was only built in 2001, not in time for my first trip in the islands when I had to take another ferry. But the sea between Eriskay and South Uist is shallow (hence the shipwreck in *Whisky Galore*), so they were eventually able to build the causeway with relative ease. If you are confused by my two-part trip that day, you certainly would find it even more confusing making sense of the CalMac timetable. Having the map in your head is a must.

SOUTH UIST

For a long time I would tell friends that my favourite Scottish island was South Uist. It is a long lozenge of an island with a north-south spinal road and single-track roads to both the west and the east of the island. To the west are sandy beaches and machair, and to the east there are hills and a coastline of rocky creeks and coves, of offshore islets and skerries. The highest hills drop down to the sea as cliffs and precipitous slopes. There are very few footpaths.

Corn marigold

In the south of the island is a fine museum, Kildonan, which among other exhibits contains material pertaining to Margaret Fay Shaw. Having arrived there just before they closed, there was no time to look at these. I met a fellow nosy parker at the museum door. He was a photographer who told me he was following in Paul Strand's footsteps. Paul Strand took some wonderful photographs of South Uist in the 1950s which have become iconic. I wondered if Paul Strand had met Margaret Fay Shaw, but have not been able to find out. From this 'follower' and from other tips I was encouraged to visit an elderly persons' residential home. Just like that.

*

There was no point in trying to ring the home first, as my mobile had no signal. I walked into the building almost apologetically. I was truly amazed and humbled by the fact that I was given permission by a care assistant to chat to a couple of ladies who were, among other residents, having a cup of tea in the huge lounge. The care assistant actually asked me if I minded if she spoke to them in Gaelic to see if they were happy to talk. What wonderful manners! I introduced myself to the women and said I was interested in their memories of school days.

Morag (not her real name) told me she was 103 and wasn't sure whether she went to school in Edinburgh or South Uist. Shona (again, a pseudonym) was a bright, cheerful 97-year-old. My own mother was that age when she died, having retained all her faculties and good health. Shona went to school in Howmore around 1925 and told me that at school they had a cup of cocoa for lunch with sandwiches brought from home. She had three miles to walk to school, but local people used to give them lifts to school in vans. 'The island people are very close together,' she said.

While we were having our serious conversation, we were being observed by a third lady who had said she didn't want to be 'interviewed'. This didn't stop her from listening in. 'What's she doing?' and 'She's writing a book about you,' and 'She's writing it all down about the...'

Shona had had enough of this after a time. 'Keep the nose out,' she said to the interloper. I sensed I shouldn't stay much longer, although I did offer to play the piano that I'd spied in the corner of the lovely lounge – this fell on deaf ears (my offer, not the piano). I bid my farewells. The care assistant, who had got a whiff of all this, told me that the interloper was in a bad mood as she'd missed out on an organised trip that day, and the male resident she had 'taken to' 'wasn't up early enough this morning and she was annoyed about that!'

*

Listening to residents of the isles, like these women in the home, is fascinating as they always give an extra personal 'take' on island living, and a glimpse into the past. In South Uist I was to chat to Betty, the warden of Howmore hostel. Howmore is a little village (Tobha Mòr – The Big Well), which I might have ignored if there hadn't been a hostel there, next to a ruined chapel to the west of the spine road.

The hostel, now much renovated, is one of three in the Western Isles owned by the Gatliff Hebridean Hostels Trust, which is part of the SYHA family. The Gatliff Trust was founded in 1961 by Herbert Gatliff who was an early enthusiast for the outdoor movement and youth hostels in the 1930s. Who knows, my father might well have met him as a fellow YHA pioneer.

The Gatliff Trust is dedicated to encouraging young people, especially those of limited means, to experience, explore and appreciate the British countryside. There are now just three hostels, all of which I have stayed in. They are more 'basic' than SYHA hostels, and all are in the Outer Hebrides.

I was delighted when Betty took time to tell me a little about herself. She was looking in on the newly arrived guests and checking that they had paid for the night, so I asked for five minutes of her time. I told her that in the last century when I'd first stayed there, my sleeping quarters were in a shed with a dirt floor. This is now the cycle shed.

She told me that she had taken over the job from her mother twenty years before, and that her parents had previously owned the hostel building. Herbert Gatliff himself had asked her parents 'if the trust could have it', as it was empty. I've heard since that Gatliff had a crisp RP English accent, spoke only English and very fast, and the islanders he negotiated with had little English. There were some difficulties with communication, but the deal was struck.

Betty told me that she and her mother really enjoyed being wardens. They both loved meeting people, and I had the impression that Betty was very tolerant, never turning anyone away for lack of bed space, for example.

As we were chatting, a couple of cows were wandering around a few feet away from the hostel. 'They belong to a local farmer,' said Betty. 'He's over eighty and with two sticks, and sends the cows 'to the hills' in the morning, and in the evening he comes along and puts them back in a field behind the church.' At least they didn't try to enter the building.

All kinds of people stay in bunkhouses and hostels rather than bed and breakfast, and for different reasons. I stay in them because I like to cook for myself and not pay for meals out (which are often unobtainable in small islands anyway), and also because I like chatting to others. At Howmore I speculated about a group of London media types who were filming locally; surely they would have the means for more upmarket accommodation? Their boss, a slick woman with attitude, was not the kind of person I usually felt comfortable with.

One morning I got up early and went to the kitchen to make my breakfast. The 'boss' was at another table telling her deeply personal sorrows to a man whom she'd obviously just met in the hostel. They were immersed in a counselling session. I can't give any details of what they said, because I worked as a counsellor and psychotherapist and could tell that these were genuine problems. I was

One of the Howmore hostel buildings

astounded that (a) they paid no attention to the fact that they were being overheard by someone just a few feet away, and (b) no one else came into the kitchen. I said nothing, and ate my muesli mystified.

*

One evening on an earlier visit, I walked from the hostel to the lovely coast. Just north of the hostel, behind the low dunes next to the sea, there is a huge area of machair grassland full of flowers, especially in May and June. It was one of my first experiences of machair. The whites and yellows of ox-eye daisies, kidney vetch, bird's foot trefoil, yellow rattle and lady's bedstraw bowled me over, and I discovered that later in the year there would be the pinks, reds and purples of red bartsia, early March orchids, common centaury, knapweed and ragged robin. A cornucopia!

The bed of machair
In the lee of the scraggy skerries
I hear the corncrake's croak;
He's peek-a-booing with the seal-pups,
from his Hebridean garden.

A pink path of thrift paves my way
until, scare-bombed by a bonxie bully,
I blindly dive into the machair,
soft landing on the speckled carpet,
spread-eagled.

Orchids join the corncrake's game;
the early March shrugs,
Heath-spotted looks away;
both wary of intruding.

Bird's foot trefoil finds my fingers;
I stroke its yellow petals,
linger with pinky lousewort.
Tendrils of dark blue tufted vetch
curl their way into my hair.

My skin drinks the machair essence
until the ego melts and merges,
and there's no longer I, but We.

Once or twice I have arrived at a place on the islands where I feel curious and yet quite sad. I see them as 'end of the road' places. One such place is around the old pier at Loch Sgiopoirt.

One of the side roads off the main road leads past Loch Druidibeag, a nature reserve, and ends up at the coast at Loch Sgiopoirt. Here there was once a great deal of activity; steamers from Glasgow unloaded their cargoes, and sheep would be taken from Uist to market. The tarmac finishes just short of the coast, and a track leads through a man-made gorge, down a hairpin bend and thence to the dilapidated pier. On one of my excursions I'd come across a dangling wall just above the old pier, and on revisiting several years later, I'd been desperate (not too strong a word) to see that the wall hadn't collapsed further. I wonder why I want things to stay the same; is it that any change reminds me of ageing?

I recorded my thoughts on my phone as I walked along.

I'm excited. I've just parked at the side of the road about 200 yards away from the pier which is invisible at this point. A Land Rover passes me, and I wonder where he's going to park. The track is full of overflowing puddles and I have to negotiate them by treading on the soggy grass to the left. Mud, I don't know how deep it is, it looks very deep. A tiny bit of blue sky shows itself. Striding back on to the road, I can now see a little bit more of the harbour; there's a mast or something on the left, on the top of the little hillock. The track becomes steep between two unexpected cliffs on either side. The cliffs bemuse; they can't be natural?

This must have been a much more important place many years ago, to have made this road through here. As well as my crunching footsteps on the small stones, I can hear an engine, it's probably a boat. Although it's been pretty grim weather this morning, some impressive hills are visible on the horizon. If it's the mainland, it would be Skye. The track, which is quite wide, is turning to the left. I hear my own breath; a sharp intake – 'I can see a wall! Is it The Wall?' I should be so sad if that jutting-out bit has gone, I wouldn't be at all surprised. It isn't there! Oh no! But here's another twist in the road. I can't believe it! It's there just as it was years ago. Relief!

Dangling wall

I'm fine, who needs a base?
I was put together by experienced hands;
they knew what they were doing back then.
Mortar, stone, elbow grease –
it's years now since that storm
washed away part of the road
and gave me a flying buttress,
proud.

Loch Sgiopoirt, South Uist

A few yards further on, the old track finally did end with the old pier, again untouched since my last visit.

Old pier at Loch Sgiopoirt

I had another 'end of road' experience, this time at Lochboisdale, which I reached by taking a side road towards the south of the island. It was once a major herring port, and is the main settlement of South Uist with a population of approximately 300.There is a parade of shops at the end of the road, with a three-storey architecture not often seen in the islands.

Lochboisdale shops and apartments above

Just one shop seemed to be open; this was on a Friday. This hardware shop's owner was standing outside hoping for a customer. He told me that the flats above the shops were occupied, but the shops were not, because, he said, all purchases were now done by the internet. (Large delivery vans from a ubiquitous food store ply the roads of the Western Isles, but not the smaller islands.) But in the past few years a huge new development project has begun, called the Lochboisdale Harbour. This aims to provide 'world-class facilities' for the tourist industry, fishing and aquaculture. I heard that millions had been spent on the new harbour, including a big pontoon, a crane, a new quayside, and showers for the sailing community.

I felt ashamed I'd nothing to buy from this man, and despite the sunny weather my shame turned to sadness and loneliness as I saw practically no one on my wanderings that afternoon.

Sadness is part of the history of this township. There were unhappy scenes in the mid-nineteenth century. Colonel John Gordon of Cluny, the owner of a large estate comprising the major islands of Benbecula, South Uist and Barra, carried out one of Scotland's most brutal clearances. Almost 3,000 of Gordon's tenants were forced to emigrate. In August 1851, the ship named Admiral was anchored at Lochboisdale to take people from the islands to Canada. The Coddy, mentioned in my Barra chapter, tells of the agony that happened on the Admiral at the time of leaving. People who were staying behind had boarded the ship temporarily to say goodbye to their relatives. The captain ordered his men to erect a fence on deck with the ones who were emigrating on one side, and the family and friends on the other. He gave orders to the sailors to 'lash out' at the ones who were staying behind; 'and the sailors got rope and lashed the poor men and women into their boats back home, after parting with their nearest and dearest friends.' (*Tales from Barra, told by the Coddy;*[7] also, *The Highland Clearances*[8].)

There was yet another poignant event in Lochboisdale in the 20th century. Peter May's *Hebrides*[9] includes an account of the arrival, on the pier, of 'homers' who were orphaned children sent by the Catholic church, mostly from Glasgow, for adoption by local people in South Uist. The practice continued up until the early 1970s. Peter May learnt about 'homers' from Alyxis Daly, whom he cast in the role of Mòrag in the Gaelic series of Machair, in the 1990s. Alyxis's father happened to have been a homer. After arriving at Lochboisdale these children were left standing on the pier with the names of the families who were to become their keepers written on cards hung from their necks. There were no background checks on these families and many children were treated little better than slaves.[10] This account reminded me of the 'boarded-outs' whom I mentioned in the Tiree chapter.

Although these accounts of children being parcelled out or dumped are shocking according to present-day mores, I guess we should take the long view and put some of these events into a historical context, and remember Kindertransport, child evacuation at the start of the Second World War, and such like.

The new harbour represents hope for Lochboisdale's future, but in these Covid times there can't be much activity going on, and I have fears that trade, tourist traffic and businesses will take a long time to pick up again. The harbour had to cancel two regattas in the spring of 2020.

One much happier end-of-the-road experience happened a few miles north of Lochboisdale. The three times I've visited this place, I've been entranced. After driving for about fifteen minutes from the spine road, the single-track road ends at a croft and a small car park for about four cars. A stile welcomes you to explore a woodland by foot. The whole area has a deliberate air of secrecy. Next to the stile at the entrance to the wood there is a helpful map of the croft, called 'Croft no. 8.'

According to the map, the path leads to a place called Àirigh nam Bàn, or Arinaban, which means 'A woman's shieling.' I did a little research that involved putting 'bed and breakfast' into Google. I phoned a woman who had an establishment just up the road from this car park, and apologised that I was after information rather than asking for a bed for the night. She told me about the crofter. He lives in the house behind the car park and has enhanced the native woodland. He has made his whole loch-side area a place where quiet types like me can wander, with tables and benches to sit on, and a little area from which to spot otters. There are one or two viewpoints in the wood, one being along the main path 500 metres from the entrance, where he has erected a bench from which you have a great view of the Minch, looking east. Further on, over a stile past the wood, you can walk as far as a substantial hill if you are so inclined.

The crofter, who is now in his seventies, has spent thirty years building paths through rough, quite hilly terrain, with his own small digger, sometimes with forestry students to help him, and planting trees and other shrubs in all weathers. He has won an award, and has had grants from SNH (Scottish National Heritage – now NatureScot), which has paid for him to plant the trees, both deciduous and coniferous. It takes a huge amount of dedication to plant and maintain a woodland in these parts. Cold winters, peaty soil denuded of nutrients, whipping winds.

The first time I went to this secret woodland I found the otter hide and watched for a short while with no luck. On my latest visit I took a small path to the shore through a large patch of conifers. It was quite dark under the canopy; the trees were closely planted, so that I couldn't see what I could hear – a racket of herons. So there must have been a heronry above

me. The racket went on and on, and I recorded their shouts, but never found out what they were complaining about. There was an ivy-infested old ruin there, too, just enough stones to whet my curiosity as to what it used to be. Apparently there are cuckoos and meadow pipits seen on the moorland fringes of the wood, and otters are regularly spotted, even from the car park. I even failed this last time to find the otter hide.

The secret woodland

Interestingly there is no sign of the woodland on the 1:250.000 OS map, but if you screw your eyes up you can just see a deciduous symbol on the 1:50.000 map. This is one of my favourite serendipitous finds ever. Places like this are treasures for those willing to hunt for them!

*

To the west of the main road just south of the causeway to Benbecula, there's a cemetery at Ardivachar, or Àird a' Mhachair. The

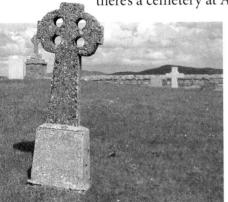

surrounding area is labelled 'Danger Area' on the OS map, but on an early visit I wandered around, after parking the car, and as usual inspected one of the loveliest machair patches in that area. Most cemeteries in the Western Isles are situated near the sea, because the soil is sandy and therefore easier to dig. This cemetery contains the grave of Angus MacPhee.

Cemetery, Ardivachar

A friend lent me Roger Hutchinson's book, *The Silent Weaver*,[11] which tells the story of Angus. There's a strong historical link between the machair plains, particularly of the Uists, and horse culture. For centuries crofters relied on horses, and men learnt to ride, often bareback, at a very young age. Young horsemen on the Uists and Benbecula took part in 'Oda' (Gaelic odaidh, or horse races) which were festivals once linked to the Catholic faith, held once or twice a year on the machair until around 1820. After the Mass, there would be food and drink, horse races and man races, and proud young lads would hang around with their pony, accompanied by their girl.[12]

Horses were numerous in farming communities right up to the advent of motor vehicles and beyond, especially in places like Benbecula and South Uist. The building of the road causeways in the mid-20th century to link Benbecula to North and South Uist was instrumental in the decline of the usefulness of horses – the horse was able to cross the shallow waters of the fords where a car would not have been able.

Angus MacPhee was born in 1915 near Glasgow. From the age of seven he lived in a croft in Iochdar, which is only about a mile from where he was buried. MacPhee's crofting youth was in the 1920s and 1930s, and he loved horses. They pulled the ploughs and all other farm machinery, and for him horses were a source of pride, status and recreation.

As a young man Angus was one of a select minority of men who joined the Lovat Scouts just before the Second World War. As it transpired, horses were rarely used in the conflict, although some were used for the transport of troops and supplies. A few cavalry units were employed as scouts. The Lovat Scouts were the last representatives of this equestrian culture that had flourished on South Uist for millennia. They formed part of a battalion of horse soldiers in smart battledress who cantered down the machair on South Uist as volunteers to board a boat in Lochboisdale to join the war. It must have been an incredible sight as they could ride with speed with very few barriers to jump over, the machair being two miles wide in places, and about twenty miles long. Angus and his fellow soldiers eventually arrived in Beauly in northern Scotland which was the Lovat Scouts' regiment base. Later he went to the Faroes where the Scouts were stationed in order to keep the Germans away. There, in 1940, he suffered a breakdown that he never recovered from, and spent fifty years, hardly ever speaking, in a psychiatric hospital near Inverness.

He had learnt, as a young man, how to weave horse collars, bridles, reins and halters, and make baskets with marram grass collected from the dunes. Marram grass, or 'bent grass', is the only plant that can grow in pure sand, and the Uists were referred to as Tir a' Mhurain – the land of the bent grass. Making the horses' gear from marram was much cheaper than buying leather ware.

He also plaited ropes made of a mixture of this grass and heather gathered from the hills on the eastern side of South Uist. It was time-consuming, but the pleasure he got from this skill never left him.

In the hospital he eventually found his own therapy. During his fifty years' residence there he found consolation in being able to weave objects of all kinds including clothes, with natural materials, sheep's wool and beech leaves, with no thought of keeping them as mementos or works of art. Luckily his skill was discovered by an art therapist, and a few of his wonderful creations have been preserved. These include a

*Angus MacPhee's 'boots' –
exhibit in Pittenweem*

jacket, trousers, pony nosebags and a pair of boots that went on display in Pittenweem, Fife, in the Art Extraordinary Gallery. The boots may not quite fit my feet, but they are a wonderful work of art.

A few of his other creations are in the Kildonan museum, but I was unaware of his story when I visited it. Angus died in 1997, and is buried behind the low stone walls of Ardivachar cemetery. It seems right that his final resting place is surrounded by acres of machair and marram.

Marram Grass
Ammophila, friend of sand,
marram grass, bent grass,
designed to thrive in gales and wind,
your matted roots keep at bay
invading deserts, arid land.

When heading for the sunny strand
I've trodden on your prickly spikes
which weave and wave as the breeze sees fit
and children make their swords with it!

I think of what was made from grass
in days when men and women dried
and stitched and plaited, wove and twined
brushes, ropes and sacks for grain,
baskets, backpacks, seats for chairs,
horses' collars, saddle pads,
when bothies' roofs were thatched with grass.
Marram grass, friend of sand.

BENBECULA

An area of very shallow sea coloured yellow, not blue, on the OS map, denotes the ubiquity of sand around the south causeway linking South Uist to Benbecula. The causeway is less than two miles away from where Angus MacPhee grew up, and he would often have ridden his horse, high or low tide, to Benbecula. This island lies between South and North Uist, and is joined up to both islands by causeways.

I have a twenty-year-old memory of sitting in a bus that went over this causeway. The bus, which was carrying my bike too, was hovering outside the Benbecula airport building on our way from Stornoway to South Uist. Two American women, fellow bus travellers, offered me a couple of mints. I was amused by the name on the tin, Senior Moments. They told me what that

Warning sign at a Benbecula causeway

meant, and at that point I didn't know! But afterwards, as you do when you hear of a new medical complaint, I began to suffer from them.

I didn't see any otters either on or from the causeway but seventeen years after I started to have senior moments, on Benbecula at South Ford, I turned left to follow the shore, passing a school, museum, a temple and small jetty until I arrived at Nunton House, which was my hostel for a few nights. The house had been the home of the MacDonalds of Clanranald who used to own Benbecula and South Uist. The family moved to Nunton House after their former home, Ormacleit Castle in South Uist, was burnt down in 1715.

I was welcomed kindly by Catherine the warden and placed in a small dorm for women only. Two of my dorm-mates were from Hoy, they said. I was puzzled, but told them I'd been to Hoy (in the Orkneys) and liked it very much. It turned out that I'd misheard them. They were from Hawaii. Quite a difference.

*

In the late afternoon I went across the road for a wander over the dunes, shore and the headland. A smart notice in the dunes, near an expanse of machair, informed me about Machair Life, a four-year project that ran from 2011-2014.

The project, like the one in Tiree, aimed to conserve the unique habitat of the machair. It was a partnership between RSPB Scotland, Scottish National Heritage and the Scottish Crofting Federation. It encouraged the continuation of traditional crofting practices of working the land, a wildlife-friendly approach; using seaweed to fertilise the ground, spring cultivation and sowing, late harvesting of grass and corn silage crops, and crop rotation where the ground was left fallow for two to three years between crop-growing seasons. These methods encourage birds and insects such as the corncrake and lapwing, and the great yellow bumble-bee, to thrive among wild flowers such as corn marigold, long-headed poppy and stork's bill, which grow along the crop margins.

To me, machair in full bloom is a magic garden. Seventy per cent of the world's machair occurs in west Scotland, mostly in the islands. Since seeing it first in Howmore, I've marvelled at habitats in Colonsay, Lewis, Harris, all the way down the Uists including Benbecula and Barra, and on the mainland near Durness: all have expanses of machair. I had heard that patches of machair were found in Ireland too, and was delighted to discover some in Derrynane, County Kerry, while walking the seashore nature trail. (The leaflet of this trail, produced by the Office of Public Works, is full of information, but never uses the word machair at all!)

On top of one of the dunes I could see the beach, totally devoid of people, as is usual in the Western Isles. But there was a man about 200 yards away, skulking around a cleft in the dunes. If I did any thinking at all, I assumed he'd gone for a swim. After a while I found a dune-top path. Then out of the blue, I received a tremendous thump on my back. For two seconds I was terrified. I turned around – there was a large dog; it was the man's dog I'd seen ten minutes before. I'd had no warning of this, not a bark, nor a sniff, nor pawsteps – sand is totally soundproof. Now facing me, the dog continued to jump up at me, but I screeched at it. Running down to the part of the beach where I thought its owner would be, I found him lurking, and screeched at him too. 'I thought it was a person attacking me', I bellowed. I can't remember any of his response, but my guess is that he justified the dog's behaviour by saying 'he was only being friendly'.

I reflected on this episode as I continued to wander along the sands, and realised how quickly my fright, once it disappeared, turned into anger. But my anger abated slightly when later I came across some unusual sand/wave formations on the same bit of coast.

There are hippopotamus heads in there, I thought. The dog knows about them hiding under the sand. Maybe they are all out to get me, plotting another attack on me...

I shook myself, labelled this paranoia and decided it was time for dinner. On returning to the hostel, I was greeted by Catherine who told me that her neighbour Alasdair was looking for one extra person to go on a private boat trip the following day to the Monach Isles. I jumped at the opportunity; I'd never otherwise have had the chance to visit these islands, which many people have never heard of. And the weather forecast was good. So with great anticipation for the following day, I made my evening meal and enjoyed the sociable atmosphere of two cheerful Spanish families.

I was picked up early the next day by Alasdair, and taken by Land Rover to Kallin (Ceallan) pier. A boat was to take us to the remote and uninhabited Monach Islands, sometimes called Heisker, or Heisgeir, which lie four miles west of North Uist/Benbecula and are a National Nature Reserve. The small launch called the *Mary Anne* set off at 8.30am, with fourteen of us, including the crew of two, a collection of geologists and a wildlife expert with a drone. Kallin is on Grimsay, an island to the north-east of Benbecula. To get to the west coast, the boat wove through many tiny islands in the North Ford (Faoghala Tuath). Timing was critical for the whole day. To get under the low bridge of the main causeway it was important for the tide to be neither too high (we wouldn't get under) or too low (we'd scrape on the sandbanks). We made it!

Crossing under the causeway at high tide, with Mount Eabhal, the highest hill in North Uist, in the background

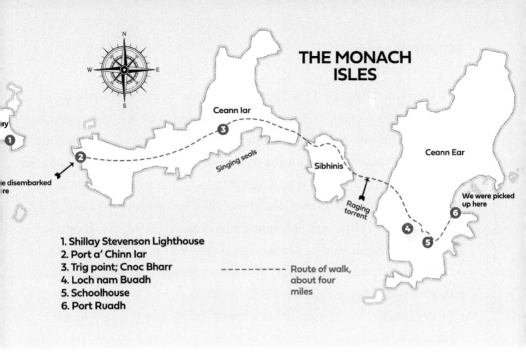

THE MONACH ISLES

Ceann Iar

Ceann Ear

Singing seals

Sibhinis

Raging torrent

We were picked up here

We disembarked here

1. Shillay Stevenson Lighthouse
2. Port a' Chinn Iar
3. Trig point; Cnoc Bharr
4. Loch nam Buadh
5. Schoolhouse
6. Port Ruadh

– – – – – – – – Route of walk, about four miles

We walked from Port a' Chinn Iar to Port Ruadh – around three to four miles

The crossing was fine until we reached the open sea – I started to feel queasy and went out from the cabin where I'd been sheltering. I felt better in the fresh breeze.

We made for Shillay (Siolaigh), the lighthouse island. On the low-lying land stood two beehive-shaped stone cairns, leading lights that helped the skipper find the correct place to land. The launch rose and fell in the swell and the crew skilfully tied up the boat to make it safe for us to jump on to some very seaweed-slippery rocks that you could only loosely describe as an old stone jetty. Not for the faint-hearted or lame. H. Haswell-Smith states: 'navigation around the Monach Islands requires great care as there are many hazards.'[13] Perhaps an understatement?

Our boat moored off Shillay

As soon as we were safely on the Shillay beach, my eyes fell upon two aluminium buoys gathering dust in the grass between the leading lights and the lighthouse. A good omen for me despite the fact that they both had broken 'ears'. I was beginning to see myself as a grey float collector. My eyes were then drawn to the two lighthouses which were adjacent to each other. One man knew a great deal about their history and gave us a short talk. The taller, brick-built lighthouse was built by David and Thomas Stevenson in 1864. During the Second World War it was closed down. After the war it was declared 'not of value to general navigation' and was discontinued 'permanently' in 1948.

In 1997 three new 'minor' lights were established in the west of the Hebrides, to aid laden tankers to use a 'deep water route'. These new lights included the construction, on Shillay, of a new light which is short, squat, box-shaped and white. However, in 2005 there was a review of marine aids to navigation, and it was decided to increase the range of the Monach Isles' light from 10 miles to 18 miles. This would best be done, it was argued, by upgrading (putting in a new optic) the old Stevenson lighthouse which had been standing doing nothing for sixty years, rather than by refurbishing the newer square one. So in 2008 the new one was defunct and the old one shone again, now fully automated.

We spent just half an hour on Shillay, where the grass was easy to walk on, then headed back to the boat. One of our party offered to carry 'my' two buoys to the

Stevenson's brick-built lighthouse, and the 'new' lighthouse behind, looking tiny

boat which was precariously tied up among nearby rocks. It was no mean feat to scramble heavily laden on to the boat, which was nodding viciously between the seaweed-slimy rocks.

The launch soon landed and disgorged us on Ceann Iar – just a couple of minutes away across the Sound – the landing place is named Port a' Chinn Iar on my special Monach Islands map. We were not to see the boat again until it came to collect us on the furthest island, Ceann Ear. Our mission was to walk across three islands.

These three Monach islands, taken together, form the shape of a butterfly – Ceann Iar, the west 'wing', Sibhinis the 'body', and Ceann Ear the east 'wing'. Iar and Ear are Gaelic for west and east. Ceann is 'head'. Sibhinis links the two 'wings' at low tide – so if you don't keep an eye on the tides, you could be stranded at high tide on any of three islands. Again, good timing was essential that day.

Once on Ceann Iar, we were left to our own devices and people just scattered. There were no paths, except for a sprinkling of sheep tracks. I walked on my own for the most part, keeping an eye on a few people who seemed to know the way. The going wasn't easy and I regretted not having brought my walking pole.

Occasionally I came across ruins of dwellings or farm buildings. The islands were inhabited from 1000 AD. There was a nunnery that had connections to Iona, on Ceann Ear, in about the 13th century, and the lighthouse on Shillay was the site of a monastery. (The name Monach refers to monks.)[14] Lady Grange, whose kidnapping had been arranged by her estranged husband, was imprisoned here for two years in 1732-4, before her better-known imprisonment on St Kilda.

The population never rose above 140 – in 1695 Martin Martin stated that there were eighteen families and 1,000 head of cattle and sheep. There were seventeen houses in 1891. By 1933 almost all the people had left, but one family returned for four years – between 1943 and 1947 – and it would be fascinating to hear about their experiences.

Besides cattle and sheep, the land was used for planting oats, barley and rye, potatoes and vegetables. Though there was a crofting system, it was managed communally – so that there were group decisions about areas to be planted or grazed. The inhabitants fished for lobsters commercially, and also trapped rabbits for sale to mainland game dealers. They collected shellfish on the shores and used lines for catching fish for their families. There were no trees, but driftwood was gathered and made good use of.

The islanders often ate birds. Ewen Nicholson tells a story about bird-eating when out on the islands with a friend. They 'shot a cormorant, tied a string round it, slit the skin off in a 'oner' (which is easier when the bird is warm) and chucked it in a pan of boiling water, and had eaten it within the hour.'[15] Apparently eider duck and mallard are tasty to eat and there was a soup, 'still longed for in Grimsay,' made of shag with barley and onions. Barnacle geese that overwinter in the islands were also eaten by the islanders.

Another reference to food is from Alexander Carmichael, who wrote a description about the preparation of seals for eating, including pressing blubber to extract oils. He recalls tasting the flesh of a young seal on Heisgeir and that it was 'very agreeable and like venison.'[16]

*

I picked my way through the marram and tussocks, often two feet tall, on Ceann Iar. Storms had caused a huge loss of soil, and some of the marram grass had been deliberately planted to stabilise the soil. It was cut for thatching the houses, like on other islands. I made it to a trig point nineteen metres high (the islands are low-lying) to get my bearings, and from then I was able to see where to drop down to Sibhinis.

The Monachs were once joined to North Uist. H. Haswell-Smith refers to a stretch of sand 'which was exposed at low water and which linked the entire group to N. Uist. In 1607 an enormous tidal wave, the same titanic tsunami which formed the Sound of Pabbay, swept away the sand-banks.'[17] While looking over to North Uist it was difficult for me to imagine this;

from where I stood the sea looked incredibly deep. The views were stunning – small islets with collars of seaweed, a dark blue sea, skerries and other rocks jutting out at random. But the highlight was the sound of grey seals singing. I couldn't see them, just hear their chorus, which accompanied my whole walk from west to east. The seals are hauled out on rocks, skerries and shores of the islands, especially in the autumn, and it is one of the biggest grey seal colonies in the world.

Walking over the sand from Ceann Iar to Sibhinis was uneventful. The sea seemed miles away. It was easy enough picking my way around the shore of this very small island, but now and then I had to traverse rocky outcrops.

But the tide was coming in. At the east end of Sibhinis I faced a tract of sand over to Ceann Ear, but a racing torrent of incoming seawater had to be crossed. I noticed that all the other people in the group had crossed the torrent already and were dawdling on the other side. I took off my boots, dangled them from my hand, and waded, knee deep, to the other side. I spent twenty minutes cleaning and drying my feet and putting my boots on again.

Looking over to Ceann Ear from Sibhinis

Now more or less regrouped, we slithered up sand dunes and walked over slightly easier ground. This island is grazed by the resident flock of Hebridean sheep, but they were not showing themselves. I passed a small loch, Loch Nam Buadh, the Loch of the Virtues, which is the subject of an old legend that A. A. MacGregor recounts.[18]

The loch was regarded as the abode of an evil water-horse, each-uisge, which got up to nasty tricks. The islanders were so afraid of the monster that they considered abandoning the island altogether. However, a certain islander, Mrs NicLeòid, had been feeding up a powerful bull in the hope that one day he would overpower the water horse. She led her bull to the loch shore, and he 'tore at the sod with hoof and horn', until the water-horse emerged and faced the bull.

A vicious fight ensued, causing such a huge amount of spray that the islanders couldn't see what was happening. Eventually the commotion stopped and the next day a pair of lungs was seen floating in the water; no one could tell if they belonged to the bull or the water-horse. But that was the end of both creatures, and the islanders stayed.

It is said that you can still see, on the shores of the loch, the 'marks made on the sod by hoof and horn', where the bull was getting ready for the fight. Unfortunately I will have to wait for my next visit to check on those marks as I had no idea of this legend when passing the loch. I was looking for flowers. Much of the islands are covered with many of the sand-loving machair flowers, the most obvious being silverweed which was growing in profusion in small ditches.

*

I was one of the last of the group from the boat to reach the schoolhouse. (The school itself was in ruins not far away.) We had been asked to congregate in the house, which has been kept intact because it is occasionally used as a bothy by fishermen overnighting. Inside, we were shown the living room, the bunk room and the kitchen.

Some of our party included men who had relatives who had lived on the

Kitchen in the schoolhouse bothy

island. These included a grandmother who had emigrated to Canada and made a great success of her life. I collected a couple of stories from these men, two of whom I noticed had taken chairs either side of the unlit fire-grate, a habitual place for storytelling. I was advised not to relate the stories in my book just in case their descendants thought the subject matter sensitive.

One story, however, is well documented; two lighthouse keepers were drowned while collecting mail from Ceann Iar, and their sister kept the light going until a replacement keeper came. More recently, in the 1940s, the final entry of the school log states that the last teacher, Anne Morrison, taught her brother Archie.

*

Graffiti on one of the school house walls caught my attention, written by young visitors from Benbecula who were stranded in the house. I quote: 'Sgoil Lioncleit, Grimsay Boat Building Course were here, 16 +17 June 2006 – too windy to leave until 18/6. Chopped, collected a lot of wood and played a lot of football.' Then six boys' names (the 'S' team), and three more, and then 'Mary'. I expect she had her work cut out.

Climbing back into the boat at 4pm was tricky. It was anchored at Port Ruadh, which was the main jetty on Ceann Ear, a few hundred yards from the school house. Many of us had trouble negotiating the seaweedy and barnacled rocks again. But we were in safe hands. The boat was anchored, but it still needed two men pulling a rope to keep it near enough a rock for us to high-step or jump off it, and then on to the boat. This, and the action of ducking under the boat's railing, caused me a moment's rush of anxiety.

Once we were on our way, the sea crossing was lovely; full sun, warm, calmer than the outward journey. We held our breath when we came to the Benbecula causeway bridge but we made it with no scrapings either at the top or the bottom of the boat. It was one of the most memorable and fascinating days I've ever spent, anywhere.

*

The day after the Monach Isles trip, Monika, my Austrian roommate in the hostel, told me she was keen to scale Rhuabhal, the highest hill of Benbecula, a lofty 124 metres, so we decided to go together. We parked at a landfill site on the spine road about four miles north of the southern causeway, and walked along a good track, which would have eventually ended on the east coast of the island to Ròisiniss from where Bonnie Prince Charlie and Flora MacDonald set sail. That destination will have to wait until next time.

At the third loch, Loch Bà Una, just before a small quarry, a path uphill to the left was easily visible. I'd heard that there were two ways of seeing Benbecula: 'Big land, big water'; or 'big water, lots of islands'. I've yet to discover whether Benbecula has more acreage of land or water.

We tramped across the rough grass, rocky knolls, heather and mud. On reaching the plateau at the top, we had wonderful views; a sparkling watery landscape crossed with islands, lochans and magical rainbow colours, as dark rain-filled clouds vied with sunny patches. Monika and I took each other's photographs, and many more of the distant views.

View from the top of Ruabhal

There is no shelter on top of Ruabhal. Bonnie Prince Charlie, just before his famous voyage 'over the sea to Skye', is said to have spent several days and nights up there, probably crouched in a makeshift shieling, scanning the horizon for unwelcome visitors. We don't know if he was a birdwatcher, but he could have seen hen harriers, merlin or short-eared owls, as these birds commute long distances between moorland breeding sites and the rich machair grasslands.

*

Grimsay is the island from which I had taken the boat to the Monachs, and you pass over it while driving or cycling from Benbecula to North Uist. I was still staying at Nunton House hostel when I drove one morning to Kallin, but not for a sea trip this time. The main road with its series of causeways links several tiny isles and you wouldn't necessarily notice that the road nips over the north-western tip of Grimsay. At this tip you have the chance to turn right and explore a circular road around Grimsay, with the settlement of Kallin (Ceallan) on its east side. Here there is the pier mostly for fishing boats, and a

The prettiest rubbish dump ever

seafood factory. On finding the factory, I was staggered to see, just outside the building, that there was a massive area of huge scallop shells piled high next to the water. The penny dropped. This wasn't a beach, it was a modern midden; a place to dump the unwanted shells.

Later, I was told that these shells were there for the taking – people needing crushed shells for drive-making, for example, would come and scoop them up. Recycling at its simplest.

I was once more on the lookout to find willing islanders to interview, especially about their childhood. Someone on the Monach Isles trip had suggested I talk to Hector, the manager of the seafood factory, and we chatted just inside the building. He was one of the many Stewarts on the island of Grimsay; this family are the descendants of the Stewarts of Appin who fled to the Western Isles after the battle of Culloden – they were dispossessed of their land because they had been on the Jacobite side.

The Stewarts in the Benbecula area were shepherds, joiners, boat-builders and, later, fishermen. They were so plentiful in Grimsay that when Hector went to primary school, Stewarts numbered a quarter of the school population.

After primary school at Kallin in Grimsay, Hector went to Bayhead School in North Uist for his secondary education. (The secondary part of this school is now closed.) He mentioned the 'belt' or tawse that many teachers used. The tawse was a leather strap with two or three prongs at the end. It was used a great deal in Scottish schools, as well as some English ones, even until the 1980s. It was designed to hit the hands of the recalcitrant pupil, but not draw blood. The tawse was banned in Scotland in 1987.

Hector had a way of telling tales of the tawse which drew laughter from both of us. All through secondary school, 'a teacher who thought that he wasn't all that good at administering the belt would send the pupil to one who was better at it,' he said. But there were funny moments. He witnessed one teacher just about to strike, but the child in question moved his hands away just in time, and the teacher struck herself on the legs. Hector said that she did it lighter next time. You could get the belt (as they often called it) for such misdemeanours as forgetting your homework, or coming in a few minutes late.

*

As a youth Hector would go with his father in the school summer holidays, along with four or five boat crews, to the Monach Isles, and stay from Monday to Saturday in a shieling which was used by fisher people.

220

It's now a ruin near the lighthouse. Another four or five crews would be on Ceann Ear at the schoolhouse.

'The fishing wasn't as intense as it is now – there was a lot of time for chatting and talking,' he said. They talked about where they'd caught the catches, where they'd set the creels. He then told me about the names the fisher people had for every bit of shoreline; 'names passed down for hundreds of years,' he said. There would be a name for a feature, rock, pool, skerry, every thirty or forty yards away from each other. He was able to remember most of the names in the Monachs. As in Islay with a big rock called 'OK' in Port Charlotte, I was reminded of a quotation whose provenance I've forgotten: 'Every meadow, every spring, every hillock, every change of atmosphere, has a name in Gaelic.' Hector reminded me that many of the Monach place names are Norse. His favourite name in the Monachs is Reisgeer – the name of a particular-shaped rocky skerry due south of Shillay, which the boats used to take their bearings from.

I have a copy of a map of the Monachs first published in 1860. On it are marked no fewer than eighty-one 'land names' and ninety-one names for 'sea' features, just off the coasts of these islands, such as individual rocks. This is astounding given the small area – very roughly four miles by one.[19]

*

I wasn't surprised that Hector knew Ewen Nicholson, who was 'somewhat older than me'. A book I found in a Mallaig second-hand bookshop tells of the memories of this 'Hebridean skipper' who was born in Grimsay in 1935.[20]

Ewen writes: 'People were kinder in those days. Perhaps they had to be, you might never know when you might need your neighbours' help.' As a youngster he liked visiting people, even older people, and many houses were called 'taigh ceilidh' by the locals – a ceilidh house. 'Myself and my friend were very keen on visiting the old bodachs and cailleachs in the area and having a ceilidh with them.' (Bodach is old man and Cailleach is old woman, as I learnt in Gigha when I visited the famous stones thus named.) It came as a surprise to me that youngsters actually sought to go to older people's houses, so they must have loved hearing the old tales. I was beginning to see how deeply storytelling is ingrained in Gaelic culture.

From the month of March until October children used to go barefoot. Maybe the sandy ground helped. Ewen writes of contests to see who would be first to put their boots on as winter loomed. I presume that this person got the booby prize for being soft.

I love the picture that comes to my mind on reading how Ewen, as a young man, swam across the ford from Grimsay in order to attend dances in Benbecula. (This was long before the causeways were built.) 'I'd take off my clothes and tie them with my braces in a package above my head to keep them dry and then make the crossing.'[21]

Ewen goes to town with his tawse stories. He tells of tricks the children would play on the teachers in his Grimsay primary school, to get their own back. It wasn't the same school as Hector's – at the time there were two primary schools on the island. The pupils, including Ewen, would sometimes hide the tawse and, in Ewen's case, in the school oven!

'Imagine my horror when the belt was discovered, and worse still, realising that I was to be strapped with the now extra hard piece of leather.' However, Ewen was not to be deterred. 'I rolled the belt up, placing it in an empty can of syrup, and pressed down the lid.'[22] The mind boggles as to what happened next, and Ewen does not tell you.

The tawse

I googled 'tawse' and came across this quote. 'Based in Lochgelly, Fife, John J. Dick Leather Goods were the teachers' preferred suppliers at the height of the tawse's reign of terror. The Lochgelly Tawse was made by cutting 2ft-long strips of leather from pre-tanned and pre-curried hides. The leather would then be dressed and cut halfway up the middle to form the tails. The particular design of the tails provided the searing nip when it struck the student's hand. However, the Lochgelly method was preferable in that the tails were 'edged' in order to prevent drawing blood.'[23]

As the reader may well know, the tawse wasn't just administered to boys. I have spoken to at least one woman who, when a youngster, received regular beatings from the tawse on mainland Scotland in the 1970s. Corporal punishment was not confined to Scotland; the cane was used liberally in English schools until the 1960s.

*

I was grateful to Alasdair for two things – one for picking me up in his Land Rover to take me on the Monach Islands trip, and the other for agreeing to be interviewed. We stood outside the Nunton hostel one morning for our chat. Alasdair is a native of Benbecula, where several generations of his family have lived and worked for some 350 years. There were no nurseries in his early years. He started at primary school at five years old, and went to the old Balivanich school. He was 'reasonably academic', and left home at twelve years of age to attend secondary school in Fort William – Lochaber High School – where there was a hostel for youngsters, particularly ones who lived on the islands and obviously couldn't get home at nights. Between the ages of twelve and twenty-two he spent the best part of those years going to school (including further education), backwards and forwards, from the island to the mainland.

'I spent the whole term in the school there. Despite there being a mid-term break, a long weekend didn't give you sufficient time to get home and back again. So we were away from home from mid-August till the third week in December, and the same again after New Year, until Easter.' There was no way of going home until the end of term. As well as islanders there were mainland youngsters in the hostel. 'They could go home at weekends, but we were boarded right through the term.' This was similar to other islanders' experiences I'd heard of, such as Effie's in Islay.

He was homesick but appreciated the school being excellent as far as education and facilities were concerned. 'My parents wanted us to have a good education; that was the priority.'

*

Alasdair has been beachcombing much of his life, 'which is a bit of a hobby, even an obsession.' Driftwood is always welcome. 'There are no trees here, no timber, so people always relied on driftwood for firewood. I dry it in my shed and use it for fuel.'

But more exciting things can turn up. 'In my young days we used to play around a Second World War landing craft that was washed up on the shore at the back of our house.' The war created a huge amount of flotsam and jetsam. The landing craft became a perfect piece of playground equipment for the young boy and his mates. 'My father found it in October 1942. I know the whole history, where it came from, where it was built. Over the years it deteriorated. We didn't chop that up for firewood, but scrap merchants would come along and take bits and pieces from it, particularly the more valuable bits, like copper and brass. It gradually rusted away, and by about ten years ago, storms and high tides had pulled it apart. It's gone now,' he added wistfully.

Marine mammals and cetaceans get stranded on the beach from time to time – seals, dolphins, big whales. The whales arouse a lot of interest, from fairly large sperm whales to the smaller pilot whales. We spoke about the eternal rubbish washed ashore. 'I never walk past a plastic bottle or tin can on the shore. I collect that stuff and recycle it. You would be amazed, even horrified, at the amount at the back of our house. In one period over Christmas and New Year I remember counting up 1,800 items. I worked this number out by what I could cram into a bin liner. I know how many bags I had, and I averaged them out – seventy items in each bag.'

I was impressed by Alasdair's account. It's good to use precise numbers

Buoys with broken 'ears' in yet another new place

to inform people. As a youngster, he collected grey aluminium fishing net buoys washed ashore. He knew a dealer who would pay him two shillings and sixpence for one old buoy, and he saved enough to buy himself a pair of jeans. He might have been envious of my discovering two buoys on Shillay, but he hadn't said anything when he saw 'mine' safely stashed in the boat, in a shopping bag. These grey buoys are a cut above the modern brightly coloured plastic ones with which people adorn their gates and garden fences.

*

I was yet to hear tales from another man, Robert, who had been to secondary school in Benbecula. Our conversation took place on Muck as he was the manager of the Muck fish farm at the time, and we spoke in his living room overlooking Port Mòr, his young son coming into the conversation a number of times. (Since I met him, he and his family moved to Tasmania!)

Robert started at Lochmaddy Primary School, North Uist, in 1987 and was one of eighteen children in the whole school. He lived in Minish, about three and a half miles away. When he didn't get a lift to school from the cook, he had to walk. Some pupils spoke only English, like Robert. (His father was from England, his mother from Islay.) But he thought there was no differentiation between the ones who spoke Gaelic and the English speakers. 'We were at the same table and we just had to get on.'

The walls of the school playground played a key part in his memories. They were about a metre and a half high on one side and four metres down on the other. A helicopter landing pad was just outside the school. 'If there was a medical emergency, we were all allowed to jump over the back wall, and watch the helicopter land – no health and safety in those days!' Blind man's buff often ended up with someone running into the wall. Once a guy actually got hit over the wall and 'that was British Bulldogs banned; that sort of stuff happened a few times.' He grinned. That particular game involved a headlong charge towards your mates, a treacherous scuffle, and a desperate sprint to the other side of the yard.

As a high school student, Robert went to Lionacleit School in Benbecula. This school is the only one serving secondary pupils from all three islands; four, counting Grimsay. He was one of the very few people I spoke to who mentioned religion, and was keen to tell me about the significance of the meeting up of Catholics from South Uist, and Protestants from North Uist. Robert told me that in his first few days at school, which was the third secondary year for pupils from both islands, there was often mayhem; fighting between factions. They had all been used to junior schools with only fifty or sixty pupils; now they were in a big school with 300, 400 pupils. But by the time they all left in the sixth year, everyone he was friends with was from South Uist! 'Six of us used to hang about together, and I was the only North Uist person. Someone was playing a tune on their tape player at lunch, and I had no idea what it was, so kept quiet; but one of the guys got ridiculed for not knowing it was the Sash, the Protestant song.' He never cared whether a person was Catholic or Protestant, he said, but other people 'hung on to their prejudices.'

*

Robert gave me a first-hand account of a mighty storm in the Benbecula area in 2005 that had made the national news; in fact, I remember watching TV footage at the time. Sadly, two cars with members of the same family were swept away and perished on a Benbecula causeway while trying to escape from the boulders and debris crashing on to their houses. At the time Robert was a young man working on the fish farm near

Lochmaddy, North Uist. 'I ended up leaving work early because the storm was that bad; the wind was about 100mph. I just went to sleep on the sofa when I got home, and my dad rang me up to ask me if I was OK. I didn't know what he was talking about! I went to the window and opened the curtains, and a pile of slates smashed the window, and some of the glass and the slates stuck in my legs.

'Of the houses to the right of mine, at least two gable ends had been ripped off. I could see the people inside the houses, running about in their bedrooms. My chimney blew off; there were slates flying around every-where – they actually hit the kitchen window as well. The kitchen and living room windows faced the direction of the wind, but it only burst the first pane of the kitchen window. It was like a shotgun going off. There was a side door of the house; I went to the porch and took the glass bits out of my leg. I tried to detach the swinging door, and phoned up my mates that lived just a wee bit away to give me a hand because the door weighed about fifty kilos. I couldn't get hold of them. It wasn't safe to go out, but I ran down to another friend's house on the street next to the church. On the way there I could see that a neighbour's shed, in one piece, was actually airborne and flying around.

'I got hold of a few of my neighbours; they came back with me to my house, and we ended up nailing the swing door over the window to try and stop anything worse happening. I ended up living with my mates for several days.

'The day after, we went to Clachan and found that the bridge had completely disappeared. On the way there, there was a guy taking the wind speed and said it was 133mph when he lost his wind-measuring gear.

'There were large bits of debris all over North Uist and Benbecula, not to mention the damage to existing houses and other buildings. It ruined North Uist fisheries – they had just built three new polytunnels – and all three were gone.'

NORTH UIST

As the reader will have deduced, the islands of South Uist, Benbecula, Grimsay and North Uist are so joined up by causeways that they inevitably share geographical features, history and customs. Residents are always travelling, just as Robert did, from one to the other island, as if they were all one long island. The terrain of North Uist is similar to that of Benbecula. It's said that half of its area is land, and half is water. From the air it must look like a huge expanse of Nottingham lace. It has a north coast as well as an east and west coast.

An easy drive from the Benbecula hostel took me to the western part of the circular road.

I called at Balranald, the well-known RSPB reserve on the west coast, famous for its corncrakes. This time I didn't even hear them, let alone see any. The information in the visitor centre explained the importance of traditional crofting methods to enable corncrake and other wildlife to flourish. There's a circular trail going through the croft land machair, and round a headland where many species of waders congregate.

A friend told me of her own visit to the reserve in 2017 when she and her husband joined a guided group, and discovered on the shore a large collection of small human bones of toes and fingers that had become lodged in the fissures and cracks of the rocks. It is just possible that the previous day's stormy weather had unearthed a Mesolithic burial site on the shore, but there seems to be no proof yet of this. I've read that 'dislocated bones of the dead were moved around, grouped and regrouped, scattered and collected'. The human body was reduced to its component parts, as compared with Egyptian mummies having been preserved intact.[24]

My friend's story fascinated me a great deal, particularly because I'd read about human bone fragments discovered in a Colonsay midden.

*

This time on North Uist I had another plan in mind. My experience of crossing the vast area of wet sand at low tide from North Uist to the tiny uninhabited island of Vallay, or Bhalaigh, illustrates how anxiety-prone I can get as a solo, older female traveller. After leaving Balranald, I followed the road towards the north shore at Àird Glas. Here the short track to the shore on my left was easy to find because I could see on the map that it was opposite a plantation of trees behind the main road; rare in the Uists.

Vallay, just over a mile away, was clearly visible, low-lying, treeless, with a large ruined building facing east. The access track next to which I parked looked very little used, and I looked for vehicle tracks across the sand; none were visible. So not many people attempt the crossing by Land Rover or tractor, I thought. This was going to be a different and even more lonely experience compared with my crossing over from Colonsay to Oronsay, when I could see others walking on the sands. I watched the tide, still in the process of going out, and marvelled at the nuances of colour, ranging from watery blue to yellow where the water was very shallow, to dark beige, with patches of green. A lovely stippled effect sparkled in the sun close to the sandbanks. No one else was around.

The track 'leading' to Vallay over the sands

Tidal islands are sometimes known in the Hebrides as 'drying islands'. The island looked dry enough, but the sand between me and it looked very wet. I'd done the homework, found the tide times and remembered them. Or so I thought.

I dithered. Wellies, walking boots? Had I got the right times? Where were all the people who wanted to cross on this lovely day? Then a sigh of relief – a couple arrived in their car and parked nearby. We chatted. They told me they had no intention of crossing. For a couple of minutes I felt like chickening out. I was going to have to do this alone.

I took a deep breath, and plunged bewellied onto, or rather into, the wet sand. I made for the ruins of Valley House. At one point I had to veer to the left to avoid a large sandy lake. There were several places where rivulets had turned into full-blown channels, cutting quite deep into the sand. Some ladylike jumping was called for. My stick was essential as at every twist and turn in my route, I had to test the new sand for treacherous properties. The quicksand fatalities in Morecambe Bay came to mind.

I was pleased with myself when after about half an hour, I finally reached the island, stepped up onto fine green turf, and walked up to what

Valley House

230

Interior of Valley House

remained of the house. Made of cement-harled brick, the external walls still stand, but the doors were inaccessible, so I wasn't able to enter the partially collapsed interior. I wandered around the exterior of the house and marvelled at the high walls, the lichen on the stones, the abundance of wildflowers, and wondered about those who had lived there.

Valley was once home to more than sixty people. It is still farmed (cattle have contributed somewhat to the poor state of the house ruins) and is also an RSPB reserve, but there are no permanent residents.

The house was built between 1902 and 1905 by Erskine Beveridge who was the owner of a successful linen mill in Dunfermline. He was a wealthy man and devoted his free time to archaeological excavations and photography – both of which he excelled at. He is probably best known for his archaeological studies of the Hebrides, one being a large dig of the Bac Mhic Connain wheelhouse, within sight of his own Valley mansion. The prehistoric material was carefully catalogued – awls, pins, combs, fasteners, and pottery of all sorts. As for his photography, an exhibition in 2009 in Lochmaddy coincided with the publication of *Wanderings with a Camera in Scotland: The Photographs of Erskine Beveridge*[25]. This rare book contains images from more than 170 glass plate negatives of Hebridean buildings and landscapes taken in the years 1880 to 1919.

Beveridge had often visited North Uist on holiday. Around 1901-02 he commissioned the building of Valley House to live in, and provide a base for fishing and shooting parties. It must have been an impressive family home in its day, the centre of more than 3,000 acres of land. Some remaining features reveal its faded glory such as original plaster ceilings and a differently coloured fireplace in nearly every room. There were precisely 365 panes of glass, one for each day of the year. No expense had been spared in the design and furnishings. Eighty cartloads of peat were needed each winter for central heating, and running water was piped from a reservoir in neighbouring North Uist.

Erskine Beveridge and his first wife Mary had six sons and a daughter. Mary died a year before the house was finished, and he married Meg in 1908. They had a son, Francis, who died aged six months, and then soon later another son was born, Charles. There were sad happenings in the family. Two of the older sons, Errie and James, were committed to asylums, and another son died at Gallipoli. The daughter Mary married but her husband died in the First World War. When Erskine died in 1920, only four sons out of eight were available to carry his coffin.

Erskine's son George inherited Valley House. The family linen business went into decline, George turned to drink, and sold off the family silver, possibly to fund his habit. In 1944 George, aged fifty-two, rather the worse for wear, drowned while attempting to cross the strand; whether this was by foot or by boat, I've not discovered. The house has been gradually declining since 1945.

I noticed a couple of older ruins near the house, including farm buildings and a chapel. I was surprised to see a modern house tucked behind, out of sight. But I regret greatly that I was too nervous to stay longer. I was the only person on the island, and anxious about the tide. I now know that I would easily have had enough time to explore the island further. I missed a sandy bay on the north coast called Bàgh nan Craobhag, with a good chance of sightings of greylag geese, snipe and oystercatchers. On the far side of this bay there is a path on to Orasaigh, a little headland jutting out into the sea. There a pile of stones marks the remains of a chapel called Teampull Orain, which Erskine must have spent hours examining, along with the wheelhouse. But these delights on the north of the island had to be left until another visit – I didn't explore further than the ruins on the south side.

A cousin of Erskine who visited Vallay House and helped with the dig was Sir William Beveridge, who is best known for his 1942 report 'Social Insurance and Allied Services' that laid the foundation of the welfare state and gave us the NHS. I found a 1919 photograph on the internet of the two cousins and other members of the Beveridge family, standing in front of Vallay House, the photo being one of very few personal photos of Sir William and his family that exist. This is ironic because Erskine himself was such an accomplished photographer. The photo evokes sad memories, a sad house, a tragic family history.

*

I dropped down onto the strand again, and as I headed back I saw two figures approaching me. Here were two women who had the daring to start to cross the strand a good hour after I had started out, and they obviously thought they had all the time in the world! I felt foolish that I had opted out of further exploring, but I asked them to take a photo of me – I'm not into selfies yet.

Back over the sands, Vallay House in the background

I arrived back at the car with dry feet. My wellington boots had stood the test of a number of raging torrents in the shallow waters. I learnt later that some time ago one woman drowned while crossing – she became disorientated when a mist descended, walked round and round in circles, and the incoming tide engulfed her.

*

Here I make a link between Beveridge and my discoveries on Tiree when I ventured on the cliffs at Ceann A'Mhara above Balephuil Bay (Chapter 4). Next to St Patrick's Temple, or Chapel, there are two stones that are carved with Latin crosses on both faces. When I looked up this building on the Canmore website I discovered that Erskine Beveridge had visited Tiree in 1898 and had taken a couple of photographs – one of the two stones, and the other of the temple itself.

*

Once or twice in my Uist travels I have mixed up Lochboisdale and Lochmaddy. They both begin with Loch, both are ferry terminals facing east, and both are roughly the same size. For example, in Lochboisdale I was certain that on an earlier visit I'd walked out of the village to go to a camera obscura in a hut. I'd remembered a swing bridge on the way. So I went looking for it. It wasn't there; rather late in the day I realised it was just outside Lochmaddy. Similarly in Lochmaddy I looked for a cafe with a pink roof that I'd vaguely remembered. It wasn't there, it was in Lochboisdale. One of the ways to tell them apart is to remember which island you are on. If you are on North Uist, it's Lochmaddy and if on South Uist, it's Lochboisdale.

In 2017 I was once again in Lochmaddy and just to make sure that this was where I could walk out to the camera obscura, I checked in the museum called Taigh Chearsabhagh. I was reassured when they told me I was in the right place.

I confidently found the footpath leading to the Hut of Shadows (Both nam Faileas), which is on the coast near Sponish, a big house that I just

234

glanced at. Chris Drury, an English environmental artist, constructed the hut in 1997. It houses a simply designed camera obscura that hints at the relationship between land, islands and water.

To get to the hut I'd walked past an outdoor centre, and trod nonchalantly across the narrow suspension bridge over the entrance to Loch Houram, an inland loch. Around here were some rocks named, in Gaelic, Big Dog and Little Dog, and not far away was Surly Dog. Perhaps they were there to keep an eye on lone explorers.

The Hut of Shadows

Camera Obscura
A small, cairn-shaped bothy
near the dazzling shores
of Lochmaddy.
Roof of turf, walls of stone.

Duck through the entrance
round the curved passage
into the dark;
blacker than black,
glasses slow to adapt.

Feel for the bench,
sit down and wait.
Trust in lens and mirror
that project onto a wall
the blurred image of sea
flecked with tiny islands,
birds and seals
and a passing fishing boat.

I took the same track on my way back, and only then, just before the bridge, did I see a notice totally hidden from view in a thicket: 'Danger, do not cross the bridge.' But I'd already crossed the bridge to get to the hut, and had to get back to Lochmaddy. This time I trod warily, but got across safely, so the Rock Dogs must have kept an eye on me.

Suspension bridge, not fit for purpose, near Sponish, Lochmaddy

BERNERAY

The north coast of North Uist looks across to Harris, forty miles away. The island of Berneray, very close to the Uist coast, is now the stepping stone you must arrive at to catch the car ferry to Harris.

On my last-century visit I put my bike on a small ferry from the north coast of North Uist to get to Berneray, the only way to reach the island at that time. I stayed two or three nights in the Gatliff Hostel facing east – with the rocky shore just metres away.

On walking along the vast sands of the north-west coast of the island, I'd noticed otter tracks in the sand where he'd dragged his tail, and suddenly an otter appeared out of nowhere. Unfazed by my presence, he lolloped nonchalantly by my side for quite a while – probably my best-ever experience of otter-spotting, despite the sighting on Islay. That night in the hostel annexe, which was as clean as any really old building can be, I had an encounter with another creature. A cockroach scurried across the floor of my room. This reminded me of the kitchen I shared with cockroaches in Sierra Leone in a rather dilapidated house in the late 1960s. Any time after dark, you would switch the kitchen lights on and see and hear the scrabbling for shelter of any number of the creatures that had been looking for crumbs or other titbits on the floor. You got used to cockroaches quite quickly, just as you had to get used to mosquitos. But African cockroaches are huge, and this Scottish one was puny in comparison. I'd not seen one knowingly, since.

I hear that the hostel had a wonderful makeover in early 2020, including a new roof for both buildings thatched with marram grass. 'During lockdown a thatcher locally sourced the turf, arranged for the harvesting of marram, and was able to continue his skilled activities observing a social distancing approach which was agreeable to the local community and all other parties concerned.'[26]

My room in 1999 and 2012. The otter on the roof is not the one I befriended on the beach

I haven't stayed overnight in Berneray since these animal encounters. In 2017 I'd left the Benbecula hostel very early one morning, and driven all the way to the most northern tip of North Uist. There a causeway was built between North Uist and Berneray in 1999, to replace the ferry that I'd taken all that time ago. The causeway was 'opened' by Prince Charles who has visited the island many times.

I made straight for Borve at the south end of this small island, not knowing then about the causeway underparts. Like Muck, Berneray has no rabbits, and never had any, but to prevent any invasion from would-be immigrants from North Uist, the causeway was made rabbit-proof with clever fencing. They also made special culverts for otters to get from one side of the road to the other. I hope the otters will stay safe near and on Berneray so I can see one or two of them next time I go.

*

I realise how much I have mentioned causeways in this chapter. It isn't really surprising as they provide complete accessibility to most of these main islands. And you do notice when they are not there – it's quite a faff to put your car on a ferry.

As for the northern Western Isles, I have spent some wonderful moments on Harris, Scalpay and Lewis, which are islands to the north of North Uist. On Harris I watched my toddler granddaughter Helena inspecting daisies at Hushinish; on Scalpay I trod boldly around the island in one of the worst bogs for feet, but one of the best bogs for views; and at the Butt of Lewis I enjoyed both the lighthouse and the machair behind it. But as far as this book is concerned, I am not following geographical logic, so have decided to stop at Berneray and go back again to Muck, which incidentally is of a similar size.

CHAPTER 7
RETURN TO MUCK

I had been looking forward very much to this 'final' visit to Muck in March-April 2019. Normally I let aspects of an island unfold to me as I wander. But for this return to Muck I had a particular project in mind, which was to learn more about three enterprises – the farm, the fish farm and the shoots – which so far I'd known a little about but not taken much interest in. I figured that I couldn't appreciate the island fully unless I learnt more about them. They are important as they contribute greatly to Muck's economy, occupying most of the working adults.

On arrival I had a cup of coffee at with Rosie at the Craft Shop, now known as the Tea Shop. Between visits, Eddie and Sharon had taken over

Bay at Gallanach

the running of the shop but Jenny MacEwen was still baking bread for it, getting up at the crack of dawn to do so. The couple had given the door a bright yellow paint job, which was a marked change from the old green. The outside seats and tables remained unaltered. They had no plans for any other immediate change apart from the door colour, as it was doing so well under Jenny's reign. Sharon was proud of her good coffee, soup, toasties and cake at lunchtime, and in their first year their nettle soup was a hit.

Tea Shop with school behind, unchanged in many years except for the door colour

They grew their own vegetables in two polytunnels up the hill past the school. When I peeped inside one of the tunnels, Eddie showed me some tomato plants in tubs, full of good-quality bought compost, planted deep into the surrounding soil. I couldn't tell the difference between the soil inside and outside the tubs. 'Muck soil is very fertile,' Eddie said.

But I have heard that they recently gave up the shop and it has been taken over by Bruce and Pam. Bruce is a chocolatier and during my second 'last visit' in 2021 (the explanation of this is at the end of the book), I was able to make room for some tasty treats.

*

The 'new' bunkhouse was smart and comfortable. It seemed weird the first time I stayed there, as it was built on exactly the same footprint as the old one and on opening the front door you went into a hall rather than the kitchen – plenty of space for hanging coats, changing wellies and the like.

One large rectangular room incorporated the kitchen and sitting area and an eating 'island' with high stools. From this big room, six other doors led to three small bunk rooms and one double room, and two loos, one with a shower. It was an excellent use of the space. My only grump was that the windows in the sitting area overlooking the estuary were a bit too high for an average woman to look out of when sitting on the sofa. It was just as cosy as the old one, and wi-fi was a great addition to the facilities. Still no television, thank goodness.

*

This was April, lambing time. Despite all my visits in spring, it was still a surprise when on my first walk I happened upon this sight.

Lambs just born

A few moments later I came across Ruth zooming around the farm on her quad bike, two dogs helping her to look for any lambing problems. Ewes are gathered from all over the island and checked earlier in March. The ones who are likely to lamb first are put in fields closer to the farm, so that it is easier to keep an eye on them. Once they have produced offspring,

241

the mothers and lambs are put together in fields set aside for the purpose.

The ewe flock includes Blackface, a few Jacobs, and a good proportion of cross-Jacob and Cheviots. There are two more 'crosses' – including Black-face and Blueface Leicester. I read in Lawrence's Short Guide that when a black-and-white Jacob ram (tup) mates with a white Cheviot ewe, the lambs are always black. This accounts for my initial disbelief when I saw a white mother with a black lamb near Godag.

There is a little cultivation on the island, but none on the wilder west side. Nearly all crops provide winter fodder (silage) for the sheep and cows. There are some game crops sown for the shoot, too.

The cattle stock consists of forty-five cows and two bulls, and are kept outside all year. Most of the cows are Luing. Their calves are born in winter when their mothers are fed with big bale silage made from grass cut between June and August. They too like pottering on the Gallanach beach. I trod carefully on the road near Gallanach to make sure I wasn't walking between mother and calf. Cows used to venture free-range up to Port Mòr, but I see them there a lot less frequently than I used to.

Both sheep and cows are 'sold for store'. This means that youngish animals are sent to market on the mainland. Other farmers, mostly from the mainland, buy them and grow them bigger for slaughter. Both the main flock of sheep and the main herd of cows are 'self-contained', and only rams and bulls are bought and brought to the island.

Pinned on a gatepost at Gallanach, just outside the farmhouse, there's a notice about Horse Island (Eilean nan Each). In September, weaned lambs are 'driven over the causeway' to spend the winter there. I've heard that getting the sheep over to Horse Island is an interesting task. From the headland at Aird nan Uan, the sheep are driven down to the rocks at the shore, then up a tricky and steep rocky outcrop onto Lamb Island. This island is the starting point of a 'causeway' made up of big jagged stones that the sheep have to negotiate at low tide to get to Horse Island. No easy sandy crossing for visitors here, such as to Oronsay from Colonsay, or to

Vallay from North Uist. Some visitors do manage this crossing, but Esther, a young visitor, told me: 'We all tried to get to Horse Island at low tide. We started off fine – a bit of scrambling on the rocks which were covered completely in seaweed and very slippy. We had to help each other over the rocks. There was just this pool of water to get to the island but we were in wellies… so we couldn't get there; yeah, it was really disappointing.'

I've yet to make it across, but failing that I'd love to witness the sheep procession. 'The sheep remain on Horse Island for their first winter and graze down the long grass until mid-April when they are returned to Muck,' says the notice. This practice manages the smaller island and maintains the diversity of its summer grassland which supports many flower species. It may be the nearest thing to machair on Muck.

*

For many years, as I have mentioned, Muck was farmed by Lawrence MacEwen and his wife Jenny. Some time ago they handed over the main responsibilities to their son Colin and their daughter-in-law Ruth. The older couple are still hands-on and you often see Lawrence on his tractor, or wading in the mud to feed the cows on the beach just outside the farmhouse at Gallanach. Over a super lunch in their kitchen I asked Lawrence and Jenny what had been, or still was, the most difficult aspect of their job. Lawrence said he hated having to slaughter injured animals. Jenny said the paperwork was a big headache, as it was now much more rule-and-regulation-bound than it used to be. Every animal has a passport, and on it there is a great deal of information, not all of it particularly relevant.

*

At one point in the past twenty years I've come across a tale involving a Stone Man in a stone circle and I've always associated it with the circle and the cairn at Aird nan Uan, facing Horse Island. But even Lawrence says he's not heard of such a tale. I cannot have made the story up, so it may belong to another Horse Island. This is my retelling of the tale.

The Stone Man

The Stone Man stares out, leaning on the turf-green, ragwort-yellow, thrift-pink, jagged promontory.

He looks across the choppy sound to Horse Island, where sheep and puffins wander undisturbed by men and seals.

His crudely hewn retinue of headless menhirs were brought by Bronze Age men from sixty miles away. Each stone was two metres high, three tonnes in weight, dragged on rollers, hauled onto rafts, and brought to the promontory. They were then placed in a circle, some with their backs to Horse Island.

But Stone Man is younger than the menhirs. Two hundred years ago Ethan, the village head mason, chiselled a head in memory of his father who had drowned while fishing. He toiled at night, scraped, scoured, scored and carved. The face took shape, a noble nose, squinting left eye, a wry grin. Once worked, he placed the head upon the tallest standing stone, to look over to Horse Island.

Years later, the villagers woke up late, their throats and legs sore after a long ceilidh. Word soon got around that Ethan's father's head had vanished. So what had happened during that moonless night?

A fisherman from the Isle of Mull, watched only by snipe and eider duck, landed, crept up to the menhir, and severed Ethan's father's head. He carried it back to his boat, put it on the prow, rowed back to Mull, and boasted to his fellow Mullians of his stolen figurehead.

A few weeks later, his unmanned boat was found by the Muck villagers, thrashed to pieces, washed up at high tide, in a tiny cove on Horse Island. The stone head was intact and brought back over the causeway. They put the head back onto the menhir-body, and held a ceilidh in the open air.

And now, among the menhirs, Stone Man stares out again, looking over the squally sound to Horse Island.

Whether or not the boat in the Horse Island story belonged to Muck or Mull, or any other island, the importance of a small island's boats cannot be overestimated. I wrote a little about Muck boats including *Wave*, in the

Stone circle looking across to Horse island

first chapter. This used to be a busy boat and was the island's flit boat. One of its other uses was to bring animal feed for the farm. It's now retired, but it's still bobbing up and down in Port Mòr harbour. Recently I have been more curious about the regular ones that come and go.

*

So I am imagining myself sitting on a well-placed bench opposite the pier slipway. Here's the main CalMac boat, about to arrive in a few minutes at the pier at Port Mòr. The Loch Nevis, brought into service in November 2000, still comes to and from Mallaig (where it spends the night), and the other Small Isles. It may not even set out for Muck in severe weather, so the island can be cut off in winter for up to three weeks. But today the weather is typical for April. The boat is having to negotiate a series of skerries including Dubh Sgeir, and in certain blustery conditions the boat has turned back without docking, in full view of all those waiting to board it, causing great frustration to everybody. I've been told that this retreat sometimes depends on which skipper is in charge. The boat carries passengers, a handful of cars (it's rare to see a car disembark at Muck), and general supplies to the island. We, the people waiting above the slipway, breathe out a sigh of relief as it passes the rocks with ease. It doesn't stop for long at Muck.

Recently a hole was discovered in the Lochnevis, and CalMac has sent the Loch Bhrusda instead. This much smaller boat has a deep keel, and the skipper is probably concerned that it might scrape on the slipway. So it's directed to the wobbly and narrow floating pontoon fifty metres away. We have been reassured that the pontoon will be mended very soon. I watch as people, some not looking too confident, offload themselves, their luggage and boxes.

The fish farm Mowi (formerly Marine Harvest), about which I write later, has built the pontoon and allows private boats to use it for a small donation. Mowi has its own boat, Beinn Airein, named after the main hill on Muck. Specially built, its duties include net cleaning and general site work. I don't often see it at Port Mòr.

But I do see Ronnie, who is a well-known figure on Muck. He and his boat, the Sheerwater, are often to be found at the pier. Ronnie, who has thirty-five years of service, still comes five times a week in the summer from

Negotiating the pontoon

the village of Arisaig, eight miles south of Mallaig. His boat is a great alternative to the CalMac ferry as he acts as a guide to wildlife sightings during the trip. If you're lucky you see whales, porpoises, dolphins and sharks. Ronnie can often land on Muck when the larger CalMac ferry is not able to. The Muck shooting parties charter the Sheerwater in the winter months to get from the mainland to and from the island.

I am delighted today to see the Spanish John 2 in business. I witness its crane being used to offload heavy sacks for Toby onto the slipway, aided by his son Archie. I've often wondered who this boat was named after, and have looked him up. 'Spanish John', aka Colonel John MacDonell, was a distinguished 18th-century army officer who lived for a time in Knoydart and emigrated to Canada. As he suffered many hardships and survived, it's not a bad idea to name a boat after him. The Spanish John 2 plies the seas around Mallaig and the Small Isles and carries large supplies such as building materials. She also brings and takes away the council skip lorries with refuse and recycling skips. I really felt like an honorary islander when, on my visit to Knoydart, a local man mentioned this boat. I nodded in recognition. Other tasks include fish feed and livestock delivery (it even took an alligator to Rum once), towing fish farm cages and barges – the list goes on. I'd love to go on her, but I'd be no use as a shipmate.

*

There's a man called Pete whom I've never met, and he hasn't made an appearance today either. He and his two boats serve two very important functions. Every other Friday during the school term Pete brings the

*The Spanish John 2; a senior moment prevents
me from explaining the floating pink sack*

island's youngsters who attend Mallaig High School back to Muck on Orion, the school boat. He leaves again about 3pm on the Sunday. These young people stay in the Mallaig school hostel during the week and every other weekend. Pete's other boat, Amelia, which used to be the island lifeboat, brings the GP whose practice is in Broadford, Skye, every two weeks. The doctor holds his Muck surgery in the community hall. It hasn't always been easy to recruit doctors for the Small Isles. They need to be happy to brave the waves on stormy days.

But Sandy, the island's fisherman, often has to brave the waves. I have now left the viewpoint at the slipway and walked round to the sheltered side of the old pier, where Sandy's boat Quiet Waters is often to be found. On an earlier visit I watched him spruce it up at low tide. Seaweed gets encrusted under the water line, and he had to scrape it off manually before giving the whole boat a hose-down and repainting it. He was lucky that year as the weather was calm and clear, suitable for its MOT.

*

That evening I talked to Sandy and his wife Vicky, in their house, their baby joining in with comments of her own. Sandy's poster said 'creel-caught lobster, crab, prawns/ langoustine, squat lobster, line-caught mackerel, pollock and saithe', so I asked him about these fish. He told me

that prawns were delivered live. Having no notion of prawn fishing, I was advised by him to watch a YouTube video. Which I did, later. It showed prawns being 'hauled up' on to the boat, selected according to size, and placed speedily in trays with tiny compartments, each prawn being put upright in one cell. Kept alive in the sea water in the trays, they are then ready to be transported. Sandy sells seafood locally, to visitors and island folk. The bulk of

Sandy cleaning his boat   his catch is sent to Skye through an exporter.

248

*

Salmon is not on Sandy's list of catches, but this fish is now farmed, as I have mentioned, by Mowi in the stretch of sea between Muck and Eigg. During one of my earlier visits, Robert, the fish farm manager, and I had chatted in his house on Muck about his childhood on North Uist. His office here on Muck was in the green 'shed' (more like a hangar) next to the pier, and it was here where he and I talked over cups of coffee. I learnt about salmon fishing – a totally new subject to me.

Prior to the farm being constructed, he said, discussions were had on Muck involving all residents, about ecological matters as well as benefits to the island. The islanders had voted on whether to have the farm or not, and practically all were in favour. Fish farms were being talked about all over the Small Isles. Robert told me that there was a new farm on Rum – and the communities on Eigg and Canna were 'thinking about it'. Eigg residents are proud of their reputation as a green island so they had concerns that a fish farm would not be eco-friendly.

The Muck salmon farm opened in 2014 with a view to creating six full-time permanent jobs on the island and building three staff houses. I was delighted to hear that one of my ex-pupils was working for the farm, but sadly wasn't able to chat with him. Workers' schedules are two weeks on, two weeks off, so they regularly go to the mainland in off-time.

The farm is stocked with salmon smolt grown in the Mowi hatcheries in Loch Ailort and Loch Lochy. It comprises twelve circular pens, each one about 400ft in diameter, which are moored on massive anchors together with the feed barge. Up to 5,000 tonnes of salmon are grown for three years in the pens. Once fully grown, the salmon is transported by well-boat to the harvesting station at Mallaig. A well-boat, in layman's language, is a boat with two swimming pools of fresh water, and lots of dials to keep the fish at the correct temperature. After harvesting, the fish are taken by road to Fort William for gutting, packing and distribution.

The company is committed to ecological matters, sustainability and salmon health and welfare. According to one Muck resident I'd spoken to, the Muck farm has a very low environmental impact. I think that in this case he meant visual impact from the island itself. You can only see the pens from a small section of the unfrequented east coast of Muck. It's clearly visible from the ferry from Eigg to Muck, but is by no means an ugly sight.

As for the health of the salmon, I had heard of the prevalence of sea lice in fish farming. Lice graze on the surface of the fish, eating the mucus and skin. Large numbers of lice soon cause the loss of fins, severe scarring and often death. This sometimes results in fish farms adding to the cages chemicals that are harmful to the environment. Robert was proud that the occurrence of sea lice on Muck was well

Fish farm with two of the pens

down. In his office he showed me an impressive intranet graph of sea lice population. 'Muck has the third lowest mortality of deaths per pen in the UK,' he said. He also mentioned the positioning of the farm. It is classed as having 'high energy' currents (large waves and strong tides), so fish waste is distributed more widely than in sheltered sea lochs, for instance.

A recent environmentally conscious decision was to add two new pens. Up until recently there were ten, and now there are twelve. This was not to add more fish to the farm but to reduce the number in each pen (there are roughly 90,000 fish in one pen), contributing to a lower density and giving them more space to grow. Another initiative is to synchronise production cycles across geographical areas. For example, the farms on both Muck and Rum were stocked with smolts at similar times. After harvesting on Muck, the plan was to let the Muck farm lie fallow for six months, to minimise biological risks and contribute to protecting the seabed and wider ecosystem.

Besides the Beinn Airein mentioned already, Mowi has two other boats, the Polar Cirkle, and the Black Pearl, both small launches. I was thrilled when Robert, having gained permission from his bosses, agreed to take me in the Black Pearl to see the fish farm at close hand. He pointed towards some heavy-duty sailing gear hanging up in his shed, which I donned. After negotiating the pontoon I heaved myself into the small boat which was waiting for us. It was a lovely sunny day and not much wind, or so I thought. Round the corner of the island a north-east wind came into play; angry waves surged over the boat sides, reminding me of my trip to the Monach Isles. Robert slowed down a bit when he thought I might be suffering, but it was exhilarating rather than scary.

We made a circuit of the twelve cages. There was strong netting around and above the cages that stopped predatory birds from diving down and helping themselves. I'd been curious to see, in Robert's shed earlier, a large black 'kite'. This was used at one time in the same way as you might want to stick the outline of a big bird against your window to stop birds from flying into it. I noticed a number of salmon leaping up in their cages, and was concerned about the fish having enough space, but remembered that they had a huge amount of space under the surface.

The 400-tonne feed boat, anchored on the site, is a squarish structure built to withstand all elements, and isn't particularly pretty. Robert asked me if I wanted to land on it, but I saw the ladder and declined. The barge pumps the feed into the cages via white plastic pipes, 500mm in diameter, and which float in higgledy huddles outside the cages. Robert explained the importance of their colour. 'White reflects the sunlight and therefore they stay cool. As it goes down the pipe into the pen, the feed won't lose any oil. If the pipes were black, there would be a potential for the feed to lose oil, eventually catching dust, and possible consequence for blockages,' he said.

The company has established a community fund to help support local projects. Visitors' boats using the pontoon, as I have mentioned, are requested to donate £5 a time and this goes into the school fund – each year an excess of £700 is donated.

Alas, Robert was shortly leaving Muck as he had found a job as general manager of a fish farm in Tasmania. There were no sea lice there, he told me.

*

The fishing industry will never dispense with floats or buoys as long as it uses nets. The words float and buoy are used interchangeably, but technically floats keep the net just below the surface, buoys mark the position of the net, and metal or stone weights keep the bottom of the net down. Old floats are ubiquitous flotsam wherever you explore island shores, but most are inferior brightly coloured hard plastic or polystyrene ones. Prize discoveries on shores would include floats made of green or brown glass, wood, cork or even leather.

Many years ago, on the wild west of the island, a number of metres inland from the coast, I discovered a collection of aluminium buoys half-hidden in the soil and long grass, still heavily entwined in the original fishing net. This collection of floats had remained undisturbed for some years.

Until I came along.

I managed to prise one of them from its fellows, put it in my rucksack and stagger back to the bunkhouse. It now features, along with four others – two of which are the Shillay ones – prominently in my back garden in Leeds. The remaining floats, about twenty, are still, as far as I know, stuck together on Muck with heavy-duty, scrambled net-rope,

Nest of buoys

half–buried in the turf. I've tried to get one more on recent visits, but to no avail. Alasdair from Benbecula would understand my frustration. It is awe-inspiring to imagine the gale that threw the whole collection, in one piece, inland for several metres. They are very heavy. I feel possessive about this nest of buoys, which I suspect hasn't been seen by many other people. So I've been moved to write this poem.

The Nest of Buoys
I'm stuck on Muck,
with twenty siblings
thrown in by a storm,
forlorn.

At least I'm not strangled by number eleven
who's been cheek by jowl with number twelve
for four years.

Choked by the knotted rope-net
by the growth of sticky turf,
we were never meant to be
so useless, ignored by fisher folk.

Except that buoy-collector
and she's no use.
She'd not even got a knife with her
last time she came.
She tried in vain to pull me away,
what a weakling.

I need to be needed,
in the sea again.
Feel the fish around my skin
and the net outspread.
I'm stuck on Muck.

Floats and buoys cannot move of their own accord, but young game birds are at least free to roam after release from their pens. Seven-week-old pheasant poults (chicks) and twelve-week-old partridges are brought to the island once a year. They need to be fed, watered and looked after in their release pens until they are set free to roam. Wherever I trod on my walks, I would unsettle a pheasant – this is the commonest bird that the visitor sees on the island – or a partridge from its cover. This unmistakable sound and flurry of wings reminded me of walking on the grouse moors and heath in my usual stomping grounds in West Yorkshire. I've never been on Muck during the shooting season, so I've not yet had the chance to see or hear shooting in action, but it was high time I found out more about the Muck shoots, hence the third important 'motive' for returning to Muck that April.

Toby and his wife Mary (Lawrence's and Jenny's daughter) have been organising shoots on Muck since 2006. They have a lovely lodge overlooking the beach at Gallanach, where Mary cooks famous meals for their shooting guests. I talked with Toby, Mary, Lewis and Dave and others about their roles. Toby and Mary's guests shoot pheasant, partridge and duck – lots of mallard on ponds made bigger for the purpose – and to a lesser extent, greylag geese, wildfowl, snipe, woodcock and pigeon.

The birds wouldn't survive without vegetation. Fifteen acres of game crop are sown each year consisting of about twenty-five types of seeds including barley, high-seeded edible mustard and linseed. This provides the birds with shelter during the winter, cover from predators during the spring and a significant food source at all times of the year. The crops link areas of land where there are no natural transfer points such as hedges or ditches. These fields of what we, the uninitiated, might call weeds, are unharvested. In addition to the crops, 60,000 trees and hedges have been planted. I've been fascinated by the burgeoning of small saplings. The hedgerow trees include alder, blackthorn, dog-rose and hawthorn. On one of my walks this visit I spent some time marvelling at a new mixed hedge-

New fencing/hedge planting

row running north-south in the middle of the east side, with stout wire fencing protecting the saplings from being nibbled by sheep, and I looked forward to the time when I could return to see it in maturity.

After their time in the poult cage the birds are freed, often into a wood. They require a fresh water supply, and I noticed with interest the huge amount of work that had been done on the stream beds to clear them of rampant plant-matter and to make the water run more freely. The fully

grown pheasants and partridges feed from blue and black barrels, or hoppers, scattered around the island. I asked Lewis, who works full-time for Toby, how the birds actually fed from them. Depending on your proximity to the barrel, you can't always see the tin 'udder' (my word) under the barrel which has holes in it.

The birds learn, in poult-school, how to tap the tin, and thus release the feed from the barrel on to the ground. I still haven't seen

Poult cage

game birds feeding from these, but have noticed robins and blackbirds lurking near them, waiting for me to walk past so that they can take their pick of the residue. This supply of food is an attraction for rats, so rat traps

255

are set near the feeding barrels. Lewis's tasks
include maintaining these traps, and teaming
up with Mary to help in the beating line during
the season. At other times he is busy planting
crops, cleaning and tidying ditches, clearing
brambles and bracken, and maintaining
fencing. Traps could be a problem for other

Barrel of pheasant feed

rodents besides rats, but there are none of these species on Muck, nor are
there foxes, squirrels or stoats. Rabbits pose no problem as predators on
Muck, because a previous owner banned their import. (Canna has rabbits
to contend with but I saw not one rabbit on a recent trip there.)

*

But in spite of the traps, rats can still be a challenge if there is a mild
winter, because a female rat can give birth after only nine weeks of life. On
the islands of Canna and the Shiants, the rat population spiralled beyond
belief. The devastation of wild birds' eggs and chicks led to millions of
pounds spent on rat eradication. And to date the Canna rats have not
come back.

On Muck the shoot team has managed to control the rat population. In
the Muck shoots' first year they killed more than 1,500 rats using traps.
This is in the region of 80 per cent of the rat population per year. The
shooting parties also shoot crows, which can be real pests – hooded crows
love a tasty chick. Common birds' eggs and chicks are surviving much
better with this reduction in predation.

But a pheasant or partridge still has to be on guard, particularly near the
feeding stations. Large birds such as buzzards, sparrowhawks and a pair of
golden eagles (which are now resident on Muck) would normally need a
much bigger territory than this small island to roam to feed, but they are
attracted, like the rats, to the pheasant hoppers.

There's a kind of symbiosis that can occur and which favours the farm,
the shoot and wildlife. Both Toby and Colin, the farmer, share the upkeep

of fences and hedgerows. The shoot uses woodland and hill ground that aren't priority land for sheep and cows, and cows 'poach' the land. Poached land, which I mention earlier in the book, is ankle-breaking muddy troughs and puddles that occur, often at field gates, where cattle like to tread. Insects are drawn to the puddles, and multiply, and the increase in local mini-ponds becomes a wetland habitat for wading birds.

*

Dave, a long-term resident, was the island's expert on wild birds, and also helps with the shoots. 'Since the start of the shoots, the number of songbirds has increased dramatically,' he told me. 'The game crop is at its best in late autumn and therefore the best time on Muck to see wild birds.' The shoots have had an economic effect that wasn't particularly obvious at first. Before Toby and Mary started their business there was little opportunity for some residents to earn money in the winters – but now they, including children, can be paid as beaters. Beating involves driving birds in a given direction so as to become targets for the shooters. Beaters are paid by the day, and a five-year-old girl once earned five pounds! Like the fish farm community fund, the shoot business has a commitment to helping boost the school's funds. It is based on a forfeit system. A few white pheasant and white duck are released each year. 'Anyone who shoots one of these has to pay a forfeit. With some teams it's £100, with others, if you shoot at it and miss, you pay a fine, but if you shoot it successfully everyone else pays between £10 and £20,' Dave said.

   The result of this boost to the school fund has meant that the children have had the opportunity to go on residential activity courses on the mainland, such as the one at Abernethy in Nethy Bridge. But I doubt that they learn how to shoot there.

*

Besides the game birds on Muck, there are now many more finches, collared doves, rock dove, blackbirds, thrushes, and shore birds such as oystercatchers and snipe than there used to be. In Shetland and other islands of Scotland's north, the noisy oystercatchers are sometimes called shalders, and great skuas are called bonxies, which I mention in my first chapter. Oystercatchers shriek whenever they are annoyed or disturbed, which is often. In Gaelic the cry of this bird is said to be *bi glic, bi glic, bi glic*, meaning 'be wise', 'be prudent', 'take care', according to A. A. MacGregor.[1] That could be an injunction during the Covid-19 lockdown.

In the poem below I make reference to birders but I have not encountered them in large numbers on Muck. So I take poetic licence imagining them lining up with their telescopes to watch bird action on one of the beaches. As for being clouted on the head by a great skua, this happened to me on Mousa, one of the Shetland islands. It thought I was walking too near its nest. Skuas seem to know that they must attack you from behind, otherwise you could see them and ward them off. The advice is to wear a hat, or keep your hood up. Once a great skua threatened me on a wild Muck cliff, but missed.

Some time ago I watched with great dismay a snip of TV footage in which a very well-known bird expert roamed around Mousa carrying his unprotected young daughter on his shoulders. He knew there were bonxies around and I feared greatly for his little girl.

The Shalder's Shouting, or Pecking Order

You blustering birders
with your scopes and your tripods;
it's rude to keep staring,
piss off from my patch!

It's my sheltered beach, this;
you think I can't see you?
Your camouflage useless,
pathetic, inept!
And down with dumb dunlins,

take cover, ringed plovers;
scram, scurrying sanderlings,
clear off, creepy curlews!
You're turncoats, you turnstones,
you've snaffled my cockles,
a rocket of hackles
has made my beak raw.

My feathers dishevelled
I'm shrieking and screaming!
You've not got the message?
I'm king of the shore!

Argh, here comes a bonxie!
Flown down from the cliff, sir?
yes sir, three bags fullest
I see you mean business.
You've ambushed that gannet
and filched his fish supper
such talons, such talent!
your prowess is boundless.

Of course you're the monarch,
the superstar skua,
you glower, we cower
when you're on the beat.

But may I remind you
those birders are twitching.
It's they who could do with
a clout from your feet!

The pair of skuas on Muck normally keep well away from people and aren't interested in eating crops. However, Muck had a problem with gangs of greylag geese that recently devoured a whole field of neeps (turnips) and left just the 'shells'. Greylag geese numbers are growing and are resident all year round, causing havoc with crops and grazing land, not only on Muck but on many other Hebridean islands.

They quickly learn to steal from the pheasant feeders. 'They did huge damage to the neeps when they were grown for animal feed, eating the whole vegetable so only a shell was left below ground-level. Quite an achievement for a bird,' Dave told me. They are listed in Schedule 2 of the Wildlife and Countryside Act, so they can be culled.

In the following poem I mention the corncrake, which is an elusive bird, as I remarked in my chapter on Colonsay. There are just about two pairs that come to Muck in summer from the sub-Saharan regions of Africa.

The Latin name for greylag is *Anser anser*, and for the secretive corncrake – it's *Crex crex*.

The greylag (Anser anser) and the corncrake (Crex crex)

Crex crex!
Not content with pheasant feed
you greylag bent on evil deeds,
you're stripping bare that field of neeps
meant for cattle, not for creeps.
Crex crex!

Anser anser!
We're hungry so we'll eat these neeps.
All you do is croak in reeds –
what a stupid hiding place!
Scared to show your ugly face?
Nothing like our orange beaks!
Anser anser!

Crex crex!
Watch it, mind your Qs and Ps,
they'll shoot you in that field of neeps
and sell your tasteless meat to eat
and we'll live on, our secrets keep,
loved by all who hear us creak.
Crex crex!

Corncrakes used to be called landrail, and I'm reminded of a verse from John Clare's poem 'The Landrail': ''Tis like a fancy everywhere/ A sort of living doubt/ We know 'tis something but it ne'er/ Will blab the secret out.'[2]

*

During this 'last' visit, I still had the time to meander around the island with no fixed motive in mind. If anyone had asked me if I was interested in how people replaced worn-out wooden posts, I would probably pull a 'not really' face and shake my head. But solo island-exploring can encourage you, when you see something unfamiliar, to stop and wonder, be cheeky and ask questions, in a way you wouldn't behave in the melee of a big city. I'm afraid that I do it when on my island journeys, because it adds to my appreciation of the wonders around me. However, there's a danger of being seen as a nosey-parker, or worse. After all, I'm not in the habit of collaring road drillers in Leeds and standing by them for half an hour asking inane questions. And if I were working in my own front garden and a stranger passed by, leaned over the gate and asked me how I was mending my fence, I'd possibly be embarrassed, or worse, distrust his motives. So I am grateful to Sandy who let me watch him at work. Unlike my watching the woodcutters in Knoydart, I felt more as if I was a part of the event.

I came across Sandy replacing a substantial but decrepit post, just above the bunkhouse. His mother was there as a right-hand woman. The gatepost held the end of a fence which was in good enough condition, but the old post needed to be hoiked out of the ground and a new one put in.

261

Lifting a post

One of the things I like about Muck is that although there are fences on farmland where necessary, they usually aren't too scary and I haven't encountered a great deal of barbed wire. A shortish woman like me can hop over many of the Muck fences with ease. (On the wild west there are hardly any.) This 'ease' has morphed over the years into 'wobbly ease'. Openable gates with stout posts are always welcome.

For Sandy's job, two motorised vehicles and a collection of tools were required. First the soil and stone around the dead post were chopped away with a punch bar and breaker bar so that the post became loose. Sandy loosened the top wire of the Rylock fencing which was in good shape and surrounded the post, but didn't unpick all the other wires, hoping to lift the post vertically out of its cage once it was free. He tied one end of a rope to the bucket of the digger and the other end around the post at earth height. With Sandy at the helm, the digger then lifted the post out of its circular cage of wire. It came away easily and he cast it on to the ground. He was confident that the new one would last longer than the old one. 'The creosote coating is superior,' he said. But putting in the new post wasn't quite so easy, despite its having a pointed end.

He attached the rope around this post, and tied the other end of the rope to the digger bucket. Positioning the crane so that the post would go into, and slip down, the cylindrical 'cage' of wire, was tricky business. It looked as if the fence wire was too short – it seemed to be pulling the post away from the hole all the time. Getting the tension of the wires right was crucial. The digger bucket didn't seem to be able to keep the post vertical so Sandy couldn't slot it into the wire cage.

He decided to use his ATV (quad bike). Attaching one end of the rope to the back of the ATV and the other end around the bottom of the post (which was by now just about in the hole, but wonky), he drove forwards gently and let the ATV do the pulling. This positioned the post correctly. After a brief inspection he jumped back into the digger to use the crane, and dangled the bucket so it was poised just on top of the post, and used the bucket as a hammer to force it down to a distance of about a metre below ground. Then all that was needed was to re-tension the wires and put stones and soil around the base of the new post. About thirty minutes' work – I was well impressed.

*

Another of Sandy's jobs is the 'station officer volunteer coastguard' on the island. If someone is taken badly ill on Muck with its forty-five inhabitants and no doctor, the repercussions would be frightful, so during lockdown residents were self-isolating as far as possible. So what happens in a medical emergency 'normally'? And other emergencies?

One day in my early years on Muck I was busy in the bunkhouse and heard the sound of a helicopter. I didn't go out to look. Later Rosie appeared with some bad news: a resident had been taken ill. There is a space for a helicopter to land next to the community hall and the patient was airlifted to hospital in Inverness, an hour away. Usually when there is a medical emergency a lifeboat is sent, so an airlift is really serious. Thankfully, in this case, word got round later in the day that they were out of danger.

Walking wounded can go to the Belford hospital at Fort William, via the ferry, but if there's a big swell and you have a broken arm, you have to be careful of knocking it, so the choice could be a lifeboat.

The community on Muck works well together as a team, as I discovered long ago watching the sheep-shearing. Another example of teamwork is that there are occasional meetings with coastguard officials and Fire Scotland who come to the island to give residents information and hands-on training in first aid, search and rescue techniques, and firefighting. If there was an incident, the Muck coastguard team would respond, as they are trained to do.

Fire Scotland has some strict regulations about the fitness of volunteer fire people, which don't take into account, sadly, the special circumstances on a small island. They could have had eight out of a population of sixteen adult volunteers, but only two passed the 'fitness' test because the criteria are so strict. Failing the BMI criterion was one reason why an incredibly strong islander failed the full test.

For a heath fire, the aim is to stop the blaze from spreading to a building. But if there is a house fire, the volunteers are to do nothing at all. To tackle a house fire you need to have breathing apparatus, and far more crew.

*

Fences and forts are built to keep creatures out, or in, whichever way you look at it. In the case of forts they also kept human beings safe. I've come across many forts and brochs in my Scottish travels, as well as other historic constructions such as the remains of villages, standing stones, crannogs, stone circles, chambered cairns and so on. Muck has only a handful of these types of ruins. John Hunter remarks in his book, *The Small Isles*, that these four islands 'have become islands without memories, islands ungrounded from their pasts'.[3] Nevertheless there are some relics that so far in my Muck pursuits I'd just seen as part of the landscape, but which do have stories to tell. And I discovered more as I returned to Muck.

*

I wanted to explore Toaluinn, and tried hard one sunny morning to locate the 'large building among the reeds, difficult to find', which I'd read in Lawrence's Muck guide. This Norse building is situated on marginal land near Port na Lice, not far from Godag House. I had read that Toaluinn had walls just over two metres thick and the building was thirteen metres long. The shape of the building is like that of Norse houses found elsewhere in the western coasts of Scotland. Its location on a former storm beach, next to good land with easy access to fresh water, is typical of a Norse settlement. Added to this, there is a rock-cut slipway and, together with the fact that the site is isolated, Hunter comes to the conclusion that these remains could represent a farmstead from the earlier phases of Norse settlement in the ninth or 10th century.

The name Toaluinn is probably derived from Thulain – meaning 'stony ground under the hill'. My own source of information regarding its location, Catriona, a relative of the MacEwens, wrote to me in an email: 'The ruin is fairly close to the west of the natural and stone dykes, which are on the east of the field. It's north of the fence which cuts the tussocky ground off, and so it's not grazed.' Canmore website has sadly not much to add to these notes, and more archaeological exploration of the site needs to take place.

It was ankle-breaking trying to find these ruins – I had to keep my eyes on the ground, pacing forwards and backwards on the only field it could have been in. I wished that I had a guide with me. I didn't find the ruins.

Near Toaluinn

In contrast to Toaluinn and its low profile, the 'castle' is hard to miss. Its name in Gaelic is Caisteal an Duin Bhain, meaning Castle of the White Fortress, and is a fort in an imposing position on the west side of the entrance to Port Mòr, six metres above the level of the headland. No one seems to know how this fort was used.

At some point in the Iron Age this natural stack was fortified by the construction of a thick wall at the summit, the interior being occupied by turf-covered ruins of a rectangular house or two, with rounded angles, and with traces of lazy-bed cultivation around them. The entrance on the east side has mainly fallen away. The fortress probably remained in use in medieval times but there is no obvious water source nearby. There still hasn't been excavation and research on Caisteal, or for that matter, on Toaluinn, to help us with questions that they pose.

On a sunny early April evening Caisteal looked very impressive, even startling.

Caisteal

This trap is V-shaped. At the apex of the V just above the low water mark was a sluice where the fish were collected in a net or trap

I had heard of Muck's 'beach of the fish trap', or Camas na Cairidh, which is the sandy cove facing north below the road where it bends sharply to the left. Perhaps this was the first fish trap on Muck; it is now invisible. But at Gallanach at the head of the first sandy bay beyond the road, there is a line of stones, or boulders, extending in a gentle arc joining two natural outcrops of rock. Now after my Lismore experience, I was a good spotter of fish traps. After so many visits over many years to this beach, including once taking a dip here, I saw the line of stones for what they were. I reminded myself of the quote from T. S. Eliot: 'We shall not cease from exploration/ And the end of all our exploring/ Will be to arrive where we started/ And know the place for the first time.'[4]

So this bay is a fine example of a fish trap, unusually big, and unlike the Lismore trap it isn't disguised by seaweed.

*

Also known as A'chille, the ruins of Keil village are easily seen just past Port Mòr on a plateau above the road. I like to walk along its main 'street', which is still very obvious, and wonder about its history – and on this visit I did it once again. It is an old township, with a chapel and burial ground. The houses include older buildings, some that were only built at the time of the clearances around 1830. The MacLeans, the then owners of Muck, evicted people from the island in 1828, when 150 people emigrated on the St Lawrence to Cape Breton. (This was before the first sheep were introduced to the island.) The remainder of Muck tenants were allowed to build houses in Keil, where they tried to make a living from fishing but with little success. Between 1821 and 1831 the population had halved. By 1835 these families had either emigrated or migrated elsewhere in Scotland. So the houses, around thirty of them, were only occupied for a few years. There must have been many sad households among them – families missing relatives and friends who had left, anxiety about making a living from the sea and not from the land, and worry about the future.

The name A'chille means 'the church'. This building, dedicated to St Finnan, a contemporary of Columba in Iona, has almost vanished, but had earth and stone walls. The present graveyard above Port Mòr is an extension of the original site higher up the slope. Today the low ruins

Keil village above the road out of Port Mòr

of the houses and their enclosures survive. Much of the stone used in their construction has been reused for dykes. A sketch-plan of the ruins was made in 1976, and an archaeological survey was made in 2000. As well as the cemetery and houses, sheds, groups of buildings around enclosures, hen houses and kilns were identified.

A stone with a carving of a ship was discovered from a rock pile during excavations, and recent digging has disturbed a midden deposit with limpet shells and china. An early medieval carved cross-slab survives as a headstone in the graveyard, and I've admired another displayed in the Tea Shop. Two querns (ancient grain-grinding devices) found in 1998 when a trench was dug for the wind farm scheme, were originally on show in the Tea Shop public loos, where a number of people would see them!

*

Still on the look-out for historical relics and unusual natural features, I've spent many an hour wandering around the rough land opposite Dùn Ban house on the north coast and this time was no exception. Not only is it a good area for seal-watching, but there are long stretches of rocks at right angles to the shoreline, interspersed with sandy and small-shell channels to explore. These are 'dolerite dykes' such as Port Chreadhain, which means 'the harbour of the clams'. This time I wanted to photograph a recent relic, an unfinished project. At low tide you can see an old stone jetty and iron tramway from which boats would be launched. There are four pairs of rusty iron bogeys tangled together but still intact, having been dislodged from the rails.

Derailed bogeys

I have tried to find out about how the set of bogeys would have worked but to no avail. There are four sets of two-wheelers, not obviously joined together. There might originally have been a cradle for the boats to which the bogeys were attached. The bogeys date from the 1970s. All I've discovered so far is that the rails were taken from Fort William when the railway station was moved to its present site.

But the jetty is much older; at one time it formed the best landing place for boats on Muck, as it is more sheltered than Port Mòr in the south.

*

In the early years of my visiting Muck I'd been told of a rock whose shape resembled the profile of Queen Victoria, as she was once depicted on coins. I then forgot all about it. On my latest visit, I happened to look up at the rock face near Gleann Mhairtein just after I had turned the corner from the east side to the west. There I thought I'd found her, looking down at me, her chin resting on the face of a chimp. That was two for the price of one.

Seeing faces in everyday objects is a very common phenomenon, I discovered, and is called 'face pareidolia'. However, when I sent this photograph to Catriona, she told me that this was not the 'real' Queen Victoria. On second thoughts I realised that my Victoria was much more

Profile of 'Pharaoh' but not of 'Victoria'

like a pharaoh. The 'real' one is like a dog looking out to sea, but the muzzle is her bun. Apparently she is situated near Port na Luinge, where you look up to the cliff and the queen is free-standing, facing the cliff twenty or thirty yards from the point. 'It was our family name for the place – the name dating from the 1930s,' she wrote.

Yet it strikes me that the two 'Victorias' are as old as each other. 'Muck is made mostly up of basalt lava flows of the Tertiary Age that have emanated from volcanic centres in Ardnamurchan and Rum,' according to the Isle of Muck short guide. This can result in a step-like landform. My photo shows these sharp steps.

I am determined to find and photograph the 'real' Queen Victoria, so I will have to wait.

*

Muck has its own equivalent of the ruined corrugated-iron buildings I've seen on many an island, especially in the Outer Hebrides. Just above the bunkhouse is the Old School, built in 1925 and costing £395. Mary, the daughter of Jenny and Lawrence, was the last pupil to study in this build-ing, with a teacher all to herself.

By the 1990s it was dying a death. There are complicated reasons why it's not yet been demolished, but its continued presence is a reminder of how things used to be. I'd be very happy if the Old School was never pulled down, but I expect my view won't be taken into account.

The Old School

On this visit I was excited to be going back to the (new) school to teach music. I'd had some welcoming emails from the Muck schoolteacher, Helen, and my visit would coincide with the last week of the Easter term. We arranged for me to go into school one hour a day for five days and for us to have a presentation for parents and friends, on the Friday, the last day of term. A school of six pupils from Primary 2 to 5 is not uncommon on small islands and there has recently been a spate of babies – this delights everyone. But they're not ready for school yet. School population is seen as a good indicator to the viability of an island population.

It was wonderful to be back again in the airy classroom, light coming from windows on three sides, surrounded by children's drawings, paintings and other works of genius. But children grow up and this was a totally new bunch, now equipped with laptops and gazing up at the smartboard. Fond and happy memories of ten years ago flooded back to me. After an introduction to each other, we hauled out of the cupboard a selection of percussion instruments including tambours, chime bars and xylophones, so that they could practise handling these, and the keyboard was waiting for me – a lovely welcome from Helen.

I enjoyed, as usual, teaching rhythm games to the pupils, clapping at first, then launching into a cacophony of percussion instruments. We sang a song that I'd made up ten years ago on my first musical project on

Muck. 'I love Muck,' and 'Come to our super school,' were easy enough phrases for them to learn by heart. This time I added all the children's names towards the end of the song and they seemed delighted that they were officially part of it. I was a little disappointed that I'd not thought of that idea all those years ago.

School classroom

Another song became an instant

272

hit. It wasn't mine, but I'd saved it for ten years. It's about dinosaurs, often a popular subject matter.[5] Helen helped me introduce it, and we asked the children to mime each dinosaur. One boy interpreted 'Pterodactyl flapping, long beak clacking, big teeth snapping' by lying face-down on the floor, kicking his legs up and down (clacking beak) and waving his arms (the wings). Brilliant ingenuity.

I was also keen to teach my own new song, 'The Green-Vested Boys.' This has the same melody of the songs I'd taught in the primary schools of Gigha, Tiree, Colonsay and Lismore. This was deliberate. Early on, I had high hopes that each island school would, at some time in the future, be able to meet up, possibly by Skype. They could sing their song to each school, learn all the other songs, and thus share, and hopefully delight in, all these folk stories, I hoped. Who knows if this could ever come about?

Prior to my visit, Helen had already introduced the story of the green-vested boys, and the children had made up a small play about it. One happy coincidence was that although they didn't initially seem to know the meaning of 'flotsam and jetsam', the children had just had an expedition to Camas Mòr to do a beach clean, so were able to relate to the context in a very real way.

I'd read the story in *The Peat Fire Flame*. It is Muck-specific and is called 'Two Tiny Boys with Green Vests.' In the early part of the 20th century the Reverend Alexander Fraser told this story to A. A. MacGregor.[6] Mention is made of a knoll, and Pier House. Some of the older residents would be able to relate to the knoll, which according to Catriona would probably be the mound opposite the estuary, upon which Ewen built Port Mòr House. Apparently children used to play there before the house was built. Pier House, which was built just next to the old pier in the latter part of the 19th century, is familiar to all.

And Pier House is the house from which, according to the story, two boys set off on their search for driftwood. In the first chapter of this book I retold the story about Diarmad, Fionn and Grainne and wrote that 'real' folklore had more or less died out in the Small Isles – but this tale, based on Muck, may have one or two elements of 'real' history in it. Here is my version.

A certain resident of Muck who lived in Pier House, Sandy Macdonald, had two sons, or possibly more. The boys went to search for driftwood on a small peninsula near Port Mòr. There, beside a green knoll and a narrow cove, they found a tin that had never been opened. Not having a tin opener to hand, they went to a rock to strike it. They eventually managed to make a hole in the tin, but two tiny green-vested boys appeared behind them before they had time to inspect what was in it.

The green boys asked the brothers (in excellent English) what they were trying to do. The brothers answered in Gaelic that they wanted to see what was inside the tin, and that they thought that it contained paint. The Macdonald boys were charmed by the green boys, who proceeded to ask all sorts of questions about their family. The brothers noticed that next to the cove there was a tiny boat moored with a pretty cabin inside. In front of the doorway stood a wee woman, and beside her 'a fully grown dog about the size of a rat'.

This green-clad woman asked the boys to come and have tea with her before they went back home. This they were reluctant to do, perhaps because they were afraid of the dog? So the woman gave them a few loaves of fairy bread, each about the size of a walnut. They were delicious.

The green boys then told the brothers that the fairy boat was about to depart. They should wait by the shore until they saw the boat pass Dubh Sgeir (the black rock); then they should return home. The boat and fairies would not return, they said, but 'others of our race will be coming'.

Their elder sister came looking for them. 'What are you doing here?' she cried. The sound of her voice broke the spell and they went home with her. The brothers had been in a kind of trance all this time. They reported how happy they had been under the spell, and went on for several years to relate the unvarying story to family and neighbours.

Song of the Boys in Green Vests
(Chorus after each verse)

Let's go to the shore, there's driftwood to find
and maybe a boat tied up on a rock!
Just hope for some luck!
Macdonald's sons saw two tiny boys,
there's fairies on Muck!

1 Hector and Neil were seven and ten
and lived in Pier House just close to the shore.
They went to the beach to gather some wood
and flotsam and jetsam from yesterday's storm.

2 They saw a wee boat tied up on a rock
and found a wee tin unopened nearby.
They wanted to find out what it contained,
but two tiny boys appeared at their side.

3 These boys with green vests and Hector and Neil
in English and Gaelic they chattered and said,
'Come meet our mum and dog on the boat,
you'll have some tea, Mum's been making her bread.'

4 Hector and Neil said, 'Sorry, we can't.'
The fairies went back to their boat and their mum
and threw pieces of bread to the boys on the shore
who picked up the bread and ate every crumb!

5 'We're off right now,' said the boys in green vests,
you'll not see us again, we're going away.
But more fairies might come, they could stay in that knoll
which is just up the track, where kids like to play.'

(musical score in appendix)

My song is rather wordy (not the first time this has happened) and they struggled a little fitting the words into the tune, but at the final performance with parents, I urged the parents to join in the chorus (words for all to see on the smartboard), to give the children a boost. The more they were familiar with the words, the louder and clearer they sang. The performance was an informal affair, which included the pupils acting out the story.

*

The Muck Community Hall, scene of a lovely discovery of mine, is a huge building dwarfing other buildings in Port. Long before the hall was built, I attended a memorable ceilidh in the huge barn at Gallanach; a great deal of clearing out of stuff, including tractors, had to happen. But now big and small gatherings take place in the new hall, which was funded in part by the Big Lottery Fund, built in 2011 and opened in May 2012. Visiting speakers give talks, and meetings and ceilidhs are held here.

Just behind the hall's main door, you will encounter the inevitable wellies and waterproofs strewn on the floor; woe betide if you haven't brought your indoor shoes – in that case you wander around in your socks. Islanders and visitors can make use of the hall as they see fit, visitors paying a nominal amount of money to use its facilities, which include, on the ground floor, indoor football and badminton, washing machine, kitchen, toilets and showers. The hall has been a great addition to the social life of Muck and I have made good use of it myself, including giving a talk to residents about my island travels, and using the wi-fi and good phone signal.

Part of the hall has a first floor where there is a pool table, a couple of computers, wi-fi, a small library of books and a heritage corner. This is somewhat small, which reflects the fact that Muck is largely peopled by incomers with little Gaelic heritage. It's such a contrast to the An Iodhlann centre on Tiree, but a population of 650 is much more likely to be able to make a greater contribution to a heritage corner than a population of forty.

*

On this departure from Muck in 2019, having ten minutes to spare before I needed to be at the ferry, I popped into the community hall. Displayed on the heritage corner wall was a large-scale map of Muck, with numerous Gaelic place names stuck on it with home-made labels. In a green folder on a table, these names were translated into English with a few interesting notes. I am very grateful to whoever put these two treasures up in the centre – the map and the green folder.

Gaelic names, once so prevalent (I quote) 'would embody much local history and tradition. For instance that particular rock halfway to a certain peat moss, conveniently sited and shaped, where the homeward-bound carriers sat for a moment to ease their burdens, has suffered with the rest. The name that named it, that very likely commemorated its use and value, has disappeared.'[7]

My travels, experiences and encounters with people and the landscape I have walked in have made an indelible mark on me. They have whispered to me and I've listened. Quiet islands have given me more space to take in the environment. Just as in the 2020 Covid-19 lockdown many of us were touched by a tiny encounter with nature: for example, a burgeoning leaf bud on a tree the name of which we've had to look up. We have 'grown' with this knowledge; it has made us more appreciative and given us pause for thought. By knowing more, even by researching after the encounter, our experiences become richer. And going back to Muck, as exemplified in the quote from T. S. Eliot about the fish trap near Gallanach, I experienced the island 'as if for the first time'. After all, I was a different, 'grown' person after twenty years or so – or was I?

Of all the knowledge I have gained during my travels, one of the most exciting things has been to discover the wealth of Gaelic place names in all their linguistic, cultural, geographical, historical and folkloric glory. About seventy Gaelic place names survive on Muck, and in the following poem I celebrate them once again, with their English translations.

Walk on the Isle of Muck (from translations of Gaelic place names)
Let's sing the song of the Beach of the Fish Trap,
the Harbour of Whey, the Harbour of Clams,
the Hill of the Goat, the Grassy Lochan,
the dark green shade of the Fank of the Dockens!

We'll pass the Hollow of the Bolls of Meal
where sore-throated corncrakes tease and breed;
which leads to the Bay of the Brow of the Hill,
the inlet blasted by gannets and gulls.

Our ears will be soothed by our singing seals
hauled on the red-brown crotal skerries
in the breezy lee of the Hill of the Bellows
and the spurs of the grey-blue Rock of Turmoil.

We'll turn our backs on the whipping waves
and stride inland from the north-east shore;
from the Field of the Crag to MacAskill's Hillock,
a stiff climb up to the Hill of the Herdsman.

The trig point's proud of its view of the Cuillin,
the Sgurr of Eigg and Rum's grim peaks;
I'll plunge through bog near the burn of Glen Martin,
you'll scramble up to the Rock of Mare's Leap.

As we wearily trudge to our Port Mòr bothy,
a bird on his passage from Mull to Skye
deigns to descend to the Harbour of Willows;
this white-tailed eagle with a sunlit eye.

Let's sing the song of the Beach of the Fish Trap,
the Harbour of Whey, the Harbour of Clams,
the Hill of the Goat, the Grassy Lochan;
the dark green shade of the Fank of the Dockens!

After this visit, during the Covid lockdown, I put this song to music, and a friend has arranged it for voice and piano. I hope to go back to Muck and teach it to the schoolchildren before long. *(Musical score, with piano accompaniment, in appendix)*

AFTERWORD

I discovered Victoria at last! After some serious inspection of the rocks above me on the wild side of Muck, there she was lurking within a few tens of metres from the Pharaoh. Complete with the bun in her hair, she was facing the vertical cliff edge. And depending on which way you looked at the formation, her bun could be equally be construed as a dog's muzzle, as Catriona had told me.

Victoria

Muck had drawn me back yet again in spring 2021 as one of the first visitors welcome to the island after the coronavirus lockdown. I was still excited, even elated, as I made my way back to the east side of the island, along the track. Approaching me was a young woman. I blurted out, 'I've found Victoria!' She had no idea what I was talking about, and I continued on my way, so pleased with myself that I didn't explain my outburst. I later realised she was a total newcomer to the island. What must she have thought? 'I came across this mad woman on Muck, who said she'd just found Victoria. Who on earth was Victoria? A long-lost friend, a pet tortoise? Do all small islands harbour crazy women?'

Further east along the north coast of the island, I was wandering around Port Chreadhain, near the farm, when I came across Wave hauled up onto dry ground, well above the high tide mark, next to the old bogeys. I was told later that the boat had come to the end of its life. She had needed a complete refit, which would have been more expensive than the other option of replacing her. I would like to think that someone really keen on doing up boats could buy her as a project, take her away for a refit and live another useful life, perhaps on a sheltered loch as a tourist boat.

Another surprise awaited me on my way from the bunkhouse past the Tea Shop – something wasn't in sight any more. The old school buildings had vanished! Just a large flat piece of grass remained, with a few sheep grazing placidly on it, and not a single scrap of corrugated iron to be seen. Eddie, who lived very near the old school, told me that the whole island population had recently pulled it down. 'It was like ants crawling all over it. The tall people did the high bits, swarming over the roof, and the short ones the low bits – split-level working. It was like peeling an orange,' he said. To keep them fortified in their endeavours they were brought bacon sandwiches, tea and cake from the Tea Shop. I really wish I'd been part of the demolishing party, if only to feel part of the community – I understand they all had a great time.

Wave hauled up for good?

But I was sad about the loss, too. I had come to think of the buildings as works of art, or a memorial. What is it about the tourist's eye that sees rusty buildings as quaint features of a landscape, yet local people see them as eyesores, let alone dangerous places for children to play in? As a Leeds resident I might be the first to pester the local

Sheep grazing where the old school used to be

council to get rid of a rusty building in my own suburban street.

But the present school still flourishes. I was welcomed by the teacher at the school as a visiting music teacher. Pupils and I met outside, as Covid regulations still didn't allow me inside the school.

The keyboard's extension lead stretched long enough to be plugged in through the open door at the side of the school and we managed to clap, use percussion instruments, and even chant some of the phrases of my song 'Walk on the Isle of Muck.' A few pupils remembered the dinosaur song from my 2019 visit, and because we were outside, chanting the words soon

Outside the school, May 2021

morphed into a conga dance on the school lawn, as they improvised on the theme of 'The Prehistoric Animal Brigade.'[1]

I watched them from a few yards away as they clung to each other, forgot to chant the words, and fell laughing in a heap on the grass. I was happy to have enabled them to do something totally impromptu.

These changes since my 2019 visit could go towards a summing up of changes, and some non-changes in myself, over the period of my Scottish adventures. I can still adapt creatively according to circumstances and not be set in my ways, as I've discovered particularly in my work in the island schools. At the Lismore school, I 'allowed' the youngest children to lie down on the floor as they were so tired, for example – which I would never have let pupils do in the city schools I taught in.

I am becoming more aware of my advancing age. Just as I hope *Wave* will find a gentler lifestyle on quieter waters rather than the open sea, my own physical activities will sooner or later be reduced. Hopefully these will be replaced by increased cultural interests – for example in the Gaelic language and heritage, including folk songs, place names and music, such as I was lucky to come across in Lismore and Colonsay.

A definite tendency to garrulousness and increasing lack of inhibition is also obvious to me – a well-known feature of old age. This could help with any future encounters with strangers, helping to provide more relaxed communicative and richer responses from others (as long as I explain myself when necessary, and not run away as I did after finding Victoria). Another really common old-age phenomenon is forgetfulness – which has increased substantially over these years, such as nearly forgetting to mention that I lost my camera on Colonsay.

But I am still curious to explore the world around me, like an infant discovering the world beyond her mother's knee. Child psychiatrist John Bowlby's Attachment Theory, which I mention in my first chapter, explains that the young child keeps on returning to her Secure Base (in my case, Muck), for affirmation, but explores the world around (other islands) to learn that she can be affected by, and have an effect on, the environment – a sense of agency – from curiosity, interest and joy.

I offer a final quote from Samuel Johnson: 'Curiosity is, in great and generous minds, the first passion and the last.'[2] I do not see myself as having a 'great and generous mind', but I am still open to surprises around any corner, and to enjoying the fun that can still be had.

And that's why I keep returning to Muck.

CREDITS

Photos

Page 61   Sloc an Leim, Gigha – Keith Wilson

Page 65   Cara Island – Marion Stevenson

Page 57   Horlick's gardeners 1971-2 – Malcolm MacNeill

Page 122   Crime Scene, Tiree – David Naylor

Page 143   Skerryvore Lighthouse – Jason Engels/dutch-engels.com

Page 280   Victoria – Phoebe Haigh

Drawings

Page 53   Giant's Tooth Stone – John Hesselgreaves

Page 66   Brownie's chair on Cara Island – John Hesselgreaves

Page 71   Brownie on bench – Anita Lucas

Page 105   Seal Lady – Anita Lucas

Page 163   Glaistig – Anita Lucas

Page 176   Beothail – Anita Lucas

Page 205   Angus Macphee's boots – John Hesselgreaves

Page 222   Tawse – John Hesselgreaves

Maps reproduced with kind permission of OpenStreetMap

NOTES

PREFACE
1. Boswell, James, *The Journal of a Tour to the Hebrides with Samuel Johnson, 1785,* Collins, 1955
2. Frostrup, Mariella, *The Times*, August 26, 2019

CHAPTER 1
1. Bowlby, John, *A Secure Base*, Routledge Classics, 2005
2. MacDiarmid, Hugh, 'The Bonxie,' from *These Islands, We Sing*, ed. Kevin MacNeil, Polygon, 2011
3. McCaig, Norman, 'Ringed Plover by a Water's Edge,' from *The Poems of Norman McCaig*, Polygon, 2009
4. McEwen, L.T., *The Isle of Muck: A Short Guide*, 2002
5. Boswell, James, *op cit*
6. Swire, Otta, *The Inner Hebrides and their Legends*, Collins, 1964
7. Hunter, John, *The Small Isles*, Historic Environment Scotland, 2016

CHAPTER 2
1. Munro, Neil, *The Vital Spark, Para Handy*, Lomond Books, 1999
2. Martin, Martin, *A Description of the Western Isles of Scotland, circa 1685*, Birlinn, 2014
3. Haswell-Smith, Hamish, *The Scottish Islands*, Canongate, 2008
4. www.communitylandscotland.org.uk/2019/03/19-year-old-director-for-trust-board
5. Haswell-Smith, Hamish, *An Island Odyssey*, Canongate, 2000
6. Anderson, R.S.G., *The Antiquities of Gigha*, The Galloway Gazette, 1936
7. Martin, Martin, *op cit*
8. Haswell-Smith, *An Island Odyssey, op cit*
9. MacGregor, A.A., *The Peat-Fire Flame*, Ettrick Press, 1947
10. Czerkawska, Catherine, *The Way it Was: A History of Gigha*, Birlinn, 2016
11. Anderson, R.S.G., *op cit*
12. Haswell-Smith, Hamish, *An Island Odyssey, op cit*
13. *Glasgow Herald*, heraldscotland.com/news/12297948/cara
14. MacLeod, Kenneth, *The Road to the Isles*, Black, 1956
15. MacGregor, A.A., *op cit*

CHAPTER 3
1. MacGregor, A.A., *op cit*
2. MacPhee, Earle Douglas, MacPhee's Tales, *Dr Earle's History of the Clan MacPhee*, www.clanmacfie.co.uk
3. Swire, Otta, *op cit*

CHAPTER 4
1. Martin, Martin, *op cit*
2. aniodhlann.org.uk
3. Isle of Tiree website, www.isleoftiree.com
4. MacGregor, A.A., *op cit*
5. canmore.org.uk
6. Macfarlane, Robert, *Landmarks*, Hamish Hamilton, 2015

CHAPTER 5
1. Grimble, Ian, *Scottish Islands*, BBC Publications, 1986
2. https://en.wikipedia.org/wiki/John_Gerard
3. https://en.wikipedia.org/wiki/Topographia_Hibernica
4. Westwood, J, and Kingshill, S, *St Moluag and St Columba Together, Friends or Foes, The Lore of Scotland*, Arrow Books, 2011
5. Carmichael, Alexander, *Carmina Gadelica, A collection of incantations and folklore, mainly of the Hebrides*, Floris Books, 1992

CHAPTER 6
1. MacPherson, John, *Tales from Barra, Told by the Coddy*, Birlinn, 2001
2. Mackenzie, Compton, *Whisky Galore*, Vintage Classics, 2004
3. Shaw, Margaret Fay, *Eilean, The Island Photography of Margaret Fay Shaw*, Birlinn, 2018
4. Shaw, Margaret Fay, *From the Alleghenies to the Hebrides*, Birlinn, 1999
5. CD, *Waulking Songs from Barra*, Scottish Tradition 3, School of Scottish Studies, University of Edinburgh
6. Kennedy-Fraser, Marjory, *A Life of Song*, The Islands Book Trust, 2011
7. MacPherson, John, *op cit*
8. Prebble, John, *The Highland Clearances*, Penguin, 1982
9. May, Peter, and Wilson, David, *Hebrides*, Riverrun, 2013
10. May, Peter, and Wilson, David, *op cit*

11. Hutchinson, Roger, *The Silent Weaver*, Birlinn 2011
12. Carmichael, Alexander, *op cit*
13. Haswell-Smith, Hamish, *The Scottish Islands*, *op cit*
14. Haswell-Smith, Hamish, *The Scottish Islands*, *op cit*
15. Nicholson, Ewen, *The Next Horizon: Memories of a Hebridean Skipper*, For The Right Reasons, 2012
16. Carmichael, Alexander, *op cit*
17. Haswell-Smith, Hamish, *The Scottish Islands*, *op cit*
18. MacGregor, A.A., *op cit*
19. Map prepared by the Trust for Heisgeir with Grimsay Fishermen and Alick MacAuley, 2007
20. Nicholson, Ewen, *op cit*
21. Nicholson, Ewen, *op cit*
22. Nicholson, Ewen, *op cit*
23. BBC News Scotland, Feb 22, 2017
24. Pollard, Antony Jon, 'A study of marine exploitation in prehistoric Scotland, with special reference to marine shell sand and their archaeological contexts,' doctoral thesis, University of Glasgow, 2009
25. Ferguson, Lesley M, *Wanderings with a Camera in Scotland*, Royal Commission on the Ancient and Historical Monuments of Scotland, 2014
26. Joyce, John, *Newsletter of Hebridean Hostellers no. 67*, Spring 2020

CHAPTER 7

1. MacGregor, A.A., *op cit*
2. Clare, John, *Everyman's Poetry*, ed. R.K.R. Thorton, W&N, 1997 7
3. Hunter, John, *op cit*
4. Eliot, T.S., *Four Quartets*, Faber, 2001
5. M.L. Reeve, 'The Prehistoric Animal Brigade,' from *Okki-tokki-unga*, A&C Black, 1976
6. MacGregor, A.A., *op cit*
7. Maclean, Alasdair, *Night Falls on Ardnamurchan*, Birlinn, 2011

AFTERWORD

1. M.L. Reeve, *op cit*
2. Boswell, James, *The Life of Johnson, Including Boswell's Journal of a Tour of the Hebrides, and Johnson's Diary of a Journey Into North Wales*, Volume 1, Harper & Brothers, 1799

APPENDIX A
SHEET MUSIC

Isle of Muck Song
by Marg Greenwood

The melody is taken from a traditional Canadian folk song whose origin is unknown, but is related to 'My Paddle's Keen and Bright', written by Margaret Embers McGee (1889–1975) in 1918.

The Brownie of Gigha and Cara
by Marg Greenwood

A bearded wee man who's dressed all in brown, Will he be kind or

will he be mad? Just take off your hat! Just take off your hat!

Say good day Mist er Brown-ie and give him a grin, His trust you must win.

V.1 Let's go to the pier and jump in a boat, you take the oars and from

Gi gha we'll row, The sea's nice and calm and Car a's not far, We'll get there quite soon. we'll

come to no harm.

Johnny MacPhee and his Seal Bride

by Marg Greenwood

Chorus: Un der the rocks and next to the sea, On the Col-on-say coast searched

Joh nny Mac Phee, Look out for your bride Look out for your bride

She was drowned in a ship wreck, turned in to a seal and swam through the tide

V.1 When peo ple are lost in storms and gales They live a nice life as

seals in the waves The king lets them turn back to hu - man form, But

just for one night they must leave be - fore dawn!

Song of the Ringing Stone
by Marg Greenwood

Beothail of Lismore

by Marg Greenwood

Chorus: Here in Lis-more, I'm rest-less and sad, My prince is wound-ed

far, far a way! Just send me to him Just send me to him It's

lone-ly in side my - cast-le Coeff-in, Send me to Lach-lann! Verse 1 My

prince - and I used to wan-der the shore, He loved-my face, 'just like sun beams' he swore, and my

steps were like songs so loud we would sing past Sgeir nam Uan and Sloc a Muill inn!

Boys in Green Vests
by Marg Greenwood

Voice

Chorus: Let's go to   the shore, there's drift-wood to find and   may-be   a boat tied

up on   a rock!   Just hope for some luck   Just hope for some luck

Mac - Don - ald's sons   saw two tin - y boys, There's fairies   on Muck!

V.1   (..) - Hec-tor   and Neill were   se-ven   and ten, and   lived in   Pier House   just

close to the shore, they went to the beach to   gath-er some wood And   flot-sam and jet-sam from

yes   -   ter - day's   storm.

A Walk on the Isle of Muck

music/lyrics by Marg Greenwood
arranged by Richard Ormrod

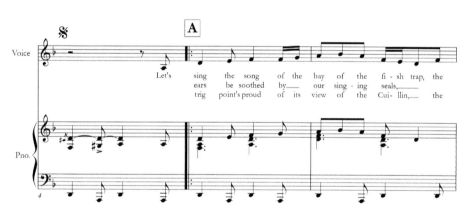

APPENDIX B
ORIGINAL GAELIC PLACE NAMES FROM
WALK ON THE ISLE OF MUCK

Camas na Cairidh	Beach of the Fish Trap
Laimhrig a'Mhèig	Harbour of Whey
Port Chreadhain	Harbour of Clams
Torr nan Gobhar	Hill of the Goat
Feur Lochan	The Grassy Lochan
Fang nan Copag	Fank of the Dockens
Lag nam Bolla	The Hollow of the Bolls of Meal
Port nam Maol	The Bay of the Brow of the Hill
Torr a'Builg	Hill of the Bellows
Sròn na Teiste	Rock of Turmoil
Achadh na Creige	Field of the Crag
Carn Mhic Asgaill	McAskill's Hillock
Beinn Airein	Hill of the Herdsman
Gleann Mhàirtein	Glen Martin
Rubh' Leum na Làraich	Rock of Mare's Leap
Port an t-Seilich	Harbour of Willows

ACKNOWLEDGEMENTS

Enormous thanks are owed to Becky Cherriman, my mentor, whose expertise and support has been invaluable throughout the long writing process; Sam Hawcroft, an incredibly patient and forgiving copy editor and designer; and Richard Ormrod who worked so hard to help me with arranging songs and composing. Also, Alasdair MacEachen from Benbecula, and members of the Leeds Writers' Circle for invaluable help and support in the technicalities of writing this book. I am also hugely grateful to family members and friends for putting up with me rambling on about 'the book', and most of all to Ken, who has read, re-read, suggested, amended, and been the most steadfast and long-suffering supporter that a writer could wish for.

This book could not have been possible without the willingness, generosity and kindness shown to me by the islanders who have given freely of their time, answered my sometimes inane questions, invited me into their homes, and taken me on special walks, trips and expeditions. I have met nothing but open-heartedness in all these lesser-known Scottish Islands.

WHERE NEXT...?

ABOUT THE AUTHOR

Marg was born in Leicester during the Second World War, and before settling in Yorkshire to raise her family, she lived and worked in France, Sierra Leone and Zambia in the late 1960s and early 1970s. She has explored mainland Scotland and the Scottish Isles as a solo traveller for two decades, publishing articles, poetry and memoirs in magazines such as *Scotland Magazine*, *Scottish Islands Explorer* and the web-based *Island Review*.

Her musical and teaching background enables her to compose songs based on folk legends of the isles which she shares with island schools. Marg is a strident walker, a very keen listener of birdsong, an appreciative flower-spotter, and an annoying but devoted grandmother. This is her first book.